D1527440

A HITTITE AND A *Shaman*

AT QUEEN NEFERTARI'S SECRET SERVICE

NAVEEN SRIDHAR

Formatting and layout: global_desing - https://www.fiverr.com/share/lY24eR

Cover Artist: CherieFox - cheriefox.com

To my late sister
Leelavathi Chandra Sekhar

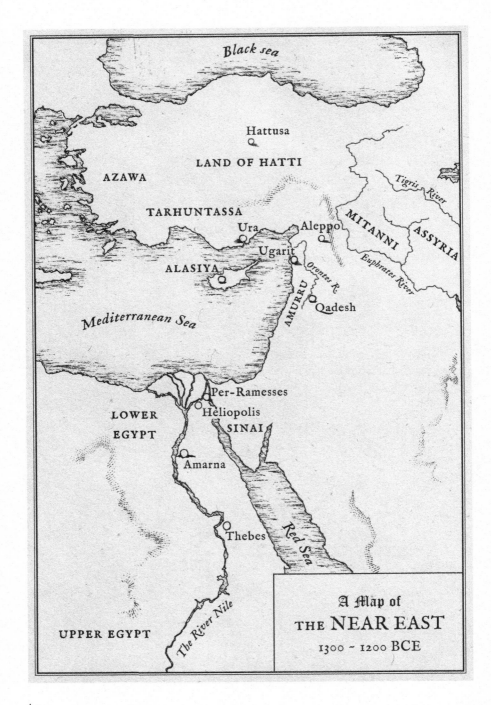

Black sea

Hattusa

LAND OF HATTI

AZAWA

TARHUNTASSA

Ura

Aleppo

MITANNI

ASSYRIA

Tigris River

Euphrates River

Ugarit

AMURRU

Oronter R.

Qadesh

ALASIYA

Mediterranean Sea

Per-Ramesses

Heliopolis

SINAI

LOWER
EGYPT

Amarna

Thebes

Red Sea

The River Nile

UPPER EGYPT

A Map of
THE NEAR EAST
1300 ~ 1200 BCE

Contents

PART I - THE SHAMAN

Chapter 1 - The Message..1

Chapter 2 - The Call..17

Chapter 3 - A Challenge...39

Chapter 4 - Oracle..55

PART II - THE HITTITE

Chapter 5 - The Mission..77

Chapter 6 - The Quest...87

Chapter 7 - The Contact..99

Chapter 8 - Comrades in Arms..117

Chapter 9 - Dreams and Plans..141

PART III - THE QUEEN

Chapter 10 - The Vizier...163

Chapter 11 - Tracking down the Truth.................................185

Chapter 12 - Conference..209

Chapter 13 - The Accord...225

Chapter 14 - In Peace..239

Author's Note..253

Personae..255

Glossary...257

About The Author...259

THE SHAMAN

Chapter 1

THE MESSAGE

1264 BCE

Queen Nefertari was an unhappy woman.

She was the first lady of the mightiest man of the times. She was blessed with the everlasting love of her spouse. She had no fears, no needs, no room for worries. Even so, she was discontented.

Nefertari Meritmut, queen of the pharaoh Ramses II, was standing on the terrace of the royal garden adjacent to her chambers and witnessing the valediction of the palace gardener. The old man was ending his service.

His boss, the supervisor of the royal gardens and orchards in the new capital Per-Ramesses, stood in the pavilion at one end of the terrace. It was an elevated structure, elegant but simple, devoid of any figurines and other decoration, with a conical ceiling for shade. It offered a podium or stage. This was the spot where the host would first stand for a brief chat with guests so they could view the scenery and absorb it before descending for a stroll.

The man was addressing the audience, composed of his peers, servants, and slaves. He closed the laud: "...and we all pray to the gods to support you, cherished Sefu, in your years of repose and reminiscence. Remember, this garden is your contribution to the peace and pleasure of our venerable pharaoh and his queen in this new city of Per-Ramesses. It is, indeed, your legacy to the world."

On his prompt, Sefu struggled up the steps and stopped before the queen. Nefertari smiled and motioned him to come closer. A maid came up to her, held out a casket, and opened it. Nefertari lifted from it a gold medal featuring the royal insignia in the middle and a floral border along the edge. This award was cherished as a sign of royal acknowledgment for lifelong service. She held it aloft for the audience's view. The stooping man bowed even deeper and held out his palms, one resting on the other. She noticed his crooked fingers and how they trembled. No smile crept through the creases of his weather-beaten face.

"May the gods bless you with a long and healthy life, Sefu," she said in a gentle tone but loud enough for everyone to hear. "I express the appreciation of your service in the name of the pharaoh. But bear in mind, you are always welcome to visit us any time you please, for this garden is also yours. All the plants here are your plants, your kin. This refuge for flowers is your creation with the blessings of the gods."

She looked up to the sky and added, *"Em heset net Ra. Em hotep nefer, em hotep.* Be in favor with the sun god Ra. Live in great peace."

Returning to her chambers, Nefertari strode to her dressing room to change. She set aside her crown and cast a look into the bronze mirror.

Before her mind's eye, the face of the old man lingered, his expression one of gratitude, pride, joy, and sorrow all rolled into one. She would miss him. Sefu was ever present in the garden, now bending over the weeds, now rustling behind the bushes, shouting commands to the juniors, and reining in his language when he sighted her. He seemed to enjoy the garden more than anyone else, laboring in the paradise of his own creation. Except for him, this was a silent world, yet the garden could be rebellious in the long run, tending towards chaos if ignored. The question could be raised: who was the master, and who was the servant? His accomplishment dedicated to the royalty was to realize heaven on earth, an abode of peace.

Em hotep, peace be with you, had also been among her last words to the gardener. True, it was the lifetime achievement of Sefu. What was her achievement in life? How could she contribute to peace in this life?

The pharaoh had been ordained by the gods to assure peace and prosperity for all in Egypt or Kemet, the Black Land, the divinely created garden. What was her contribution to that enormous task? How did she support her beloved husband? Was the role of a queen only representative? Was she to be respected only because of her marriage, celebrated and paraded only for her position? A live decorative banner?

Yes, she could pride herself as an ideal spouse, mother, and wife, just as the society expected, nay, demanded. She had been a faithful and loving wife to Ramses, presenting to him six children and heirs among them. Her occasional contribution to state affairs had won her the title "Mistress of Upper and Lower Egypt." But endowed with her abilities, skills, and position, what had she truly achieved as queen?

She came out of the dressing room. Her gaze wandered and rested on a clay envelope and a tablet lying on a small table next to the tall figurine of goddess Hathor. The tablet was a message from Hattusha, the capital of Hatti, the kingdom of the Hittites to the north, who had not been on good terms with Egypt for ages. Delivered two days before by a herald from there, the message was written in clay.

Nefertari corresponded with various queens of other lands. The most prominent among them was Queen Puduhepa of Hatti. Their friendship had not been shadowed by the cold war between the countries. Usually, such messages in cuneiform script from Queen Puduhepa were in the Akkadian language, the diplomatic *lingua franca*, which Nefertari had mastered along with the hieroglyphs of the Egyptians. But this time, the same script was in a strange language she could not identify. She stared at it. The message stared back.

"Yesterday, you called for the scribe, milady," Bennu, her lady-in-waiting, called out from behind her as if she had read her thoughts.

"Yes, I did," the queen said.

"He is here, awaiting your audience."

"You may usher him in."

Ife, the personal scribe of the queen, stood near the door, waiting. He was an elderly man, bent with age and the typical posture of a scribe over decades.

He bowed and said in a shaky voice, "You sent someone for me, your majesty?"

"Yes. I did. I need your help. Do you see the envelope over there on the table? The message reached me two days ago."

Ife shuffled towards the table and gazed at the object.

"See what you can make of it."

He picked up the envelope with both hands.

Bennu approached Nefertari. The queen raised a hand, signaling her to wait. The scribe inspected the message for a few seconds and shook his head.

"I can only say this is from—"

"I know it is from the Hittite kingdom," Nefertari said. "The insignias on the envelope and at the bottom of the message say that much. But what about the text?"

Ife frowned, hesitated, and shook his head again. "I am afraid, your majesty, the language is not Akkadian. It could be Nesite, the official language of the Hittites. It could even be Palaic, Luwian, or Lydian."

"Is it from Queen Puduhepa of Hatti? Can you say that much?"

"I could not say that, either." Ife drooped his lips.

"Strange. She always wrote in Akkadian." Nefertari said to herself.

Ife said, "Maybe she chose the Hittite tongue this time. It could be something she could not express otherwise."

The queen was a bit restless. "Or the author is someone else who presumes we can read the language. But you cannot. Who could read it and translate it for us?"

"I know none who would be reliable, I am afraid, your majesty. The only other scribe who was well versed in Nesite passed away a year ago. I will have to make inquiries."

"Do so. But of course, do not let anyone know who the author could be or that I am the recipient. Make sure he does not turn up out of curiosity."

"Yes, of course. You can count on my oath, your majesty. I will do my best, but it may take some time." Ife returned the tablet to the envelope, placed it on the table, bowed, and left.

After he had gone, Nefertari stared into her handheld mirror, adjusted her hair again, and said to Bennu, "I would like to change my dress. Get me the red one with the brocade."

Bennu walked up to the wardrobe in the dressing room.

"By the way," Nefertari called out, "how is your family getting on?"

"What shall I say, madame?" Bennu chuckled as she came up with the garment. "They are well, but right now, instead of my daughter, it is my husband who is excited like a child; it is about the upcoming celebration."

"Do you mean the annual parade?" Nefertari asked, taking the dress from Bennu's hands.

"Yes, the one commemorating the battle near Qadesh."

Nefertari held out the dress and cocked her head to the side, casting a critical look at it.

"In that war, your husband was a charioteer at the front, and I can imagine he is proud about the event," she said. "As for me, I must confess that the battle was a nightmare. I hoped day after day that my spouse would return hale and hearty from the front."

Nefertari reached to her neck to stroke the gift from her husband that she always wore. It was a collar with a pendant of pure gold in the shape of an *ankh,* a cross with a loop as the top limb. The *ankh* was a symbol of breath and life. Ramses had presented it to her before leaving for the campaign to Qadesh as a promise of his victorious return.

She strode towards the dressing room.

"It was no different in my case, milady," Bennu said, following her. "In fact, we women only fear for the lives of our fathers, husbands, and sons, not for mere victory. The battle cries we hear are the cries of wailing women. I was lucky not to be widowed, nor to face a husband returning maimed and…as a cripple".

"Yet," Nefertari said, looking back at Bennu, "let us also honor those who lost their lives for the cause."

Bennu bit her lip and spoke up after a short pause.

"The *cause,* milady? The cause we have in life is to remain hale and hearty, to survive and serve, not to mourn and moan. But all I can do is to hope there is no war. I can only fear, sigh, hope, and face fate. What else can I ever do? I am only a woman."

Nefertari sighed and whispered, "Yes, we are only women."

* * *

On the same day, in another part of the city, the bronzesmith Rai'a had laid down his hammer for a chat with his old friend. He had come out to the front of his smithy and was sitting with his comrade Sa'a on a brick bench. He had built it as a crude seat for a pause between long hours standing at the anvil. The workshop was the porch of a dwelling, before which, a road approached and forked into two paths leading to its rear.

He stretched, stroked the small of his back, and said, "Whew! When I was young, I could take a lot of the strain. Remember how we went through thick and thin at the front?"

"Sure," Sa'a said. In contrast to his comrade, he was a slender man with a hungry look. In his youth, he had been hailed as an expert bowman, renowned for his speed and adroitness in his art. Now, living in a village, he had come on a visit to the big city. "Soon we will be celebrating that famous battle."

The army consisted of infantry and chariotry, the latter being the elite branch. In the battle, Ramses had led four divisions in a campaign to the north with the purpose of conquering the vassal states of the Hittites, Qadesh being one of them. A young pharaoh only five years into his reign, he had shared all the danger with his troops at the front. He had been misled by spies, told that the enemy location was far from Qadesh. He had led his Amun division ahead, outdistancing his other three divisions and isolating his own.

Rai'a and Sa'a had been charioteers in the Ra division, following the pharaoh's. Rai'a was the driver, and Sa'a was the archer. They were surprised and attacked from the right by the Hittites, who had crossed the Orontes River to its left bank. The Ra division took a heavy toll, with the survivors getting split into a group heading south with the enemy in hot pursuit and another small group moving north to join Ramses's division and warn him. Rai'a and Sa'a were in this group.

As Ramses set out for a consultation with the military officers of his division in the far north, the Hittites closed in. With his troops surprised and fleeing in disarray, he had to act fast. Calling out to the god Amun for aid, he fought his way out and regrouped the troops to dispel the assault with success. The battle ended in a stalemate when the Hittites withdrew to the east after heavy losses.

"A great time to remember and to praise our pharaoh. Only the young know nothing and do not care," Rai'a added and pursed his lips.

Sa'a nodded. "Those days, we were also young but brave. Today's young men hang around and loiter, playing games or chasing girls."

"All idlers." Rai'a shook his head.

"On the other hand," Sa'a corrected himself after a pause, "how could they show their bravery if there is no war? They cannot pick up weapons for mock battles and slaughter one another."

The pair fell in thoughtful silence for a while.

Sa'a broke it. "The day of the celebration is also a day to mourn the dead. I think of Qali."

Qali had been a comrade in their company. In the battle, he had been hit in the chest by an arrow and had perished in the arms of his comrades.

A girl in her teens emerged from the house and entered the smithy with a carefree, jumpy gait. She would qualify as a beauty in any land of her times. She was carrying an open basket of colored grass woven to form a pattern.

"Going to see your uncle, Anat?" father Rai'a asked.

"No. To the seamstress. Mom has some work for her." She stopped, fumbled in the basket, and gasped,

"Oh, I forgot something." She set the basket on a small table near Rai'a and rushed back to the house.

Sa'a's face had been bright since her entry. He said, "You have a beautiful daughter, brother."

"Oh, thanks." Rai'a grinned. "How time flies! When I returned from the battle, she was a kid. Just imagine. She is now seventeen."

"All set to get married. Any plans?" Sa'a asked.

"We are on the lookout. Maybe she will find her match herself, the way I found my wife."

"The way *your wife* found *you*." Sa'a pointed at Rai'a.

"All right, all right."

They laughed.

"And the gods spared you from the arrows of the Hittites," Sa'a added.

"That is true. They saved me from the devils. I call them *Hyksos*." Rai'a grimaced. "They are no better than those barbarians of yore. All from the north. Aliens are by nature bad."

"What do you mean? Can you explain?"

"They have neither our gods to protect them nor a pharaoh to guard and guide, no one to teach manners. For them, life is a game, and that game is war."

Sa'a shook his head. "You generalize, my friend."

On the road before the smithy, a young man ran up to them. Out of breath, he stopped a few feet before them, paused for a fraction of a second, looked over his shoulder, and moved on, overlooking the table ahead. He stumbled and staggered. Before the men could jump up to help him, he scrambled up on his own, almost tipping the basket on the table. He turned to the men, nodded an apology, and ran off down one of the roads leading to the rear.

Then the next surprise came: two burly men from the same direction the young man had come. They were in a hurry, too. They stopped before the smithy. One made a move to approach Rai'a and Sa'a, but the other blocked him. They called out some commands to each other and separated, each taking a different route along the two roads past the smithy.

Sa'a was the first to speak up. "What is going on?"

"What do I know? The young man was being chased. Maybe he stole something."

"Were they members of the royal guard?"

"No," Rai'a answered. "The royal guard is made of soldiers from the Mejay tribe. You would know them by their looks. They are all tall and dark and come from the south. These were civilians in peculiar clothes."

"Did you hear what they were saying?" Sa'a asked.

"I could not follow. Maybe they were foreigners. There are quite a few here, mostly merchants and traders. Anyway, I must get back to work." Rai'a slapped his thighs and rose. Sa'a followed.

Anat came out of the rear and dropped a garment into the basket. She picked it up and said, "I have everything now. I must hurry." She ran off.

"Anat! Come back before it gets dark," Rai'a yelled when she was almost out of earshot, the words all elders would say to their daughters for ages to come.

Anat yelled back, "Of course, Dad," and disappeared.

Previously, the men had failed to witness a subtle move. With his back turned to them, the young man on the run had dropped something into the basket.

* * *

A week had passed since her father had sat for a chat with his comrade, one of his rare visitors. As usual, he was pounding a piece of bronze with his hammer, the routine bang, bang, bang. He returned the adamant beast in the stranglehold of his tongs back to the fire for another trip to hell. That gave him a break to wipe the sweat off his forehead with a rag.

"Dad, I am going to see Uncle," Anat called out in her cheerful voice. "I have not seen him for weeks."

"Forgot anything?"

"No. This time I have everything in my basket," she said, forcing a laugh. She hated being reminded like this, but again, she had often been caught absentminded.

"Give him my wishes, Anat!" he yelled after her and began hitting the metal with the hammer.

After a few steps along the road, a young man loitering on the other side of the road caught Anat's eye. He was tall and had a handsome face. He almost threw her a smile, or was she dreaming? Why would he? She had never seen him before. She averted her eyes and walked on. Who was that? She was used to second glances by young men, but this man's stare did not leave her mind. On turning the next corner, she stole a glimpse over her shoulder. No sign of anyone except for two kids arguing and a cat crossing the road. After a long walk, she stole another glance as she entered her uncle's home. No one was in sight.

Uncle was his usual self, beaming on seeing her. He was someone with whom she could share her hopes, worries, and even dreams. She was thankful to be able to talk to someone who would accept her with all her faults and doubts. To that extent, he was a friend. At times, she had to remind herself that he was still her uncle and demanded respect whether she liked it or not. She had often wondered if people without families of their own retained their childhood and youth all their lives.

"I have brought your tunic, Uncle. Mom got the seams sewn up. Now it is like new." She fished it out of her basket. It was a long sand-colored tunic with decorations around the neck and the cuffs.

"Oh, great." He held it up, looked at it, and nodded.

When he started his usual fuss, displaying his avuncular care and concern, Anat let him have his fun. Her parents had great sympathy for this lonesome man who was much attached to his sister Bennu and her family. Six years older than Bennu, he had often said he saw in Anat his own sister at that age. More than once, she had heard him insist before Bennu and her husband that he never wanted to discipline the girl. That was the lot of parents. He was the uncle to guide, not to drill. But she knew he doted on her.

He was not a great cook, but he made this an occasion to do his best with his mock performance as a cook and literally feed the child that he always saw in her. He would fuss a bit about Anat's selective appetite, pretending to be offended if she did not consume enough. It was partly real concern, partly his posture as a senior, partly a chosen role. She let him play his role in the drama.

At long last, after a lot of magic in the kitchen performed with great gusto, they sat down on the floor for lunch.

He said, "You are a bit late, dear. I was worried."

"Uncle, I am sorry," she said and added a white lie: "I was held up by an old friend of mine."

Her uncle laughed. It was that disarming laughter that suggested a shrug. "'Old friend'? He is not *old*." He chuckled again and said, "Nor even the friendship."

"What?"

"Your boyfriend, I mean, your admirer. Is he a foreigner?"

She swallowed, although her mouth was empty. "I don't understand you. What do you mean?"

The uncle nodded. "Just what I said, not that I mind."

"How do you come upon a boyfriend? I have none." Anat snorted, raised and turned her head, and puckered her lips.

"Guesswork, instinct, certainly no trick. Maybe plain observation. All right, I was only teasing." His benign smile gave no room for alarm. She did not fear any protest or reprimand.

"Let me explain." He tilted his head. "I noticed the new ring you are wearing is from elsewhere, not from here. Was it a present?"

Anat's head sank. She felt her cheeks getting warm and hoped she was not blushing. She wanted to be honest and said, "No one gave it to me. I *found* it, Uncle. Please do not think I stole it."

"Common, dear. You could not have *found* such a precious ring lying around somewhere. Let me take a close look." He took her hand and peered at the ring, narrowing his eyes. It was a golden ring with a design engraved on it depicting two crossed swords and an eagle spreading its wings above them. The border had an intricate heraldic design.

"You are the only one I have told about this, Uncle. My parents may not believe it, so I never told them anything," Anat said in a plaintive voice. "Honest, I found it. I did not steal it, nor did anyone give it to me. It was lying in my basket. I do hope you believe me, Uncle."

He gazed at his feet and pinched the bridge of his nose. He said with a smile, "A strange story. Nobody would discard a precious ring or lose it this way. What you say is too strange to be a lie, too incredible to be an invention. I believe you, dear. Do not worry. I won't talk about this. I am only concerned. If the real owner finds you with this ring, you may be charged with theft."

Anat stopped eating. "How is that possible?" she asked. "Do you mean I should have searched the whole city to find the owner and return it?"

"Of course not. That is the problem. Nor can anyone claim the ring, not knowing where he or she lost it. Anyway, it is a precious ring with a strange pattern, and it is quite conspicuous. But it fits you, right?"

"It didn't. It was too loose for my finger. I have a friend whose father is a goldsmith. He did me the favor of adjusting it to my finger lest I should lose it. Now it is *mine*."

"I suggest you do not display it. Carry it somewhere else." He smiled and patted his chest. "On a necklace, hidden deep in the bosom."

Anat was relieved to know her uncle was not going to make a mountain out of a molehill. She nodded. After returning home, she would hang it on her golden necklace and carry it that way, concealed. It was hers to keep.

* * *

After lunch, Anat took leave of her uncle and proceeded to the local market for groceries. It was a small market meant for the residents in the neighborhood. There were some regular shops in brick buildings, and others were just spaces in between, with their wares spread out on reed mats. Vegetables were available. Meat was, of course, not on the daily menu of the residents and could be procured only elsewhere. The fish market was near the river. Her purchases were limited to what she could carry in both hands. Luckily, this time, she did not need much.

A vendor was standing before his fruit stall, calling out to passers-by, making them aware of the delicious articles he had to offer. A woman squatting on her heels beside him passed him a few pods of carob from a basket next to her. He held them high and spoke flattering words about the product. He went on and on, even suggesting recipes for sweets to make the people salivate. His words came out in an entertaining singsong, like that of a storyteller. About ten people had gathered around him and were watching his performance with relaxed and amused looks. Serious expressions would reappear on their faces once they assumed the role of customers. Only the woman, apparently his wife, had a look of boredom. Anat walked on after a short pause to watch the man.

A cat brushed past her and ran off past a stray dog lying in the shade of a stall. The dog gave the cat a tired look but did not move, too lazy to begin a chase in the heat. There would be another cat, another day. He yawned and settled down for a nap.

After buying some peas, Anat passed a shop for incense and scents. The smell of roses and jasmine filled the hot and humid air, alternating with a few more scents she could not identify. In the sudden atmosphere of fine and delicate flavor, she slowed her pace to have a look at the vials.

A big customer stood with his back to her, blocking her view. He was talking to the seller but not bargaining. He went on and on while the vendor She had to nudge past him. He noticed and stepped aside. The seller turned all his attention to her, apparently eager for another customer. With all eyes on her, she felt nervous. She had only wanted to glance at the items. After all, these enticing goods were not for her, not at that price. She cast the vendor a smile and backed away.

After a few paces, warding off this pleasant distraction of perfumes and nobility, she looked around for the next item on her mind and then she saw him again, the same young man who had been ogling her before the smithy. Or was it only her imagination? She brushed aside the image and kept moving.

The last stop in the market could also be smelled from a distance, the new spot for onions. The silent vendor squatting with a balance before him was surrounded by heaps of onions of different sizes. Anat could imagine the vendor was proud of his wares, which signaled their presence far and wide. The neighboring shopkeepers took it in stride, for the cause was no mystery, and all kinds of smells were the pride of a market anyway.

Like two or three other customers, Anat hovered around the wares putting on a slight frown. This was the standard expression for a customer, either judging the product or showing some displeasure or disgust so the vendor would reduce the price. Any bright expression suggesting enthusiasm or excitement would only spoil the bargaining position. She showed mild interest in a variety of onions, her body turned in profile, and asked the price in a half-willing manner.

As usual, she did not accept the vendor's first offer. Haggling seemed to lead her nowhere. The fat man scoffed at the final price she proposed, refused to bargain anymore, and got up. He turned his back on her to rearrange some onions already well organized in a heap. That was a clear signal for her to give up and retreat. She hesitated and was at the point of settling for a cheaper variety when the man turned back to throw a glance beyond her. His frown turned into a relaxed smile.

"Ebo, aren't you asking too much for those onions?" she heard a man ask from behind her in a friendly but assertive tone.

Before she could look back, the vendor said to her, "Oh, I am sorry, girl. I didn't know you were a friend of Harti. Of course, in this case, I will make an exception for you. How about just one deben? A special offer."

She produced the copper piece, and he bent down to pick up the balance to weigh the onions.

Anat turned her head and saw the same young man as before. He was well dressed, not barefoot; above all, she was impressed by his erect and confident posture. He winked at her and threw her a smile. Confused, she looked back.

The shopkeeper was weighing the bulbs on his balance. One of them rolled off his hand and hit the ground. While she looked around to spot it, the young man was quick to stoop and pick it up for her. She thanked him.

After the purchase, they walked a few steps together. A bit thrilled and confused, she decided to take the plunge. That led to a chat. He spoke with a pleasant voice but had an accent, and he often paused while searching for a word.

"You are not from here, are you?" Anat asked, cocking her head to look up at him. She could not control her curiosity anymore. It overcame her demure diffidence.

"No. I am from the far north. You noticed it, I am sure."

He said he was a trader from somewhere in the north. Questioned further, he revealed he was employed as a scribe by a textile merchant from his native land. His work also involved store management and helping the merchant with the local language.

She had nothing much to say, but he was polite and nodded on hearing she was the daughter of the smith.

"Oh, yes." He nodded. "I know the smithy. I have never been there. I only mean to say that I know where it is."

She was on the point of asking him why he had been watching her earlier, but she bit her lip.

Three young men sauntered past the pair, and one of them called out, "Hey, are you coming to the game tomorrow?"

"Yes, of course," the young man called back over the shoulder.

Anat and the young man had hardly resumed their chat when two girls, around fifteen, came from the other direction, giggling as they walked past and throwing a glance at them—at him. Anat glared at them and shook her head.

After quite a long talk, she felt she ought to cut it short and prove her modest womanhood. She excused herself with the customary, "Now, I have to hurry."

"It was so nice talking to you. I have few friends here who would care to spend time with me like this."

Really? She held her breath. Then he reacted the way she had hoped.

"Maybe we can meet again." He smiled and made a slight bow.

She lowered her head, smiling, and waited.

"Tomorrow at this time, right here?" he asked. "Then, from here, we can walk up to the riverbank, where it is quieter."

"I will try to get some time off," Anat replied. She paused. *Never sound too enthusiastic, dummy.* "You know, I have to run many chores for my mother. I may have to find an excuse."

"I will be glad if you can make it. Please, Anat." He smiled and turned away. She stood in a daze, bewildered by how he knew her name. Yes, of course. Her father had called out to her when she had left home, and the man had been within earshot.

What had that fat man called him? Was it Hari or Hara? She walked on. Deep in thought, she rubbed her ring and mused: *This gift from heaven has really brought me luck.*

All of a sudden, she realized she was walking in the wrong direction. She continued until the young man was out of sight and then turned towards home.

* * *

The big man at the perfume stall was Suppilamus from Hattusha. He was a visitor scouting the possibilities of trade in precious goods. The variety of such goods in this big city impressed him. His visit to the market was neither as a seller nor as a customer, but only as one snooping around for information. He was getting a quick introduction to the products and prices. His approach with the vendor, promising to purchase large orders for his homeland, had led nowhere. He had to admit he was not convincing, for the vendor had shown no interest. As a novice, he had to learn a lot. After all, the whole posture as a trader of goods was only a façade.

He strolled through the marketplace with the real purpose of the visit nagging his mind.

Chapter 2

THE CALL

In the past weeks, Bennu had noticed a change in her daughter's mood. She was getting sloppy in attending to household duties and running errands, always finding some excuses, procrastinating, or even forgetting facts and appointments. But whenever she left home to meet her "friends," she had a special, jumpy gait, and she often returned humming a tune. This was no more a mere sign of growing up and casting off the last vestiges of childhood; it was more than that. There were enough indications for Bennu to know what was going on.

Instead of preparing for a big, mother-to-child chat with a wise prelude, she decided to ask Anat bluntly.

She walked into the kitchen and saw Anat squatting in a corner. The girl was in tears.

The mother smiled, walked past her daughter, and stopped at the window. She took a moment to find the right words and turned around.

"You have cut enough for now, dear. You can stop now. That is enough for today. I would like to talk to you."

Anat sniffed, pushed the darned onions away, and, with a smile, came up to the window for fresh air.

Bennu asked, "Anat, how is that man you are dating?"

"What?" Anat looked up at her mother.

"I know, dear. Now you know that I know. Tell me about him."

Anat took a step back and lowered her head.

Bennu regretted shocking the girl with such a serious question. Maybe she should have begun with a more cautious tone, lady to lady. The girl stared at the floor, sticking out her lower lip as if she had committed a crime and been caught lying.

"You are old enough, dear," Bennu said, trying to smooth over the subject. "And as your mother, I would be glad to hear that a young man is interested in you. I presume a man of your choice." She laid her hand on Anat's shoulder.

Anat cocked her head and began twirling a lock hanging over her ear. She swung to and fro on her hips and, after a pause, cooed with a sideward glance, "Do you really want to know?"

"Of course, I do," Bennu affirmed, turning back to the onions to avoid a stare.

"His name is Harti. He is from the north, Mom. He is decent, helpful, gallant, and all that. I think I am in love. I hope he loves me, too." She sighed. Was it a relief to have spoken out, or was she in despair?

Bennu did not stop to think along these lines. "Fine. But what is he? What does he do for a living?" Bennu faced Anat again with her hands akimbo.

"Oh, he is working for a merchant from the north. He helps the trader in deals, in keeping stock, and so on. Of course, he speaks our language, too. Otherwise, it would have been impossible for me—"

"I am glad to hear he is settled and is earning his bread," Bennu said calmly. "All right. How about introducing him to us?"

"What?" Anat's mouth gaped.

Bennu was slow to realize that she was banging on Anat's door again. This was her second incursion into her daughter's intimate life. But Bennu was the mother, and she could not just wait for the girl's future to unravel as if she were a motherless child. It was Bennu's right to know where her daughter was heading. After all, the relationship between them had always been open. She would have felt put off if Anat had found some pretense to avoid an introduction. She took one step forward.

"Don't get me wrong, Ani. If you are so serious about him, is it not high time you presented him to us? Also, your dad would be interested."

Anat took a deep breath and gulped. "I don't know, Mom. All right. I'll try."

* * *

Bennu wanted to invite the young man for lunch. Rai'a was of a different opinion. For him, this would be too much of an honor for a youth the daughter had just met, even if the child had lost her heart and head. In the first meeting, it was enough to look him up, and if he were agreeable, later on, a social relationship could develop. Bennu felt that Rai'a was not only skeptical about his daughter's choice, in line with the usual stance of "father knows best," but also maybe even jealous, reluctant to acknowledge his child could seek out and see a hero elsewhere. However, she gave in. There would be no great reception bordering on a celebration, only a casual chit-chat, an appraisal of this candidate applying for their daughter's attention. A possible intrusion into their family would remain an unspoken prospect until he was found worthy and accepted. It was their choice, not Anat's.

Although no lunch was called for, Bennu insisted on offering snacks. The variety she prepared amounted to a lunch. She would make her husband happy by avoiding a regular lunch and her daughter happy by offering its equivalent. Good food could bode a good mood.

They lived in a simple house, typical of the dwellings of most citizens. In their case, though, the customary sheltered porch was also the smithy. After crossing this space, the front door opened to the living room at the front. Behind it was the kitchen, followed by a storeroom with a dormitory.

Rai'a was on the porch, his tools scattered on a large table, when Anat and Bennu approached him to introduce the young man. As usual, Rai'a was busy hammering an obstinate piece of metal like a furious father challenged by his rebellious child. He pretended not to hear amid the noise. Then he paused, staring at his victim on the table while listening to Bennu. He nodded and turned his head in dignified slow motion. He acknowledged the visitor with a nod and the trace of a smile and followed them into the house.

On the way, he asked the young man,

"Have we met before?"

Harti said, "No. I don't think so."

Rai'a shrugged. "I just wondered. Somehow, I feel I have seen you before. Never mind."

The young man was offered a stool in a corner, which was pulled next to a chair. He raised his hand and said, "Never mind. The mat will do."

Anat said, "But this stool is for you."

The young man waited until Rai'a took his seat.

After seating himself in his favorite chair, inherited from his father, Rai'a turned to Harti. The latter sat on the stool.

With his hands resting on his knees, the smith bent forward towards the young man and asked with a slight frown, "It is nice to have you visit us. I heard you are not from here."

When Harti mentioned the city Amurru, in the far north, where his mother hailed from, the whole chat got a boost and went off on a tangent.

"Really?" Rai'a's voice grew higher and louder. He could barely control his excitement. "That is great. I know that region. Great people. I have been all over there up in the north."

The young man raised his eyebrows. "Are you not from here?"

"Sure. But I was there as a charioteer in the battle of Qadesh." Rai'a nodded slowly. "That was years ago."

After the improvised lunch, Bennu got up, followed by her daughter. They cleared the table, excused themselves, and went into the kitchen. When they returned after quite a while, they saw the men had left the room. Anat went to the window opening to the porch and called to her mom. They witnessed the two men in an intense chat, or more accurately, a lecture by Rai'a, with the visitor wide-eyed and all ears. The smith was bending over his table, moving the tools around.

"...we were there, right at this spot, bringing up the rear." He was describing a battlefield. "Our pharaoh was ahead of us to the north in his Amun division. Our Ra division was surprised by a massive attack by the Hittites coming from the south. They had crossed the river many hours earlier than expected. Surprised, shocked, and in total disarray, we scrambled to resist and get out of the mess. They had chariots manned by three men, but ours were small and nimble, manned only by two. All the chariots had a common handicap on the uneven ground, which we all abhor. But our chariots were lighter than theirs and could easily wobble and tip over..."

So it went on, with the veteran swinging his arms and even enacting his deadly moves and the noises of the timely defense.

Bennu parted her lips and rolled her eyes. "He is in his element."

"Let him be, Mom. He has no one else to talk to."

Bennu checked herself. She could not tell her daughter that the idea of the invitation was to find out all about the young man and not waste time with old stories of Rai'a and the family to impress him. Bennu had wanted a conversation on a broader scale to know more about the young man, his childhood and family.

Bennu and Anat went out to the porch, stood before the men, and waited. Bennu was pondering how to cut her husband short and move on to the themes of her interest.

At last, her husband paused to breathe. But then the young man stood up.

"It was immensely interesting and informative listening to you, sir," he said. "It gives me plenty of food for thought. I am so glad you invited me, and I feel honored. It was a great moment for me to get to know the cherished parents of dear Anat." He looked at Bennu. "Anat's cherished mother." Then he addressed Rai'a: "Her venerable father. For me, it was a pleasure, indeed. Please do not find it impolite of me, but I have to leave now because my boss will be waiting for me. There is a lot of work to do." He looked again at Bennu and then at Rai'a. In his eyes, there was an appeal for dismissal.

Rai'a smiled and nodded. Bennu stifled a sigh. She blurted out as an afterthought, "Excuse me, young man. You said you speak the language of Hatti. Is that right?"

"Yes, I do," he said with a slight bow.

"Can you also read and write that language?"

"Of course, yes. My mother taught me. She is from a region that is now under Hittite control. I have been trained as a scribe for both languages, Akkadian and the Hittite tongue."

"I ask because the queen has received a message in a language she cannot decipher. Can you help her with that?" Bennu asked.

The young man raised his eyebrows, his eyes wide open. "Did I hear right? The queen, milady?"

"Yes. You may not know that I am her majesty's lady-in-waiting. I'd like to be of some help to her."

Rai'a butted in. "Wait, Bennu. Would she trust a stranger?"

"She trusts *me*," Bennu shot back, fending off the interruption. She turned back to the young man. "And I trust *you*. Tell me whether you can do it."

The young man shifted his weight and pressed his lips together. As the suspense mounted, he took a deep breath.

Finally, he said, "It will be a great honor and delight for me to have an audience with the cherished queen. If she permits, I will do my best and be of service to her majesty. If the language is, indeed, in one of the languages I mentioned."

Anat left with the young man to accompany him to the street corner.

Bennu hoped the visitor had not been exaggerating when he had said he knew the Hittite language and could even read it because he had been brought up near the border. She had noticed how he had been a bit upset when asked to prove his mettle.

Rai'a watched the pair with one hand resting on his anvil. It was his customary pose for contemplating at his workplace.

His wife stepped up to him and prompted, "Mmmmm?"

"The young man is all right." Rai'a drummed his fingers on the anvil. "I should say, I find him impressive. At least on the surface. He seems to be a mature and steady fellow, not one of those idlers everywhere on the prowl for girls. He is well informed, interested, and can get on with one and all."

"And a good listener," Bennu mocked, "to the stories of your youth. Yet I suspect there is something queer about him. He is full of contradictions. I believe that he is a scribe and can speak and write two languages, but at the same time, he has the physique of a soldier. In addition, he dresses with taste and has the grace and manners of a nobleman."

"Don't be silly, dear. All scribes are not alike."

"He is too smooth and polished. There is something sinister about him. Are all those people from the north like that?"

"Not at all." Rai'a shook his head. "They are just like us, I should say. If he were not so polished and well behaved, you would be complaining about how our daughter picked up a wayward loafer, a street urchin, or a village bumpkin."

"I don't know, dear. I have my hunch. He seemed to be a bit upset when I asked him to come to the queen to read out a private message. I hope it was not a mistake on my part. There are all kinds of aliens prowling in Kemet, I hear."

"You and your imagination." Rai'a chuckled. *Women!* "Do not see ghosts and devils everywhere. He was, indeed, surprised at your sudden request. He probably felt it was too much of an honor for a youth to be asked to meet the queen, let alone be of service to her. Tell her majesty what you know and, if you like, share your views. Let her decide. She has her own way of finding out the truth. As for now, I think you are only a bit jealous of having to share your daughter's affection with a stranger. It may also be because you like him, too." He grinned and winked at his wife.

Bennu let that taunt pass. But she was not to be silenced. After a pause, biting her lip, she shrugged and said, "I don't pretend to be wise, but I do have a hunch. Did you see how he sat on the stool, his back bolt upright, his knees together?"

"That was out of respect. Just because he is a scribe, do you think he ought to drop to the floor, squat cross-legged, roll out a papyrus sheet, and begin painting funny figures on it? You are prejudiced. You can never tell a scribe from his appearance. Can anyone tell by my appearance that I am a smith?"

"Sure." Bennu chuckled. She cocked her head away from him and threw him a sideward glance. She puckered her lips and squeezed his biceps. Rai'a laughed and slapped her bottom.

Bennu screamed, "Wow!" and covered her mouth.

Anat was in view.

* * *

Only the day before meeting the young man from Hatti, while cleaning up the queen's chambers, Bennu had noticed the clay tablet lying on the table in the same position in which the scribe had left it. She had picked it up and dusted it off with respect, cleaned the table, and put it back to rest. Poor thing. After traveling all this way, it had made it to the palace and the hands of the queen but to no avail. There it lay, in a strange land, unread, ignored, and dispirited, a bold soul holding its secret. The scribe Ife had not yet found anyone up to the challenge. With her offer of a solution, Bennu hoped to be of more help to the queen than just as a stewardess with the usual routine chores.

A few days after meeting Harti, Bennu was rid of all her doubts but one. The youth was a cultured and intelligent fellow, all right, and Bennu was sure he would know how to conduct himself respectfully before the queen, but still, she had doubted he would really be up to the task. On her request to prove his mettle, he had hesitated but not backed off. Maybe, as a mere scribe for merchants, he had been overwhelmed at the thought of having an audience with the queen, the most powerful woman in the world.

The man could have been boasting to impress the family. Any young man tends to boast to impress, all the more so if the listeners happen to be the parents of his girlfriend. Most youths have this tendency. At that age, Rai'a had been no exception. She remembered him as a loudmouthed braggart concealing his insecure soft heart. But now Anat's friend had to face the challenge and deliver.

Her majesty knew her daughter, but now Bennu had found a way to introduce the girl's choice, that young man who had stolen her daughter's heart and even that of her husband. But now she hoped to hear a second opinion about the match, a regal verdict.

Bennu picked up her daughter and the friend at the palace gate. After leading them to the reception room, she asked them to sit down on a mat and wait for the royal hostess. The queen had met Anat a few years ago, but this time, she would be seeing her as a grown-up lady.

Bennu instructed Anat and Harti how to conduct themselves before her majesty. She gave them tips, like not to sit down unless offered a seat, to always look at the queen when being addressed and when addressing her, and never to interrupt. Two more important instructions were not to leave her majesty's company unless dismissed and even then, to take three steps backward before turning around. It was not courteous to turn one's back abruptly on royalty. Bennu could be an exception, for many of these rules did not apply to the lady-in-waiting.

On her final "Any questions?" the young man, who had patiently listened with a smile hovering over his lips, said, "Yes, please. How do I address her? How does one address a queen of two kingdoms who dons a double crown? I think it is called the *pshent?*"

"That is right. You address her with *Hem-etj*, which means 'your majesty,'" Bennu answered. "But you do not have to use the phrase every time you speak to her."

In her view, the kids were now groomed and ready.

* * *

Seated on her favorite throne, covered with decorative silk, Queen Nefertari practiced on her reed flute. Usually, she would play only at set times of the day, but of late, she had begun picking up her favorite instrument on a whim. The melodies were always melancholic, but that was her taste of style in music.

When she settled for a break, Bennu hurried up to and said, "The young man has come to translate the message, milady. Anat is also with him."

Nefertari looked at her and put the flute to the side. "Oh, yes. Show them in, both. I have not seen little Anat for so long."

She rose and followed Bennu to the reception room. The two visitors greeted her in silence with deep bows. She welcomed them with the casual greeting, "*Ii-wey*," and gestured for them to sit on two simple chairs on the other side of the room. These seats were offered only to the queen's immediate associates, like her scribe and the shaman. She made an exception this time to please Bennu. Nefertari seated herself on the throne. Bennu closed the door and lingered, standing as usual.

The queen greeted Anat in a gentle manner and said to Bennu, "Your daughter has grown up to be a dazzling woman, indeed, a beauty. I am sure she is a true gem of the family."

Bennu smiled and bowed. Anat pressed her lips together and blushed.

The queen made some remarks about the last time she had seen the girl. Then she turned to the young man. The youth was seated with an erect posture. His hands were delicate and not used to hard work, typical hands of a scribe. She noticed his eyes were alert and met hers all the time, unlike the usual furtive gaze of others as their eyes sought the solace of the ground. He seemed to be looking at her as an equal, but it was not disrespectful. She liked it.

"Young man, I hear you speak our language and are in a position to read Hittite scripts, too. How do you have that knowledge? Can you explain?"

As a scribe, he was well versed with Akkadian. He said his mother came from the far north, near Amurru, which was now a vassal state of the Hittites; his mother knew the language of that kingdom, and he owed his knowledge to her. Nefertari found the background a bit unusual, but she did not broach the subject.

She smiled and offered them refreshment besides plain, cool water. It was quite an honor for the young guests, but the queen was being considerate because she had known Anat ever since the girl's childhood. Bennu was beaming with excitement. She served the drinks. Then Nefertari turned to business. She strolled to the table in the corner and brought the clay tablet to Harti.

Without handing over the document to him, she held it before his eyes, covering the lower half with her hand, and asked in an earnest tone, "What do you make of this script?"

After a quick look, Harti said, "*Hem-etj*, your majesty. It is in Nesite, the Hittite language, written in the same script used for Akkadian."

"I thought as much." She withdrew the document. "I must remind you this is a private but royal message. That much, I could make out. Therefore, I need you to swear confidentiality. I allow Bennu and Anat to be witnesses, as they have my confidence, but I do not know you."

"I have made my oath to be a scribe, but if you wish, I can swear again by divinity."

"By which god?"

"I swore by Ishhara, Goddess and Queen of the Oath."

"Oh." Nefertari raised her eyebrows. Gradually they descended to form a frown. After a pause, she smiled and added, "Your ready answer convinced me. You have my trust. Now, take a look." She gave the tablet to him.

After allowing sufficient time, she asked,

"Who is the author?"

"It is from Puduhepa, the queen of Hatti."

"I had guessed as much. Now, translate it for me."

The young man read aloud, pausing now and again, "I, Puduhepa, the Great Queen of the land of Hatti, speak to my sister Naptera, the Great Queen of the two kingdoms of Kemet, to thank you for the kind message inquiring about the well-being of our land, my family, and myself. I pray to the gods for the well-being of your kingdoms, your family, and your health.

"I write this to inform my dear sister to help our relationship progress without any impediment. The object of this message is to let you know in advance of a possible request that my husband, the Great King of the Hittites, may be posing to your venerable Great Pharaoh Ramesses of Kemet.

"It has come to the ears of my beloved husband that his deposed nephew Urhi-Tesub, calling himself Mursili the Third, has fled with his son to one of your lands. The fugitive may soon request the pharaoh for asylum. I take the freedom of our mutual trust to let you be forewarned, fearing tension developing between our lands.

"In order to thwart any mischief by the fugitive and have the matter of throne succession be settled once and for all, my husband proposes to send a request to the Great Pharaoh for repatriation of the fugitives, namely the erstwhile king and his son Hartapu."

He broke off without reading further. Nefertari noticed his hands were shaking. He licked his lips.

"What is the matter?" Nefertari asked. Her mood had changed from anxious to worried.

She stepped forward. "I notice you are upset at this point. The name mentioned after the king is that of the crown prince Hartapu. Isn't that right?"

The young man nodded.

"And your name is…?"

"Yes, your majesty." He rose slowly, raised his chin, and said, "I am Hartapu, the prince mentioned here. King Mursili is my father."

Nefertari heard Bennu gasp and caught a glimpse of Anat, whose eyes were wide open. A long silence ensued.

The queen broke the stillness. "When you mentioned the goddess Ishhara, I realized you were a Hittite. You ought to know we recognize all gods. In the name of the goddess and all that is holy to you, let me hear again. Are you really the crown prince of the kingdom of Hatti?"

"What shall I say, your majesty?" The man's lips drooped. "I swear it is true. Yes, a crown prince with no hope of a crown, the son of a king now without a throne." He looked straight at her with swollen chest despite his despair.

After another pause, Nefertari asked, "If that is true, were you lying to me before?"

"No, *hem-etj*. I would never lie to you. I do come from the far north, and what I said of my mother is totally true. She was a *hasawa*—a Hittite priestess and healer—originally from Amurru, which is now a vassal of Hatti. She passed away a few years ago, may our gods bless her soul." He paused and swallowed. "I am a Hittite and was qualified as a scribe, which is not uncommon for people of royal heritage in our land. I swore before our goddess Ishhara. Now in exile, living incognito, I labor as a scribe without revealing my identity to anyone, not even my employer. But I have never lied to anyone." His glance swept over Bennu and Anat.

"Are you sure you told us only the truth?" Nefertari asked again, bending forward, her stare fixed on his eyes.

"Yes, your majesty. Maybe not the whole truth. I had to guard my identity. We are being pursued by sleuths from Hatti."

"The message is from Puduhepa, your own grand aunt, married to your father's uncle, who ousted your father and usurped the throne. If you are what you say, I assure you that you need not fear the least here. We do not have sleuths in the palace. But again, you may be only claiming to be the prince. Can you *prove* it?"

The young man swayed, pursed his lips, and, after a pause, said in a low voice, "I wish I could. I had a ring with the royal seal, a signet ring from my father, but…"

"But what?"

The young man dropped his head for the first time and fell silent. Then he slowly turned his head toward Anat but remained silent. She raised her eyebrows, pointed to her chest, and shook her head. Then she reacted. She drew out her necklace and held out the ring attached to it.

"Is that the one?" she asked in a shaky voice.

"Yes, it is," Hartapu said after a quick glance at it. "I dropped it into a basket at the smithy, for I was being pursued. After that, the first time we met in the market, you were wearing it on your finger."

The queen scrutinized the ring with the necklace still in Anat's hand and compared the design with the royal seal on the clay tablet. She let go of the chain and went to the table to pick up the envelope and look at the insigne on it.

"They match. Now we need a clear explanation, the whole story leading to your dropping your precious ring in such a sinister fashion."

The young man felt encouraged by the queen's benign smile instead of a reprimand. He let it out.

A year ago, he had escaped Hattusha, the capital of the Hittite kingdom, ahead of his father and reached Per-Ramesses, the new capital that the present pharaoh had built in the Gizem region of the Eastern Nile delta. He had found an occupation as a scribe. His father had arrived much later with his entourage and was now residing somewhere in Gizem.

On his birthday, Hartapu wore his cherished family ring in memory of his deceased mother. At his stall, he noticed a trader from the north chatting with someone at the next booth. Then he watched this man go over to a comrade, speak, and throw his glance at Hartapu twice. He must have noticed the ring. Haratpu walked away, removing the ring from his finger, but then he noticed he was being pursued. Increasing his pace, he came to the smithy and had to decide to take one of the two ways at the fork. He pretended to stumble, dropped the ring into the basket, and rushed away. The two men chasing him never got him, for he sprinted to a wall, jumped over it, ran through a shop, and exited at the rear.

"I can understand your fear of being detected. You are here without any guards, shelter, or aid. But do you really fear being attacked or abducted in this region, so far away from your land?" the queen asked.

"Yes, now I do," he said

"Do you need protection?"

"Your majesty, I thank you for your kind concern. I have been warned that my uncle Hattusili has stretched his fingers to the Lower Kingdom. I can well imagine he wants us eliminated. But I have managed to be on my own so far. I do hope I can look after myself with the grace of our gods."

Nefertari looked at Bennu and Anat.

"Can I count on you to keep the young man's identity confidential, a total secret? Do not pass this on to anyone for any reason. Nor should anyone get a glimpse of the signet ring."

Both women replied in one voice, "Yes, of course."

"I repeat," the queen said. "This news remains here within these walls until I find out a way to help the prince. From now on, this news is to be deemed a state secret, not just a personal one. Do you understand?" she repeated, raising her voice. The women nodded.

She turned to Hartapu. "This message is a few days old." She tapped the tablet. "Anyway, I will have to pass it on to the pharaoh and warn him of what is to come. If your uncle has not reached out to him already with an official request for extradition, I will get in touch with you soon. In the meantime, rest assured we in Kemet do not believe in refusing asylum, much less to the royals of another country."

Hartapu bowed his head and thanked her with the customary words, "*Dewa netjer en etj!* I thank good for your favor."

Nefertari was impressed by his etiquette. She nodded. "Of course, our court will not be interested in getting involved in the family matters of Hatti, but again, when there is a formal demand for extradition against a formal request for asylum, this becomes a dilemma demanding a foreign policy decision."

She paused and then added, "It is an irony that, at my behest, you divulged this message, which is detrimental to your own safety. Neither you nor I knew what was on the tablet. I am obliged to you; the next time, I will not forget to receive you in an appropriate manner."

Hartpu translated the rest of the text, which was the usual concluding salutations, and then the purpose of his visit had reached its end.

"*Em heset net Hathor*. Be in favor with Hathor." With this remark, Nefertari ended the audience.

* * *

Anat and Hartapu walked out of the palace, quiet and sullen, each one in their own thoughts. They were escorted by two palace guards up to the exit. After passing through the gate, they headed towards their favorite spot, under a sycamore tree offering its shade and silence. It was a favorite place for lovebirds to hold hands, dream, or mend fences. With the tree as a host, offering its welcoming shelter and a cool place in a vast area, each couple could sit far enough away from others. Yet whispering was the norm. Voices raised meant demeanor hazed.

They reached the spot and sat on a mound of bricks that someone had arranged to serve as a bench. Ever since the audience with the queen, Anat had worn a deep frown.

Hartapu yearned to know what was on her mind. He prompted a chat: "Now, Anat, dear, you know my true identity."

Anat nodded. Her lips quivered. "And I know the reason you approached me. But for the ring, you wouldn't have wasted your time on me. Am I right?" She turned to him and fixed him with a stare. Her eyes glared. There was fury in her voice.

She fumbled in her bosom, drew out the necklace, pulled it over her head, and began detaching the ring from it. "Here, you have it."

"No, dear. It is yours." Hartapu raised his hands in protest. "I presented it to you, and I am sure you like it. Please keep it."

"What should I do with it? It is your cherished family property. I do not want to have anything to do with it. You did not present it to *me*. You threw it into a basket. That is all. I was only meant to be an involuntary custodian."

Hartapu took a deep breath. "I admit to that. I needed somewhere to hide it and did not even know to whom the basket belonged. But believe me, after coming to know you…well, you are too furious to listen, Anat. But I want to say…" He nudged a little closer.

"What more do you want to say? Has there not been enough talk?" She got up.

"Listen." Hartapu caught her hand and looked up at her, almost kneeling. "Now that I am so…so fond of you, I am glad the ring is where it really belongs. I mean to say, it is near your heart."

"Nonsense." She raised her chin, wriggled her hand free, and looked away.

"I do not know what you feel for me, Anat," Hartapu pleaded. "I can only say I am in love with you. In my heart, you already belong to my family, and the ring was ordained by the gods to be brought to the right place."

"Whatever." She looked down at him and lowered her voice. For the first time, the frown had vanished. But her eyes glittered. "Don't think you are the only person with sincere feelings. Have you asked yourself why I ever cared for you in the first place? It was not for the ring. I did not even know—"

In desperation, Hartapu raised his hand and cut her short. "I have thought about that. You knew nothing about me. But you became my friend. You did not care for me just because I am a prince, nor do you now detest me because I am a fugitive. You take me as I am. What more could I ask of you? Now, please do not spoil our dream by returning this token, which is, indeed, a seal of our friendship, of our love. Do wear it around your neck for my sake."

Anat did not budge. She let the necklace dangle in her hand.

"Anat, dear, I love you," Hartpu pleaded further. "I beseech you to do me a favor. Keep the ring where it belongs and show your feelings for me. You took me for what I am, and you conquered my heart."

At last, half a smile appeared on her face. Anat put on the necklace again, stuffing the ring down into its nest.

For Hartapu, that act was proof of her unspoken love. In the hug that followed, he sensed her melt in his arms with an almost audible sigh.

* * *

After the young pair had left, Nefertari noticed Bennu hovering in the background, hoping to hear some compliments about her daughter and maybe even an opinion about the young man, now revealed to be a prince. Nefertari could feel the need and anxiety of the mother: Anat was Bennu's only child after she had gone through miscarriages.

"Anat has grown up to be a beautiful girl, indeed, Bennu," the queen said, giving her honest opinion.

"Oh, thank you, your majesty." Bennu beamed and bowed.

"Moreover, she is growing up to be a polished woman, thanks to her upbringing. Pass on my compliment to her father as well. One day, she may begin working for me, too."

"Oh, really, milady? That would be an honor for our family."

Nefertari noted a lack of enthusiasm in Bennu's tone. She was neither cheerful nor deep in thought.

"Do you have other plans for her?" Nefertari asked.

"What shall I say? She has lost her head and heart."

"Of course, she will have other ideas and designs than what her parents plan." Nefertari still did not understand Bennu.

Bennu explained, "It is true that every girl at that age dreams of finding the prince of her life, milady, but look at my daughter. She has found one hiding and, on the run, a prince of our enemy. This is not an occasion to be joyous and to rejoice."

Nefertari gulped and winced. As for the status of the groom, it had been no different in her own case. She had also dreamed of marrying a prince. She had been a commoner, too. Her family had always wrongly claimed they were descendants of the pharaoh Ay of the previous dynasty so that she could qualify as a bride of royal descent, not only of nobility. But there had been no concrete evidence to prove their royal origin

It was, indeed, a paradox. A person of royal origin, a prince, ought to be Bennu's ideal future son-in-law. Even a commoner would have been accepted by her. Could she not accept one who was no more a prince, not even a prince of the enemy? Was this a reason to disdain a groom? Strange demands, a mother could impose on her daughter. How did she deal with her own daughters? She did not pause to get into those stories.

"Do not think only of what he is, Bennu, nor of his present situation. Think of his character and sincerity. What counts is that he maintains his composure and is guided by true love to your daughter even in these days of anonymity and misery."

Bennu clasped her hands. "I can only hope the love between them lasts forever and neither one disappoints the other. Whatever the gods may will, I fear the loss of our child to a prince of yesterday." She walked to the dressing room, her voice trailing off.

Nefertari turned her attention to her own problem. What really bothered her, even overwhelmed her, was the foreboding involvement of her kingdom after Puduhepa's message.

She was well acquainted with the ways and means of different people with different motives vying for attention and sole acceptance. After all, that was, in essence, also true of palace life, with its gossip, scandals, intrigues, and vanity, cultivated and fostered by bored ladies with idle brains, who languished in luxurious quarters granted by uxorious monarchs.

But now she was viewing a case in emergence, through a door opening to politics, even geopolitics. One could say there was fundamentally no big difference between politics and a family squabble, but in this case, the stakes were high, enormously high. This case was neither just a distant family drama nor the personal tragedy of a king losing his throne and being tossed onto the street. It was a lot more. It involved two major powers in the world, each with its own vanity and fear of loss of face. This affair, if not handled carefully by both sides, could lead to war. If what queen Puduhepa had written should materialize, the pharaoh would have to go looking for the fugitive king, arrest him, and send him back to Hatti, or else, what next? War and loss of lives on both sides?

Was she an alarmist? But again, why had the gods wanted her to be involved, perhaps even become a pivot in this affair? Was it not more than just an irony that the message sent from Puduhepa had waited for days until that queen's nephew's son had come up in all innocence and read out to her that he was one of the men wanted by the present king of Hatti, had, in essence, read out his own search warrant?

How dare the uncle Hattusili topple the crown of his nephew, who was the rightful successor of Hattusili's brother? Family affairs were now affecting two kingdoms. She felt the young man and his father deserved protection no matter what the father had done to get ousted from his throne. The prince reminded her of her husband at that age. Only her dear "Shishi" had been chosen and blessed by the gods to be the pharaoh. He had even proved his worth to the world by the miraculous way he had fought and survived the Hittite onslaught.

She could not just pass on the message and turn back to her easygoing life, telling herself that affairs of state, war, and peace were matters left to men. She would reveal only the message, which was a warning for Kemet, but she would not mention meeting the crown prince. That event would remain "within these walls," as she had demanded of the others.

Devotional by nature and education, the queen approached the figurine of goddess Hathor and sought divine counsel. She cast her glance on the solar disk on the figurine's head, representing Ra, the ultimate authority. She closed her eyes in silent prayer, seeking inspiration.

In her fantasy, she saw a parallel. Goddess Hathor was the sky deity supporting the sun god Ra in his daily travel across the sky from east to west. Hathor represented femininity, incorporating joy in life as well as violence and fury against evil. She also represented love and maternal care. Even the natives of foreign regions, like Sinai and Cana'an to the north, Nubia to the south, and Punt to the east, along the Red Sea, venerated the goddess. Likewise, with Ramses representing the supreme authority over a part of humanity on earth, Nefertari was the spouse to support him in his rule. She had been blessed by the goddess with six healthy children. Now the queen was being prompted by Hathor to direct her motherly instinct towards all humanity and not only her own children.

She began praying. After a few long breaths, she felt Hathor's palm on her head and imagined hearing the goddess's voice: "It will turn out all right. Do not worry, but decide."

She made the decision: she would protect all, not only her subjects in her realm, even strangers at the door and beyond. This resolve derived from her own reflection and, confirmed by the goddess, would not be deterred by other opinions. She would visit the shrine of Hathor in the newly built temple complex of Amun.

She called for Bennu.

Chapter 3

A Challenge

Bennu was an open-minded soul and could never keep a secret. She was highly charged with the knowledge about the identity of Anat's groom as the prince of Hatti. Though alarmed at first, she had later become elated at the thought of her daughter being courted by a prince. But having promised the queen not to reveal the news to anyone, she took this secret to heart even with regard to her own dear husband, whom she had never kept a secret from in her life. Did a promise to the queen favored by the gods have priority over her loyalty to her husband? After all, this concerned his daughter, too.

But she could imagine what a ruckus it would cause when Rai'a should come to know. It would be a family crisis. As of now, she hoped the situation would resolve itself and go away somehow, like a dark cloud swept by the wind or a bad dream on waking up. It could be mere calf love.

After restless nights, she chose a middle road, beseeching the gods to understand and hoodwinking both the regal and conjugal snakes slithering around her feet. She had reached out to her brother, her eternal friend and counsel. On that occasion, his reaction was as quiet as expected. In fact, he had no reaction at all. He was also saved by the interruption of her husband calling out to her from the smithy.

Yet, for her, the secret revealed was of a burden relieved.

Today her brother was visiting her for another exchange of thoughts on this matter. She was alone at home. Rai'a was away to another part of the city to deliver some articles, and Anat was spending the day with a girlfriend.

Her brother stood at the door with his benign smile.

"Come in, dear," Bennu called out. "There is nobody else at home. We can talk freely."

He sat on the mat nearby.

She said, "Wait," and went into the kitchen. On return, she halted at the kitchen door, holding a plate with a specialty she had prepared for him: sweets of honey and nuts rolled into balls, the "honey-balls" for which their mother had been famous in her locality.

"Oh, that is great! Delicious!" her brother shouted on only seeing them. He had not even tried them. Anyway, they were his favorite sweets, and she knew none could beat their mother when it came to their quality. For him, she hoped hers were the second best.

"The way our mother used to make?" he asked.

"Yes, of course."

"I wondered when you came with the plate. I smelled that great fragrance. It was mother's secret."

"Rose oil. A fragrance she used only for this dish."

She brought the plate to him. As he reached out to grab a ball, she snatched the plate away and giggled.

"Not so fast, dear. Wait." She put the plate on a small table and brought it to him with a decorum worthy of the memory of their mother.

After a small chit-chat, she turned again to the matter aflame in her heart. He listened attentively without interruption, keeping his mouth otherwise busy.

"As I told you last time, dear Bennu," he replied in his usual cheerful tone, "do not worry for the future of Anat. She is a grown-up girl and knows what she wants. I do not have any opinion of her groom. I have not met him. I do not have any first-hand information. You will understand that I can only maintain a neutral position."

"But we cannot sit with our hands in our laps. The situation could get worse."

"Worse for whom, dear? The worst case would be if he is a sorcerer and seducer and drops her for another girl. We can only warn her of this possibility, but we know love makes a person blind. Nevertheless, I could talk to her on this subject. Would that help?"

"It is our responsibility to protect her. She is a child exposed to a cruel world, and even her father is in the dark. To that extent, I have made her an orphan. You are my only hope. You ought to be equally concerned. You have abilities I do not, and she may listen to your advice, not mine."

Her brother had been her only pillar of hope after their parents had passed away. She had been six, and he had been twelve. All her life, he had been her guardian and counsel, the only one to whom she could turn at any time of indecision or distress. As a child, Bennu had admired her brother's gift of smelling secrets, even in games like hide and seek and searching for hidden items. The quality she cherished in him most was his insight into other people's characters and intentions, easily detecting any trickery, however harmless it might be. He had even encouraged her to marry Rai'a and talked her husband into moving to this new city where he lived. But now she was reluctant to beg him to investigate her own daughter and her boyfriend. It could not be done.

The brother spoke after a lapse. "I am Anat's uncle and shall support her choice, even if her man is a prince from our enemy land. It is character that counts. Does it really matter that Anat and her groom are from different lands and pray to different deities? Two hearts meet, and two lives want to unite. It is for them to decide, to agree or to disagree."

There was a long silence.

She was observing him. Talk and persuasion would not help. She tried to read his mind. She waited.

He sat there, motionless. He pressed his lips together and sighed.

"What else is on your mind? Speak out," she said. "Don't start playing hide and seek with me!"

"Give me some time, dear."

That was it. But something was better than nothing.

She stretched out her hand, stroked his, and said, "You are my only friend."

* * *

The next morning, after breakfast, Nefertari had a few minutes alone to share private life with Ramses. The hour of breakfast and soon thereafter was the customary time for any private talk, mostly involving the big family. Officially addressed as Usermaatre Setepenre Ramesses Meriamon, to her, the pharaoh had been Shisi since her early youth, even before marriage. This was the only time of the day when Shishi would reserve his time for private matters, with his mind being reminded after a night's repose that his private life was as important as his multiple duties and busy schedule as pharaoh. He was approachable and thankful for any suggestions from his dear queen. He was a good observer and a good listener.

This time, even before any cursory talk, Ramses bent towards her and asked, "What is on your mind, dear? I noticed after breakfast, when the servant left us while clearing the plates, that you opened your mouth to say something but then bit your lip and did not speak out. What is worrying you?" He stroked her cheek. "Tell me."

"You can read my mind and my face, dear. You are right." Nefertari felt obliged to share her news. She told him about the message she had received. She did not mention the appearance of the crown prince yet. Consequently, she did not bring up the delay in having it read and translated.

After she finished, his forehead wrinkled, and his boyish face cast the customary officious shadow. "I have not yet heard anything about such fugitives in our land. I know what is going on over there in the Hittite kingdom, but that is a palace intrigue, a power struggle, an internal affair among relatives. But the message from the queen is interesting. If it has some basis, we will be involved in this matter."

He smiled and placed his hand on hers. "Meritmut, I invite you to stay on for the usual conference we have now. You can present this message there. Let us see how our vizier reacts to the possibility. The vizier will be giving a provisional report of the situation in Per-Ramesses, this time also representing Amun-her. The next time, Amun-her will also attend the conference for a personal report."

Amun-her-khepeshef was their first son and heir to the throne. As the general of Lower Egypt, he was the chief commander of the troops guarding the northern border.

Nefertari said, "I hear our son proved his mettle and bravery as a warrior in the last campaign in the north and the conquest of Dapur. He reminds me a lot of you, Shishi." She smiled and stroked his cheek. "He has the same kind of fire in his eyes and power in his gait. I know that narrow escape near Qadesh was for you—"

"Ah." Ramses leaned back and waved his hand. "Forget it. Past is past."

Nefertari could swear this was not the case. Shishi had, indeed, escaped death by a narrow margin, and she thanked the god Amun for it to this day. But as a consequence of that ambush, the word Qadesh had become an obsession for him.

She knew the truth about the story. In that battle, he successfully repelled the Hittite army, which had retreated to the east across the river Orontes. However, Qadesh was defended well with a mighty fortress and could not be taken without a months-long siege. For such an enterprise, Ramses had not prepared in advance. Heeding his reason, he had returned unscathed but empty-handed. The phraraoh's valor in survival was not in question, but the battle had led him nowhere. Back home, the result had been claimed to be a victory and celebrated as such. The present king of the Hittites, Hattusili, had been the commander-in-chief, and Ramses had a score to settle with him. He wanted to build up the military strength in the new city as a deterrent and a launching base for his own attacks.

"Now, for Amun-her," Ramses said. "He is doing well as commander, but we are a long way off from building enough forces in Per-Ramesses for any serious defense, not to mention assault. As a youth, he is impatient."

Like you at that age, Nefertari thought.

"Where is the meeting?" Nefertari asked after a break. "In the 'war room'?"

Ramses laughed and said, "Yes. In the small audience chamber."

The royalty knew well the nickname the personnel had given this special room. It was used only if a highly confidential audience was given by the pharaoh or a very small group came together to confer. It had gotten the nickname from the large depiction of Mantu, the war god, posted on the wall in the interior.

A servant came in and stood at the door, robbing them of their privacy. The intimate hour was over. The curtain was up. Ramses took the hint, sighed, and got up to stroll towards the door. Nefertari followed.

It was a long walk along the corridor of the spacious palace all the way to the other wing. However, it was not monotonous. It was a pleasant stroll indoors, with much to behold. The walls were decorated with floral designs in brilliant colors, like a combination of blue cornflower, sunflower, and scarlet poppy, intermingled with the bright yellow fruit of the persea tree. The ceiling was decorated with flying birds, mostly imitating nature, though at times stylized. Even for the inhabitants used to the interior, there was always something to arrest their eyes as in a museum, meant to calm the nerves and heighten joy, sometimes also to offer a springboard for deeper contemplation.

Ramses, a head taller than Nefertari, walked as usual to her left, adjusting his pace to hers. Two guards followed them, many paces behind. Servants and slaves on their way stopped, bowed, and waited at the sides of the corridor until the pair had passed them.

The entrance to the conference room was conspicuous, with tall pillars decorated with images of papyrus flowers at the top and bottom. In the recess between them, two heavy cedar doors were set, bordered with dark wood. The doors were carved with designs suggesting a hunting scene. They were not as tall and lofty as others leading to more representative rooms and halls. Therefore, the two guards who opened the door did not appear as diminutive as they would have before other entrances. The doors were meant to usher the entrant to an enclosure for intimate and secret conferences of great import to the kingdom. They would be firmly closed when the meeting began. The guards would stand outside on call.

On entry, one beheld the life-size painting of the falcon-faced war god Montu, wearing a crown with the sun disk and topped by two feathers. He was associated with the sun god and also known as Montu-Ra, for he symbolized the ferocity of the sunshine destroying enemies to the cosmic order, Maat.

The room was small, though spacious due to its emptiness. The interior was as simple as that of a military tent. There were no distracting articles around. Decorative elements for the sake of representation were not called for here. There was a dais for the throne, as in all rooms for an audience. The closeness of the seating arrangement around the dais suggested intimacy, openness, and shared secrets: this was no room for ceremony and postures. Ramses motioned his spouse to a raised chair. On the opposite side were two more chairs of the same size, all with simple cushions but heavily carved backs and armrests. There was a matching table next to each chair. Ramses strode towards his throne.

Promptly, the servant announced the advent of the *tjatey*, or the vizier, Paser. An elderly man of medium height shuffled in. He wore the simple dress of a wise man, a tunic of plain linen stretching from the chest to the ankles, held by two narrow strips acting as braces that ran up to the shoulder and around the neck. He was bareheaded and wore leather slippers. On seeing the queen, he stopped and raised his dense eyebrows.

After a deep bow to his master and the queen, Paser proceeded to one of the empty chairs and seated himself. He adjusted his tunic and stroked his clean-shaven chin. He was ready for the conference.

Ramses was blessed with a wise and experienced vizier of noble descent from Memphis. He had also served in various high positions, ultimately as city governor and vizier, under Ramses's father, Menmaatre, known as Seti. Ramses had accompanied his father on his expedition to the north in the last years of the latter's reign, and on that occasion, he had gotten to know this man of wisdom and experience. Paser had a multitude of titles, and as a faithful servant to the pharaohs, he had supervised the construction of the tomb of Seti.

After a few cursory remarks about affairs of state, Ramses turned to the question possibly buzzing on the vizier's mind: why the queen was there.

"Before we go into the affairs in Per-Ramesses, I suggest our vizier should listen to what our queen Meritmut has to report." Ramses was sitting with his back erect and hands resting on the armrests. His face was motionless, with only his eyes turning towards his wife.

Nefertari greeted the elderly man with a few words and went into the message she had received from Puduhepa a few weeks ago. It was common knowledge among them that she maintained contact with various houses of royalty in the neighboring countries. Therefore, the reason for her correspondence needed no explanation. She left out details about the language used in the message and her difficulty in finding a transcription. It was the content that mattered.

Ramses threw a glance at Paser and added, "So far, we have not been approached by the new king of Hatti in any matter. Nor has anyone approached us seeking asylum."

Paser nodded. "It may be that Hattusili does no know that his nephew is hiding here and that the latter is biding his time. At any rate, your majesty, how will you respond if Mursili is hiding somewhere in our kingdom and we do, indeed, receive a request from Hattusili for extradition?"

"I have a clear answer. I am not going to comply with his request. This is an issue resulting from an internal matter of the Hittites, the usual case of relatives vying for the throne. It is a family affair in which we do not want to get involved."

"Quite true," Nefertari said.

Ramses turned his head towards her. The queen went on. "It is our policy and tradition never to turn down a person seeking our protection and asylum. We, the cultured people of Kemet, have never done that and shall never do it, be it a commoner or royalty from another country who seeks shelter. Moreover, King Mursili is, in my opinion, the rightful heir to his throne after his father. He has been ousted and may be hiding somewhere in Kemet. We are not going to throw him back to his adversary."

Paser pressed his lips together and nodded.

"What is on your mind?" Ramses asked. "We would like to hear your wise words."

Paser said, "The Hittites do not have a king ordained by their gods, even if they claim that to be the case. As your majesty knows"—he looked up at Ramses— "they fight for the throne, and the stronger one at the moment seizes it. It is a free-for-all among them, with their gods sitting back as spectators. A forlorn folk."

A mixture of sympathy and contempt lingered on his smile, and the corners of his mouth turned down. "Their squabble is not our concern. I see no reason why we should take any sides in this matter. I see no call to action."

After a brief pause, he cleared his throat and added, "Moreover, our queen appeals to human decency on our part. She is perfectly right. If we capture and send the ousted king back to his uncle, that would be his certain death. This is, indeed, a major argument she has brought to our notice."

Ramses stared into the distance. His face was not relaxed, for there hovered a light frown. Nefertari was familiar with this expression: it was a prelude to an announcement. He gave his decision. "I refuse to give Hattusili his nephew's head. I will be of no service to that usurper and mischief-monger." He turned his face away.

Nefertari had hoped for this reaction. Her husband hated the commander at Qadesh, now calling himself a king. She said, "I see we all agree. I presume this stance will be the same, even if the present king of the Hittites were to send a formal request for extradition."

Ramses nodded and clenched his fists. "If there is a request for asylum from Mursili, I am prepared to grant it."

The vizier stirred in his seat. "Once you grant it, your majesty, your word of honor is irreversible, come what may."

"So shall it be," Nefertari asserted, looking into the pharaoh's eyes.

Ramses nodded.

* * *

True to his name Userma'atre'setepenra, which meant "Elect of Ra, the Protector of Balance and Righteousness," Ramses had built a temple to the honor of his patron god, Amun, identified with the sun god Ra.

The temples in Egypt were not always abuzz with devotees. The commoners were allowed entry only on festival days to witness and rejoice in the divine glory in this abode. Instead, temples were meant for royalty to visit the deities. Therefore, the royalty had no need to have the shrine cordoned off for a visit.

The palanquin of Queen Nefertari was lowered before the entry arch. She alighted nimbly without help. The four carriers waited until she had moved seven steps away. Then they carried off the chair in a trot. Two of her personal guards accompanied her up to the arch. The temple guards standing vigil bowed deeply and moved up to her. They helped her remove her leather slippers. Now, reduced to a humble devotee, she walked barefoot with her head bent in reverence. Like the pharaoh, she was divine in the eyes of her subjects, but here and now, she was only a child of the gods, fallible and mortal.

The entry was through the massive pylon, a gigantic arch made of a pair of enormous prism-like pillars, each with four flat surfaces sloping upwards. The surfaces were painted on all sides with colorful figures and hieroglyphs selected not only for their content but also for their aesthetic contribution. They stood out brilliantly in the sunshine, resplendent with rainbow colors ranging from violet and blue to red. In addition, precious stones like lapis lazuli had been added as decoration to shine on the smooth white surface and arrest one's eyes. Gaiety could easily coexist with solemnity.

Before the pylon stood two towering obelisks, one on each side, making the visitor humble and stoop on reflex. The tips of the obelisks were gilded. The four giant limestone statues, two on each side of the arch and with their backs to the outer wall, were impressive but not meant to overwhelm. The figures stood with arms crossed in the common posture of each hand touching the other shoulder. Their crowns were decorated with inlaid work of precious and semi-precious stones as well as gold. Their benign expressions, reddish-brown skin tone, and white clothing made them familiar and endearing to the visitor. The adjoining flagstaffs were also resplendent, as were the standards they hoisted. The bottom of the entry wall was plated with silver, which was more precious than gold, for silver was not indigenous and had to be imported.

After passing the vast, sunlit courtyard, she entered the sheltered hall of pillars, with a ceiling interrupted by skylights offering dimmed lighting. As she neared the Hathor temple to one side of the complex, she could smell myrrh. She heard a gong on this visit. It indicated a worship in progress. In the stillness and solemnity of the surroundings, the sound caused a vibration on the skin of her arms. The goddess was beckoning her in various ways.

On entering the shrine, which was windowless and lit only by oil lamps, she could feel a slight chill for a minute. Although this was her routine monthly visit to the temple, never before had she noticed this sudden shift to a cooler environment. The shaman greeted her with a deep bow. He was his usual self, agile despite his age, dressed in his long, colorful woven garment with brocade borders. To her, he had always been a priest, despite his other designations as shaman and healer. On this occasion, she could not distinguish the roles well enough to say which one would fit for the help she needed.

"You are most welcome, your majesty. For me, it is always an honor to have you visit this shrine and holy abode of Hathor in the temple of Amun. You come at an auspicious moment. I was about to complete the morning prayer, and you can join me in the final phase."

They approached the altar.

A major deity in the pantheon of ancient Egypt, aside from her maternal quality, Hathor represented and promoted art, like dance and music, as well as sexuality. In short, she combined the furious and the gracious qualities of femininity, the vengeful and protective aspects. Hathor was the divine mother of all, like the queen who was the symbolic mother of the subjects, offering them peace, comfort, and solace in times of personal crises. Nefertari had come to seek divine direction and help pertaining to her role as a queen. Her problem concerned the kingdom and mankind.

Nefertari's eyes concentrated on the serene face of the divinity, a friendly face supporting her in her own venture on earth, akin to Hathor's function in the universe. The sun disk on the goddess's crown was encircled by a cobra and supported by two cow horns. The disk was the symbol of the life-giving sun god Ra, the cobra was the guardian of life, and the cow horns symbolized motherhood and fertility.

She raised her forearms and, in adoration, held her hands with the palms turned towards the idol. After a long gaze invoking help and guidance from the deity, she regarded the objects laid around, symbolizing the five elements at the altar: earth, water, fire, air, and space. Before the idol in the middle, a small plant in a pot stood for life, supported by moist mud symbolizing earth and water. On either side were two knee-high bronze oil lamps, each with five wicks. Their flames represented not only the element of fire but also air, causing their gentle sway, as well as space, which accommodated the glow around them.

She fixed her gaze again on the idol for a long while and then closed her eyes in deep prayer. At first, even the silence in the room seemed to vie for her attention, and her mind became distracted for no reason. Gradually, as the thoughts stopped racing one another, she rested in a serenity engulfed by that same stillness.

Opening her eyes after a long while, she took a few steps backward.

Sennefer proceeded towards the idol and spoke out the last part of a long prayer to complete the ritual. He turned around and offered her the blessings of Hathor: a jasmine flower and a drop of honey on a silver spoon. She was to regard, smell, and touch the flower and taste the honey at the sound of a gong in his hand, thus engaging all the five senses with her thoughts fixed on the goddess.

When the ritual was over, Nefertari took a seat and allowed herself to engage in cursory small talk with Sennefer. He was tall but thin. His beardless face, shaved head, and hollow cheeks made him appear emaciated. But his eyes, their borders painted black with kohl paste, gleamed and darted, their glances bird-like. Those vigilant eyes were not the dreamy, half-closed windows to the world typical of the wise and withdrawn. His worldly presence and vigor were that of a young man. He was elderly but youthful, active but thoughtful, solitary but not lonesome. In contrast to other mortals, he seemed to live in both the worlds, here and beyond.

After a few general remarks, Nefertari said, "I have not come in a personal matter, but I have a request dealing with royal affairs. Moreover, I have come on my own and not as a commissary of the pharaoh." She looked around.

"There is nobody here, your majesty."

"Now, please listen carefully." She paused and bit her lip, searching for words. She went into the matter of the fugitive king from the Hittite kingdom, leaving out any mention of her meeting the crown prince. Then she came to her request,

"I know, as a shaman, you are often consulted in matters of the state by my spouse and the vizier."

"Yes, *hem-etj*"

"The pharaoh could simply refuse the request for asylum, comply with the request of king Hattusili, and surrender the fugitive. As an alternative, he could resist the demand and grant asylum. This is a matter where I feel we need advice and guidance."

"I am sure the pharaoh will know best, your majesty. I wonder whether I can be of any service."

She judged his comment was borne of his curiosity; it did not sound like a protest. He was politely asking why she had come to him.

"I must admit, in this humanitarian matter, I feel personally involved," the queen replied. "I am against a betrayal of those who seek our help. Whatever led the fugitive to this result is none of our concern. For us, it is a fact that Mursili was deposed by his uncle. The real reason appears to be a family affair and the usual power struggle among the Hittites."

"That is true, *hem-etj*. They do not seem to have a king ordained by god."

"I am seeking your counsel. With your shamanic access to divinity, could you consult the gods and ascertain which course we should pursue, either to expel the fugitive or grant him asylum? What would be of better interest to our land, our people, and the kingdom, in short, to the general good?"

"In case our pharaoh refuses to comply with the request of the king of the Hittites, would that lead to war?"

"This question has not been posed, but it may arise. As of now, a refusal to extradite would definitely cause tension between the two kingdoms, but I am not sure if Hattusili would make this a reason for war and go beyond rattling his saber. He would not dare provoke us with such action. Anyway, that is my judgment. Lest I should forget to point out, please keep this matter to yourself. I do not want the pharaoh to be influenced yet. I will choose the moment to inform him of any divine indication we may receive."

The shaman lowered his head and stared at the ground for a long while. Then he said, "In such matters, the gods may give us a hint or stay away from any advice. But I can try."

Nefertari arched her eyebrows. He cleared his throat and said, "At first, I thought of presenting this question as a petition for an oracle to the mother goddess at the Hathor festival in two weeks. The usual procedure would be oral. It would be presented before the idol during the celebration and at a chosen spot where the procession stops for a while. The answer would lie in the interpretation of signs sent by the goddess. The last time, I remember, it was the direction of movement of the carrying chair when the procession continued."

The queen nodded. "I have heard of that incident."

"As this matter is highly confidential," the shaman said, "this method would not be appropriate on such an occasion, with the question being posed in public. Nor presenting it in a written form, for it will have to be read aloud. I suggest we hold a separate ceremony here for you alone and present this problem for the divine attention of our goddess, the mother figure who will consider the well-being of one and all. In seclusion and beyond the din typical of a Hathor festival, a clear answer to your question may be heard. Shall we say, next week?"

The queen had one week to do her homework: formulate the question as a simple sentence. It ought to be posed in such a way that it would neither be answered with a simple yes or no nor elicit only a divine blessing as confirmation of her own decision. She had ample time to come up with a reasonable and simple formulation to elicit a clear, or at least comprehensible, response.

Nefertari agreed.

Chapter 4

ORACLE

Sennefer had been a priest in Iunum, or Heliopolis, the city of the sun god. He was highly respected for his multiple qualifications. He was also known for his interpretation of the manifestation of divine powers. As a free priest without any obligations to a traditional system with a hierarchy full of man-made norms, he could be more innovative than his comrades. Nefertari had full confidence in the sincerity of this priest-cum-shaman now in the royal service.

When Nefertari entered the Hathor temple at the appointed hour for the oracle, Sennefer had completed his first worship of the day.

After his salutation and welcome to the queen, he said, "Your majesty, your knowledge about our deities, faith, and culture is immense. Yet, permit me to give some prelude to the ritual that follows by focusing your kind attention."

"Oh, you overestimate my knowledge. I am ready to listen and learn. Go ahead," she said, adjusting her seat, a raised chair placed against the wall. "I must confess I have only limited knowledge in this field. I am also curious as to how you go about this difficult assignment. I have only heard that this practice of appealing for an oracle has something to do with the concept of *heka*, or should I say magic? Will you please explain what that means?"

Sennefer squatted cross-legged on the ground, facing her. He had a serious look, and he took a long breath.

"Heka." He nodded and collected his thoughts. "It is, indeed, the magic of life. Fundamental to our faith, borne of nature, is this principle of *heka*. It stands for the life energy inherent not only in human beings but also in animals and plants, in general, in all 'mortals.' It is the life spirit or radiant consciousness in all beings that guides them to grow, evolve, act, and react to the environment and situations as well to connect with one's own social and cosmic consciousness, in short, with manifest divinity all around. Its intense spirituality incites thoughts and actions in human beings. *Heka* is the life source. It is the breath of life, transforming our imagination into thoughts, deeds, and experience, the process we call creativity. It is the driving force of our soul."

Nefertari paused to understand this stream of a definition and asked, "Is *heka* connected to other concepts I have heard of, like *ba* and *ka*?"

"Good question. I will try to explain. *Heka* is the soul, explicit as the life spirit in the individual. Although the soul is eternal, during our lifetime, it could be seen as being held captive by the body. But this stage is temporal, only as long as life lasts.

"If we take a closer look, we may discern two fundamental facets of this individual spirit or soul in each human being: *Ba* and *Ka*. *Ba* is the distinctive manifestation of the divinity in a living being, making it an individual. Besides this, there is also the life force, *Ka*, surrounding and guarding the life of the individual. On death, the *Ka* of the deceased leaves the body. After funeral rites, *Ba* also leaves the body for good and begins a journey to unite with *Ka* to be transformed by this union into a state called *Akh*. This state is final, enduring, and unchanging for all eternity."

She said, "I have one more question. How are all these concepts related to the state of a medium and the process of receiving oracles? How do you function as a medium for an oracle? Do your mind and soul have a function in this process? Is the mind active, or is it only a conduit, or even just a witness?"

He said, "The ritual we perform today will lead me to a state of mind that is neither sleep nor consciousness. It is not even unconsciousness. It is a different state, an enhanced state of consciousness, with my *Ba* apparently existing outside the body. This transformation or apparent liberation from the body is described as an astral journey or flight out of the body.

"By the way, this is also the condition necessary for the process of healing to mediate between the physical and the spiritual world. Only then is it possible for the healer to evaluate the symptoms of an ailment in an exhaustive way, probing the mental condition and worldly situation of the patient.

"Having reached this state, at times, a shaman might appear to lose control of the body, which may react in a fashion resembling an ecstatic dance. Otherwise, this state may not be perceptible to an onlooker. In this state of altered consciousness, the medium will be only a conduit— by no means a participant or witness—to receive and answer the question raised for the oracle.

"In the process, you will be asked several times in my voice to pose the question. Thereupon, the question will be passed on to the cosmic consciousness where gods reside, and any answer to it will be formed into words intelligible to mankind. My mind or my self will have no say in this matter. I shall be only a venue or medium. This is assured, for, in that state of mind, an individual thought process to influence an answer or modify it with one's own words is not possible.

"However, I beseech you not to speak the question you have prepared too soon, but only when asked. It should not be posed before I have reached the special state. This precaution is needed because, while hearing your question, my mind should not get involved or have any influence. Raise the question only when asked. Until then, just be ready."

He described certain procedural matters and repeated that she ought to keep her question simple, finalized, and ready. Each time she was asked, she ought to speak the same question without any variation.

The answer expressed in the shaman's voice should be clearly noted and remembered by her. After the ceremony, she could dictate it to him, and he would write it down.

The ceremony began when he approached the idol of Hathor and turned to the queen to thank her in a formal fashion, with a deep bow, for choosing him as the medium for her assignment.

He reached for a mug and, with one draught, drained some concoction he must have been sipping all the while. She smelled a waft of herbs she could not identify. Then, seated cross-legged with his hands folded across his chest and his head lowered, he began the ritual with a long prayer in praise of Hathor's maternal qualities, invoking her grace and mercy.

This call to the deity was followed by repetitive chants. Their rhythm grew quicker, leading to body movement beyond his control. He stood up, staggering, swayed his arms, and swung his legs in moves suggesting an ecstatic dance. This went on for a while, and once, when he turned around, Nefertari saw his eyeballs rolling skyward. Then, all of a sudden, he stopped all movements and collapsed back into a squat and stayed in the erect posture of a person in meditation.

After a long time of stillness, she heard his voice, which seemed to come out of a deep well: "What is the question for which you seek a divine answer?"

Nefertari cleared her throat and said, "Should our pharaoh grant asylum to the fugitives from Haiti, the previous king, Urhi-Teshub Murisili, and his son?"

For a long duration, Sennefer went back to a low murmur of prayer, gently rocking. Once again, he asked for the question, and it was promptly provided by the queen, who was alert. This process was repeated once more.

Then there was stillness.

Nefertari waited. She realized the ceremony had come to an abrupt end when he rose, stretched his back, and turned around. With eyes wide open, he bowed to her and asked in his normal voice, "Your majesty, I hope you are not disturbed by the ritual."

She shook her head.

"Did you hear any message?" he asked.

"Yes, I have got it by heart. I heard the answer more than once."

As she told Sennefer the words of the oracle, he raised his eyebrows, absorbing them as if hearing them for the first time. He repeated them slowly for confirmation.

"Let me note it down before we begin any interpretation," he said.

He hurried to a corner of the room where he had set writing material in anticipation of the words of the goddess. All the utensils were laid out on a narrow rectangular wooden plate; one could call it a palette. It carried trimmed brushes, solid soot like kohl, and a cake of ocher for black and red ink, respectively, with water in a pot beside them. He picked up his palette and some ostraca—smooth pieces of broken pottery—and squatted cross-legged on the floor, placing the palette beside him. After adjusting his kilt by pulling it tightly across his knees, he laid an ostracon on it.

Nefertari told Sennefer what she had heard. He painted the message onto the piece, stopping after each word in search of the right symbol for the next. Divine words were sacred and written up in the sacred script, the hieroglyphs. Yet, to be quick, this time, he had used hieratic cursive, the shorthand used by priests.

Nefertari bent forward to cast a look and grimaced.

"Can you read it, your majesty?" Sennefer asked with a smile.

"Yes, but with difficulty." She smirked. "Not enough to refresh my memory."

"Never mind. I will soon have it in the right script for *medu netcher*, the words of god." He bowed, touched the edge of the piece with his forehead, and read the oracle's words aloud: "A wrong king will bring a land to ruin."

* * *

As days passed by, Nefertari heard that Hattusili had, indeed, done what Queen Puduhepa had foretold, asking for the extradition of his nephew

Mursili and the crown prince. It was no surprise for Ramses, who had been forewarned, but he was vexed by the way Hattusili had presented his request. After a cursory formal address, the message from the Hittite did not beseech but demanded in no uncertain terms that the pharaoh search for, find, and expel the fugitives to Hatti. Even a threat of war had been signaled.

In addition to this development, Mursili had proved his presence in Kemet by sending a message through some undisclosed channels, begging for an audience with the pharaoh to apply for asylum. This turn of events called for a decision. A meeting was scheduled for the purpose. Nefertari chose to present the oracle on this occasion, knowing well this would raise a debate.

This time, her son Amun-her-khepeshef would also be attending the conference. Nefertari suspected his assessment of the military situation was called for, with war becoming ever more imminent. The military was divided into two commands, one for Upper Egypt in the south and the other for Lower Egypt in the north. Amun-her was appointed chief commander or general in charge of the northern command, with four divisions. Each division of five thousand men was made of twenty-five companies consisting of two hundred men.

The queen was delighted to see how her son, ever a boy in his mother's eyes, had matured in the recent past, especially after the recent campaign in the north assisting his father. Her son had the same fervor and vigor as his father. With his head jutting ahead on a slender neck and large eyes with a steely stare, he was a copy of his father from his younger days, a chip off the old block. Like him, the prince was all action and not much talk, much less debate, unless it was unavoidable. Then words would flow in a torrent. Shishi had yet to commend him for his qualities. But successful fathers like to set high standards for their sons, demanding and awaiting perfection, forestalling approval forever and forever. Her father-in-law, the pharaoh Seti, had not been different than her spouse.

After some pleasantries and cursory remarks by Paser and the crown prince, drinks were served. Once the servant had retreated and closed the heavy door, the pharaoh initiated the conference.

"We are all aware of the message from Hattusha and the petition of the fugitive for an audience. Before we begin a discussion on this matter, let us hear what our queen Meritmut has to say about the counsel she has sought from the gods."

With all eyes on her, Nefertari took the floor. She went into her initiative in consulting her personal deity, Hathor, about this humanitarian matter of great political import.

She noticed that when she mentioned the shaman, her spouse smiled and exchanged glances with the vizier. Unperturbed, she went ahead and announced the oracle, reading it from a decorated papyrus scroll worthy of the goddess's words: "A wrong king will bring a land to ruin."

She repeated the sentence slowly, pausing after each word.

There was a long silence.

The pharaoh glanced around the room and, noticing no reaction, made the first remark.

"With due veneration to the divine word, I accept the statement as a blessing by goddess Hathor. Let us first thank her for blessing us with her opinion. Yet, without being critical, one could look upon the statement as self-evident. Any king who is not up to his mark will fail his land and, in due course, cause the breakdown of his kingdom and ultimate devastation. We must therefore be careful in interpreting the statement. In the case we have on hand, this true statement points to the usurper Hattusili and tells us not to get involved in Hittite politics. It is a prompt for us to decide on our own and feel free to shelter the fugitives. Let Hattusili lead his land to ruin."

Nefertari sighed.

Paser cleared his throat. The words of the statesman who had served as vizier for so long, even under Ramses's father, Seti, had great weight.

"I highly appreciate the initiative our queen has taken and the way our venerable goddess Hathor has answered her prayers. There is no doubt that we must follow divine advice in such a political decision of great import. As is always the case with an oracle, the goddess wants us to think over, interpret, and understand her advice. But as for your opinion, your majesty"—he raised his heavy eyebrows and looked at the pharaoh— "I beg to differ."

"Go ahead with your view," Ramses replied, and then he added, "We would like to hear the comment of a wise senior."

"In my modest opinion, the oracle is explicit. The only king meant in this context is Mursili. If we harbor this king, one day, the tension between two great powers in this matter could lead to the ruin of a land—even our land. We ought to heed the clear warning and expel the fugitive to avoid any such calamity."

Amun-her grinned. "In other words, throw him to the crocodiles."

Ramses snapped, "I cannot see how this erstwhile monarch Mursili, with no powers or support, could cause havoc in our land. I must make it clear that I have no desire to please Hattusili by doing a favor to him at his behest, much less after the tone he has taken in his message, making it sound like an order. It is audacious."

Nefertari noticed the controlled fury in her husband's eyes.

Prompted by his father's anger, Amun-her scowled and bent forwards. "I can understand our pharaoh's indignation. No pharaoh would take orders from anyone, never from the enemy. With his indolence, if Hattusili is spoiling for war, let him have it. We can take this affair as reason enough to silence the Hittites forever. After all, they have been asking for it all along."

Ramses nodded in support of his son's disdain. "It is not just a matter of vexation on my part. There is a point in what Commander Amun-her says. We owe no favors to that man in Hattusha."

Paser kept calm and smiled, staring into the void. "Turning to our commander's enthusiastic proposal, shall we agree on the point that attacking the Hittite kingdom would be advisable only if we are ready for war?" His eyebrows shot up, and his eyes bored into Amun-her. "*Are* we?"

He paused and stared once again into blank space with a hint of a smile. "Now that our multiple campaigns in the north have not led to lasting success, our next and last one must bring durable results."

He was referring to the two recent campaigns in the eighth and tenth year of Ramses's reign—with Amun-her's participation in the last—both celebrated at home as a victory but of no lasting consequence. The conquered territory of Dapur had reverted to Hittite rule. Coming from the old man's mouth, the undisguised rebuke was accepted as a just assessment.

"Moreover," Paser added, "let us not forget the basic wisdom of statecraft: 'Attack your enemy only after choosing the right moment on your own.'"

Ramses took the hint and pursued the point. "Amun-her, if Hattusili does want war and is provoking us, can we proceed as you suggest, with a massive assault pushing back and pursuing the foe all the way through the terrain of their vassals and to the borders of Hatti and even beyond? Bear in mind, this would mean a sustained effort with prolonged sieges until we reach a final settlement or resolution to our satisfaction. Can you assure us we are ready for such an ultimate military campaign today, right now?"

The young commander shifted in his seat and bit his lip. After a thoughtful moment, he said in a sullen tone, "We are ready to fight. There is no doubt about it. As of now, we can defend ourselves against any incursion by the foe. But a prolonged campaign to the north with the corresponding secure lines for provision of our forces will need a separate plan, including a transfer of troops from the south in addition to new recruits. Conquered territories will also need garrisons to be stationed and duly provided with reliable and secure supply chains. I must admit, as of now, we cannot carry out a successful assault of large scale and duration. We would need at least six months of preparation."

Sensing the drift towards violence, Nefertari forced herself into the debate.

"I look at the oracle differently." A female voice seemed to offer relief and attracted immediate attention.

"As our pharaoh pointed out," she continued, encouraged by the hush, "the king mentioned in the oracle is not Mursili. May I remind our vizier that Mursili is no king at all? He is a fugitive in our land with neither a throne nor a crown to show. Nor is he aspiring to become the king of our land. He is a mere mark on the run, a hapless, cowering prey in the bush. The king meant in the oracle is the present one, Hattusili, who is on the throne. He is the king today, for his position has not been questioned by any other power nor disputed by the gods. He will only weaken his own kingdom, leading it to ruin. Unless we are provoked, we need no belligerent effort to destabilize his realm. Hattusili will cause the fall of his own kingdom. I support our pharaoh in his judgment that the oracle is not a prompt for any military action on our part. We can safely offer the fugitive asylum."

She noticed the stillness in the room as all faces watched her, but no one attempted to protest. She went on. "I understand our pharaoh's indignation at the unworthy demand of Hattusili. It is best to ignore him and let Mursili have an audience."

Then she turned to Paser. "As for war, I appreciate and extend your question about our readiness. I wonder whether Hattusili is ready for war, either. Is his rude tone mere saber-rattling, mere bravado with nothing to show, nothing in store? Could it be a panache, a cover for his own scare? How do we know if this affair of Mursili's flight is reason enough for him to attack us and lose face once again? He may be bluffing."

Paser took a deep breath with his mouth open. Then he smirked, despite his frown, and nodded. "Our queen has raised an interesting point. From here, it is difficult to say what his motives are. We can dig into this aspect after we collect more details about his disposition, not only about his military capability but also his strategy. We can expect some knowledge and expertise in this matter. We should not forget, Hattusili was a celebrated commander and war hero for the Hittites. He reached only a stalemate after the battle of Qadesh against our pharaoh, but even that result is considered a great victory over there."

Ramses grimaced. "The man has lost his head. To be charitable, we could say he is ill-advised. Let us see what our expert has to say in this matter. It is time to call in our chief informant, our spymaster, as I like to call him. He is waiting outside. Perhaps he has more information about this new quarrelsome neighbor who calls himself a king."

Ramses looked at Nefertari, and a teasing smile flashed across his face. "Meritmut, you will be surprised."

Then he cast a glance at his son. Amun-her jumped up and sounded the bronze gong nearby. Without delay, the door opened, and a guard ushered in a man, who entered with a respectful stoop.

Nefertari had to gasp.

After bows to everyone in the room, the man stood at a distance, facing the pharaoh with his hands clasped.

Ramses said, "We welcome our shaman, who is of great service to us not only in his spiritual capacity but in worldly matters." Then he said to the shaman, "We discussed the significance of the oracle of goddess Hathor after our queen Meritmut's petition to the goddess. We thank you, Sennefer, for your assistance in this respect. Now we have an official request."

"Yes, *hem-ek*," Sennefer said. "I am at your service."

"I referred to the oracle by the goddess Hathor. However, the matter now does not pertain to spiritual matters. I count upon you as my eyes and ears in various spheres beyond my physical reach. You have plenty of sources in your informants and your daily contact as a healer with our subjects and even aliens. What news have you heard of late from the Hittite kingdom after King Mursili was ousted and his uncle crowned?"

"Your majesty, I do hear a lot of gossip, as this city is full of Hittites of all sorts, from traders and merchants to displaced persons and vagabonds.

Nowadays, in addition, many subjects loyal to the previous regime are leaving their country out of fear or spite and finding their home here, feeling safer under your gracious and god-blessed shelter than that of their own illegitimate king. There are even defections by senior officials of the previous regime, who fear not only a loss of their office but reprisals and persecution, even torture and death. The ousted King Mursili appears to be still popular in the Hittite land."

"From some confidential channel, you received a request for an audience by King Mursili and forwarded it to us after verification. Do you know where he is right now?" Ramses asked.

"No, your majesty. It is rumored he is hiding somewhere in this city. The Hittite refugees have formed their resistance group, calling themselves the Black Hoods, and are protecting their king in exile. He is believed to be moved from one place to another almost daily. Opposed to that group is a small group of agents of Hattusili. They are operating here, trying to track Mursili and his son, and are called the Red Hoods."

"Another question: what is your take on the military preparation among the Hittites to begin an attack on us?"

The shaman fell silent. He stared at the ground and scratched his temple. He opened his mouth but stayed silent.

"Speak out. What do you know?"

"Nothing much, your majesty. There are all kinds of news abuzz about forthcoming recruitment in Hatti and so on, but I will have to dig deeper before I can pass on any valuable information. In fact, I did not know this point was of particular interest to your majesty right now."

"Never mind. You can go into it now and collect information. Treat this as if it is of primary importance." Ramses paused, threw a glance at his spouse, and said to the shaman, "Moreover, regarding the Hittites, I want you to work closely with our queen, who will guide you on diplomatic matters."

Nefertari gasped. First, she had discovered a re-incarnate spymaster, and now Shishi wanted him to work for her on this international issue. Was this a reward for her engagement?

Sennefer nodded, bowed, and walked backward to leave. As he made his exit, Nefertari asked him to wait for her outside.

Ramses had his final word.

"As of now, I cannot ask the petitioner Mursili to come for an audience. If I do, it would be another way of granting him my word for an asylum. I cannot invite him here and give him hope only to tell him to his face he shall be extradited and, therefore, will not be free from then on. That would be deceitful, the way of a warlord without scruples.

"I am afraid we have to gather more information before I decide. I suggest our queen and the shaman gain a clearer picture of the state of affairs in Hattusha. Amun-her shall look into the prospect of a determined and sustained defense in case the foe really means to attack us. I will make the decision about granting an asylum after returning from Waset."

He turned to the vizier. "I fully understand your objective appraisal of the situation. For the sake of the security of our land, it could behoove us to solve the problem on a low plane. By which, I mean"—he looked at his son— "simply extraditing the fugitives."

He raised his hand to block any protest from Nefertari and said to her, "Of course, it would be against our principles and, for other reasons, also against my own will. Therefore, extradition will not be an easy decision. As for the alternative, I must be careful before choosing to grant any asylum, for my word will be final and irrefutable, come what may, war or peace. For now, let us disperse."

Paser crouched, drooping his shoulders, and scowling at the ground. *No decision!*

Amun-her was pressing his lips together and tapping his foot. *No action!*

Nefertari observed the pharaoh's face. *Shishi needs help.*

* * *

After everyone had left, Nefertari stood for a while in the spacious corridor and strolled towards the window to gaze at the peaceful expanse outdoors. In contrast to the serenity the scenery offered, a storm was looming in her mind, one full of pros and cons and calling for urgent action. Could she secure peace with only information? A tall order.

She heard someone clear their throat behind her. She turned and saw the shaman politely making her aware of his presence.

"Your majesty wanted me to wait."

"Yes, indeed." She told him what went on after he had left, that the pharaoh had postponed his decision about the audience until his return from Waset. That meant, within a month from now, they had to get a clearer picture of the state of affairs in Hattusha, the military preparedness for an assault, and the strategy in general. His face went pale.

"What is the matter?" she asked.

"The time scale, your majesty. If our pharaoh wants a definite answer to his question, I need plenty of time."

"I know. But we have to make the best of the time we have. The matter is of utmost importance and urgency, for we must always stay ahead of the foe. The pharaoh wants to decide whether to risk provoking the Hittites or give in against his own will."

"What is your estimation, your majesty? How would he decide?"

"It is likely that he will cool down a bit and should no longer be concerned with the tone Hattusili adopted in his message. Paser's argument of the kingdom's interest will weigh far more. If the pharaoh learns through our efforts that the Hittites are really planning an offense against us and are, or will soon be, in a position to carry it out, he will react by all means and attack first. That would be his method of defense. If, on the other hand, Hattusili is only bluffing…" Her voice trailed off.

"I have some news, your majesty. Only, it is so fresh that it could be considered hearsay. That is the reason I did not mention it in the conference."

Nefertari waited. *One more surprise?*

"As I said in the meeting," Sennefer said, "it is true that more refugees are arriving from the Hittite land. The new king has lost many officers and is swimming, for want of advice, in a confusing situation. Only the other day, I received news of a major officer of the secret service of the previous regime who has also deserted and fled to our land. He feared reprisal under the new regime and was wise to flee. He is here in this city. This news has been verified, but I did not mention it because of the more drastic news: he is said to have brought with him documents pertaining to the military situation in Hattusha. This additional information has to be confirmed lest it should turn out to be hearsay to glorify the man. Also, we have to ascertain if he is just a spy on a mission to mislead us. We have to be very careful. The officer has to be trusted."

"If it turns out that he is not a spy and the documents can be produced and verified, would the situation become detrimental to Hattusili?"

"Yes, indeed. That is what I heard. I have to work my way towards the Black Hoods to get that piece of news confirmed and the evidence, that is to say, the documents offered to us for review."

"After due verification, could the officer present them to Mursili, which would make the case for the fugitive stronger when he appears for an audience?"

"That would be a problem. Both the officer and the king are hiding in separate places, each one being moved almost daily because the spies of Hattusili are hot on their heels. The two men are not in contact."

Nefertari was about to blurt out that she had met the prince, but she bit her lip and asked slowly, "Is the prince housed along with his father?"

"No. He is at large, but I hear the Black Hoods could find access to him."

"If the prince is moving freely, they could ask him to reach out to the officer with their assistance and procure the documents for us."

"Let us hope the officer knows the prince from olden days."

"There will be one way or the other for the prince to prove his identity to the officer." The image of that signet ring hovered before her eyes.

"Yes, I hope so."

"As of now, let us keep our activity totally confidential. At this stage, I do not want anyone in the court to know about our attempts and progress, not even the vizier, Amun-her, or the pharaoh. Any messages and new developments will be reported to others only after I allow it. Do you understand?"

"I understand."

"Now it is up to you to work for our success. We do not have much time, about a month, to check on the officer, procure his documents, verify them, and translate them. In the meantime, I will work out a diplomatic approach."

"I will do my best, your majesty."

* * *

The next morning, Nefertari rose with many thoughts running amok. She put them aside and turned to her routine at dawn of sitting before the Hathor image and praying. She had wanted to pray for a while to thank the goddess for the assignment she had received from the pharaoh in pursuance of the oracle. She had also wanted to ask for support. But this time, there was a strange interruption. She had a vision of Hathor asking her to stop praying and to act. It was in a stern tone, a command. She opened her eyes and shuddered.

To calm down and collect her thoughts, she went for a long walk in the garden. She mused about the turn of events and found it a bit cynical, even comical: two great powers at loggerheads, and if it turned out that the Hittites were as unprepared for war as her own kingdom, each fearing the other and only capable of swinging their swords for drama, that would offer a great opportunity for her. Yes, indeed, for peace. *Em hotep.*

The moment for diplomacy had arrived, the opportunity was there, and even the pharaoh expected her contribution. Then a chain of ideas came up dancing, all that could go into a message from her. She sped back to the palace.

Heading towards the chambers, she saw a servant standing guard at the door. She asked him to hasten to her scribe and bring him immediately. She rushed to her study and looked for her writing materials. She owed a response to Puduhepa, anyway. She set out with gusto, woman to woman, swinging the pen, not the sword.

She did not waste time formulating her response to queen Puduhepa. Leaving it to the scribe to add the preliminary salutations, personal compliments, thanks for the gifts, and the like. She would put down the significant points. It could be edited later for effect, and her Akkadian polished by her scribe. On that same day, a special fast messenger would be sent to deliver the message to the queen in Hattusha.

Her fingers hovered over the papyrus, but she hesitated. She had to rearrange her thoughts first. The core of this message ought to sound highly personal, by no means official. Nevertheless, it should express the danger of a war breaking out at any moment unless there was a contrary initiative on both sides. The style ought to reach the heart of the reader.

Hattusili would fear a rebellion after his seizure of the throne. A revolt could be generally expected after such an irregular succession. Sennefer had confirmed that Mursili was still popular among the subjects. She could also picture Hattusili's helplessness as a new ruler without appropriate advice, as even senior officers were deserting him. Before long, his vassals would also begin to revolt, sensing their chance to throw off the Hittite yoke. He would be getting lonely and would need advice, but from whom?

His wife?

Nefertari knew Puduhepa's background. After the battle of Qadesh, on his way back, Hattusili, the commander of the Hittite troops, had stopped at Lawazantiya to marry Puduhepa, the daughter of Pentipasharri, the local priest of the goddess Ishtar.

Now, with Hattusili ascending to the throne, she had become the queen. It was also in her own interest to maintain the royal status and power bestowed upon her. Of course, she would support her spouse by all means, come war or peace. But would she not rather have peace for her own benefit— to maintain power and security, too? Not blinded by any manly ego, Puduhepa ought to be the one to advise her husband not to pick up a quarrel with Kemet and open a front. Even in a subdued moment, Hattusili might or might not be wise enough to think along these lines on his own accord. But he might like to hear another private opinion on this matter. Thereafter, that opinion could be accepted and named as his own. That was the way leaders reacted to their experts, said monarchs to viziers—and husbands to wives.

Nefertari had to check her fantasy. She knew nothing more about Puduhepa. Was she his respected counterpart in affairs of the state? Was she a dominant spouse or a devout mouse?

Snatching up the fine brush she used as a pen, she began her letter in her customary fashion.

"Em heset net Hathor. May you be in favor with Hathor."

First, she complimented Puduhepa's husband's success and the high regard he had earned among his citizens. She also alluded to the troubles he had gone through and his concern for the safety of his kingdom. Then she dove into the subject.

"While our pharaoh is seriously considering the request your spouse has made, I take the opportunity to express my own opinion regarding the interests of both the lands. It is the privilege and duty of a ruling authority to nurture the well-being of the subjects and ensure lasting peace. The monarch of any powerful land, if threatened by a foreign power, would be ready to retaliate. So will it be on a massive scale when there should be a threat to Kemet."

After this unmistakable declaration of strength and resolve, she turned to a softer tone.

"With god's grace, we in Kemet do not have borders to worry about, neither in the south nor in the north. Even so, like you, we would avoid fomenting animosity and attempt to reduce aggression. We would join hands in resisting other monarchs threatening our land and subjects. With this purpose in mind, we, both the heads of your kingdom and of Kemet, should unite, especially

in difficult times. It is natural for both of us to seek and maintain peace, but this needs cooperation. A mutual peace treaty for all times would also relieve a burden of suspended or tacit dispute and ensure a prosperous reign in each land conducive to the subjects, for that is the god-ordained duty of royalty."

The Hittites had peace accords with over fifteen vassals and protectorates. Recalling from her memory she cited some examples.

"Your land has a history of securing and ensuring peace by way of treaties even with smaller powers, like Wilusa, Aleppo, Hapalla, and Mir-Kuwaliya, by your previous ruler Muwatalli and also of your own spouse, who signed an accord with Benteshina of Amurru. I propose, independent of the official view here, that we reach a similar peace accord, for, as major powers, we respect each other. We know well the spirit and the word of such a treaty will count forever, binding in stipulations and in oath, by 'ishiul and lingai,' as you say in your language."

The message would close with the customary wishing well to Puduhepa's land, people, and family. She read her points again and again.

Convinced of its content, tone, and style, she stretched with a sigh. She had sown the seed of a peace agreement in the recipient's mind. Now it was for Puduhepa to accept it and nurse the illusion that it was her own idea.

The girl within Nefertari giggled. She could imagine Hattusili, lying in bed, exhausted and sliding into sleep, not prone to protest, and Puduhepa preaching peace into his ear: *the lullaby tactic.*

THE HITTITE

Chapter 5

THE MISSION

It had been one more workday, week in and week out, unless interrupted by a break of a day or two thanks to a religious festival. But from the next day onward, Hartapu would be free from work for quite some time, as his employer would be going home to Ugarit to replenish his stock. Back home, there would be no language problem, and the merchant would manage alone.

Now on holiday, Hartapu was having a great time with some comrades in the late afternoon at the customary meeting point, nicknamed the "Battleground." It was a free space on the river shore, wearily presided over by the ruins of an erstwhile fisherman's stall. They had fixed a board on one of its walls and playfully threw daggers at the targets painted on it.

To make the practice more enticing, they were inventing new hurdles. The game this time was to aim first and then close one's eyes—no cheating—and throw. Two teams of three youths had been vying for victory over three rounds. It was all just a game and no great contest, just some action to let out their youthful steam after the laborious day of hanging around in stalls, grinning, and offering wares to customers pretending disdain.

Throwing knives was quite a new sport for Hartapu, but he had an advantage in that he was an expert in aiming arrows. The education of a prince in Hatti covered many subjects: administration, religion, languages, script, and of course, warcraft. Of the last, his domain was that of a charioteer and archer with some knowledge of close combat, although the latter was the prerequisite for the infantry. He had trained for years in aiming and shooting at moving objects as well as when moving in a chariot himself. The concentration needed to hit anything and under any conditions was the same. He only had to get advice on the right kind of knife, its weight and shape, and the technicality of the hold and launch. In this art, even as a beginner and not an expert, he could claim to be one of the best of the bad lot.

With dusk nearing, the game came to an end. Hattapu bid farewell to the men. Being no celebrity here and unknown to any person, he was carefree. He was a vagabond getting to know the real world and the way people were. It ought to be exhilarating not to be in a palace or in a restricted sector, like the one in Hattusha, called the Palace District, with all its stiff demeanor and polished language. He was getting quite an education in the way of life in a foreign land with no one watching, not to mention learning foul language and curses, too.

Nevertheless, he dreamed of his home back in Hattusha. The capital of the Hittite kingdom was situated in an area surrounded by lush forests that provided wood for construction—in dire contrast to Egypt, where wood was a scarcity and, therefore, precious. The region also had seven springs, ensuring an abundance of water all year round. A city wall some ten meters in height had been erected around the whole settlement. A natural rocky elevation in the eastern corner offered an ideal spot for a citadel. The city's ground stretched over two parts, one lying on a lower level to the north and the other elevated and much larger to the south. In those days, Hattusha was mainly limited to the city on the lower plane, but several projects for development had been planned for the larger area to the south, including the construction of over twenty temples.

His thoughts came back to the comrades he had just left. They were simple and spontaneous souls given to pranks and jokes, even expletives and gestures, the kind he had observed among servants and slaves when he was a child and there were no seniors around. He could imagine his own ordinary people back home were no different, simple and frank. In Hatti, such people would have been his subjects. He would have ridden a chariot with guards as his escort. No doubt, there was a barrier, a wall, rather a fort, in his own mind. With these youths, he enjoyed the company, all right. But friends? "Friend" was still a remote word for Hartapu.

To get home, he had to walk up to the next house and turn right. As he neared the corner, he heard a husky male voice from behind him whisper in his language, "You need a friend, sir."

Hartapu stopped and turned as the voice added, "And we need a leader."

A tall man a few years older than Hartapu was standing there, wearing a long gown, with a hood over his head and his back to the setting sun. He uncovered his head. He had a handsome face and a disarming smile. In contrast, his eyes had a piercing stare. He made a slight bow.

"Do not be concerned," he said in a normal tone after throwing a glance over his shoulder. "For the sake of security, but with due respect, I do not address you in the customary way you are due, but I know who you are, and I will tell you who I am."

He lowered his voice again. "I am Teremun, the head of the Black Hoods, your father's supporters. We are here in Kemet to make sure the other side from our homeland does not do any harm to him or his son."

Hartapu appraised the stranger—and the danger. The man's bare hands dangled at his sides. He was too close for a kick, but Hartapu could punch him in the belly and follow up with a second fist to his face, or better, his throat. No cause to flee.

To be sure, he stepped back a bit and said, raising his chin, "I do not know you."

"You do. I was one of your father's counsels back in the glorious days when he was in charge. You met me when I visited him. My nickname was 'the Wolf,' do you remember?"

Hartapu could clearly remember. But he raised his eyebrows, suppressing any other reaction.

"We have been watching you for your own safety," the man calling himself Teremun said. "Two months ago, you were recognized and pursued by two goons. Surely, you remember."

Hartapu had to pause. Then he nodded. "They didn't get me."

"Because we got them first. They were from the other side, agents of your father's uncle in Hattusha." Again, that glance over the shoulder.

"Did they confess?" Hartapu wanted to know.

"More than that. Now we know more about their network. We are done with the two men. We took them out."

"What do you mean by that?"

"We silenced them. They are out of business, not to be seen anymore."

"What do you really want?"

"I have some good news, and I need your cooperation—it's in your own interest. We need you to lead us all."

They walked on past two houses and turned back towards the shore. The open space offered no cover for an eavesdropper, even in the advancing darkness.

"Our activity is mainly in warding off the other side, which we call the Red Hoods, and thwarting any attempts on the life of your father, our true king. We are also on the lookout for support for his position here. In this regard, I am glad we have found a trace that will be of help."

Hartapu was wary of this announcement. It sounded like the opening call of a street vendor laying out bait. He had been hooked. Nevertheless, he was curious and wanted to hear more.

"Do you want to hear what it is all about?" the stranger prodded.

"Sure," Hartapu said. "Go ahead."

The man told him that a senior security official who served Hartapu's father had recently fled to Kemet. He was in possession of certain documents that would be of high interest to the pharaoh and could help the ousted king secure asylum. Teremun asked the prince to proceed to a place in the north of the city and meet this man and receive the documents. They had to be inspected and brought to the pharaoh's attention. He asked the prince to take the lead in this matter.

"You want *me* to do it? Why?"

"Because you are the only person suitable for this purpose. You are the only person that particular informant, a high officer of security, will recognize and trust."

"Do you mean to say…"

"You will be free for quite some time from the next week onward. We know."

The man seemed to know everything. The argument for Hartapu to take the matter into his hands for his and his father's interest could not be contested. Yet all this sounded sinister. Could it be a ruse? Hartapu would not be carried away by mere curiosity and a tall tale—from a stranger. Not exactly a stranger. He had identified Teremun, but what if he had run over to the other side, and Hartapu was being talked into an ambush?

"I am not sure whether all this is true. Plainly, I do not trust you." He looked away and half turned, hinting that the chat was coming to an end.

"How else can I make you trust me? Will it help if I tell you the name of the officer?" Teremun pleaded.

Hartapu smiled and shook his head. "You know who I am. You know where my interest lies. I am not one who has defected and am working for my father's uncle and against my own father. You spoke to me because you trust me. But I know nothing about you now or on which side you are. Tell me the whole truth in every detail. Only then can I make any move for your sake."

The man stood with a face cut in stone.

Hartapu turned away from him and said over his shoulder, "You began this chat asking me to lead you all. Why do you bother me if all you need is a courier to meet a stranger and pick up some documents for you?"

Teremun sighed and suggested they move on and settle for a chat. He pointed to a few bricks forming a low bulwark on the roadside.

* * *

They sat down facing each other, with the river to one side. Each of them could keep the rear of the other in view, watching out for passers-by. To start, Teremun told a few anecdotes from Hartapu's childhood. Building this bridge was superfluous, for Hartapu had recognized him, but he had doubts about this man still being loyal to his father and not crossing over to his uncle. Then Teremun came to the details.

"There are documents that the security officer by the name of Zananzash brought with him when he deserted the secret service of your uncle. He is here in this town."

Hartapu frowned. "Zananzash? I remember him. He was one of the counselors to the king. My father even hinted that he would become the *hazannu*, the chief administrator, of Hattusha. Why would he like to share the documents with me?"

"The sympathy of Zananzash to your father was known all along, and the officer knew that the new king would eventually have Zananzash arrested and thrown into jail. For his own security, he brought with him some sensitive material that could be of great value to you. At best, he would present them to your father. But no one is in a position to approach your father right now, not even you."

"What is the matter?"

"We know that Hattusili has sent his agents to Kemet, and they are looking for your father. They have the assignment to capture and bring him back to Hattusha. Your father's supporters are moving him from one place to another every few days. Only a few are within the network, which helps our people fleeing to Kemet know the location. You ought to be warned, for these orders may apply to you, too. Hattusili does not want any contestant to the throne he stole."

"Under these circumstances, do you want *me* to expose myself by risking this mission?"

"Zananzash is prepared to hand over the documents only to you. Only, in this case, he does not need to identify the recipient nor identify himself to the recipient. As he is an elderly man and new to this land, it is more practical for you to seek him out and receive the documents rather than expect him to come looking for you with the precious articles. You will have to make certain contacts, identify yourself with a phrase, and be led to Zananzash. If you like, I can accompany you."

"No, thanks." Hartapu was emphatic, waving his hand. "If at all, I'd like to move alone where and when I please. And now for the content."

"Of course. I will come to that. One more reason why I am seeking your cooperation: we know that you have made inroads into the royalty here."

"Nonsense."

"We watched you enter the palace in the company of the lady-in-waiting of the queen. We surmise you have established some connection and can use that to get the attention of the royalty concerning the documents. But that would be your decision, acting in your own interest and not mine."

Teremun's eyes narrowed. He bent a bit forward and lowered his voice. "There are two kinds of documents. The first kind is messages sent by Hattusili to vassal states with identical content except for the long passage addressing the recipient.

"It is a call to neighboring states for cooperation refreshing or renewing the alliance they had with the Hatti kingdom under your grandfather Muwatalli at the battle of Qadesh. In the extreme, it could be interpreted as preparation to attack and destabilize the Lower Kingdom of Kemet. This would be an answer to the military build-up in Per-Ramesses by the pharaoh with the evident purpose of organizing an attack on the Hittites. This matter would be of prime interest and concern to the royalty here."

Teremun paused. Hartapu nodded and waited.

"The next kind," Terenmanu went on, "in fact, there's only one document, is even graver. It is an internal communication to Hattusili from his security officer and viceroy in Qadesh, who was a colleague of Zananzash. It is in response to Hattusili fearing the pharaoh will grant asylum to your father and march against Hatti in support of him.".

Both men fell silent for a long while. Hartapu could not decide whether all this was mumbo-jumbo, just bait or a ruse to get him into an ambush. He decided to hit Teremun's nerve and see how he reacted.

Finally, he said, "All this may be true or made up. You may be on my side but not your informants, who may have cooked up the story. How can I know whether I will be going on a fool's errand at best or stepping into an ambush at worst?"

Teremun sighed. "If I had wanted to capture and abduct you, my men could have encircled you right here and now. Why should I be sending you somewhere, giving directions on how to reach a man called Zananzash? I have approached you alone and unarmed. Anyway, I can only appeal to your cooperation. In fact, we also need leadership in this matter, in your own interest. I beseech you, my prince. You were born and brought up for a far higher purpose in life than…"

Living as a scribe?

"…being a fugitive." Teremunu continued. "You can take your own future into your hands. But if you refuse for whatever reason, we can separate now. No hard feelings."

They sat still for a while. Hartapu noticed that Teremun did not get up, which would have signaled the end of the chat, meaning take it or leave it. The matter was, indeed, too earnest for a haggler's stunt. But the prince wanted to know more.

"You tell me where, when, and how I can meet Zananzash. If you want to send me to him, you cannot hide him from me."

Teremun nodded and gave him the details. It would be a long walk of an hour, first along the river and then turning into a locality buzzing with shops and vendors. He was to meet a vendor from the south offering tools in a shop for copper wares, situated next to the stall of a cloth merchant. Copper was a valuable material procured from Upper Egypt in the south. Such articles were usually offered in tool shops in the market. The vendors of copper wares were considered honest, as opposed to traveling vendors, who were usually thought to be trading stolen goods.

After approaching the vendor as a customer, Hartapu was to use the key sentence: "Are you from the other side of the river?" He would get the answer: "Every story has two sides. So, too, the river." The shopkeeper would accompany Hartapu to a place a few houses away and put him in touch with a contact who would lead him to Zananzash. Only this last contact knew where the man was put up that day.

Chapter 6

THE QUEST

Two days later, just after dawn, Hartapu was striding past the spot where he had met Teremun. He walked on, following the directions given. He was greeted by the birds twittering to cheer him on his mission.

After passing the fish market, with the stench lingering on his nose for a free ride, the scenery changed. More recent buildings appeared, with cultivated gardens in their front. He turned right to walk until the pleasant surroundings gave way again to huts and ramshackle dwellings. The ubiquitous stray cats scowled at his intrusion, spoiling their environment. The land of the cats. They were natives; he was alien.

Strange land, strange customs, all right, but what appalled him most was how these people spent so much time, energy, and resources on building places like tombs, temples, and palaces on the one hand and, on the other, struggled in their own misery. They were content to be left to fend for themselves, to live within their meager means, in need of health and safety, even in squalor, and seemed to look up to the pharaoh only in times of inundation. If they were otherwise content, one could argue it was not the duty of the pharaoh to make them feel miserable for not having the amenities with which he was blessed. Should a monarch take recourse to cause misery among his subjects and provoke a rebellion?

Thinking along these lines further, how far was the pharaoh, or any monarch in general, really concerned with his duties towards his subjects? Was he not always trying to satisfy his own ego, "ordained by the gods," as he would put it? As each king felt the same way, there was always conflict and war among kings, with each one, of course, claiming a divine reason. The hapless farmers recruited for the front had to bear the brunt of this and bleed.

Was it not also the case with his grand-uncle and father? His father had been the rightful heir, but in his reign, he had marginalized Hattusili and offended him to the extent that the latter had gotten the upper hand and his father had lost. Now ousted from his position as crown prince and at the hands of fortune and destiny, how would Hartapu go about being a monarch? As a first step, he had to fight his way back to recover his birthright. Among Hittites in exile, besides the group called the Black Hoods, he must look for other supporters, too. But first he must prove to himself in a foreign land that he had the mettle to become a king of a land at all.

He ended his thoughts with a shrug and quickened his pace.

Lest he should stray too far, he decided to ask for the cloth merchant. He had no interest in copper. He did not want to be too explicit with his real destination. He was about to cross the road to reach out to some pedestrians when a stocky man wearing a red and white headscarf darted out of a side street. Hartapu stopped him and asked for the cloth merchant. The man stalled a bit and then told him to turn down the alley the man had just emerged from. He would find the cloth shop not far from the alehouse.

On turning down the lane and walking a few paces, Hartapu spotted the shop for copperware next to the cloth shop. It was easily discernible. All around its entrance and high above the door, articles and tools were displayed, glittering in the sunshine. A buzzing crowd stood outside the shop, almost hiding the entrance. The shop next to it, that of the cloth merchant, was closed.

Hartapu walked on, and as he neared the shop, the crowd began to dissipate.

He heard a man tell a youth, "We should get away here. When the *mejays* come, they will arrest even bystanders just to impress the mayor."

Hartapu asked him what was going on.

"The shopkeeper has been killed, stabbed in his chest. He was found lying in his shop this morning after his neighbors broke in to see what was up. The guards will be here any moment and await the local mayor. It is no place to hang around." He rushed away with the youth.

Hartapu walked on to get a closer look. The door was blocked by two men, most likely the neighboring vendors. They were fending off the curious, fearing looters among them.

Hartapu was at a loss. His contact was gone. What now? He could not give up. He had to find a way on his own. He traipsed for a while around the area. His thoughts wandered, too. The contact was supposed to get him in touch with someone else. He had to find that next contact somehow. That other person might also be at a loss and be looking for him. Who would hear his code words?

The event in the copper shop might have no bearing on his appointment. He had made it a point not to tell Teremun when he would set off. Even Teremun did not know on which day, if ever, he would be reaching out to the copper vendor. If this timely death had nothing to do with the proposed meeting, what else was it? Was this so-called contact a criminal with unrelated problems who had met his nemesis? Or was it a simple case of burglary colliding with the day Hartapu had set out? Was this an omen?

He was used to having protection and announced appearances, and here he was, in the streets of Per-Ramesses, playing hide and seek with unknown, invisible, maybe absent pursuers, unlike the chase weeks ago. Not at all trained for this kind of sleuth's game, he did his best, darting from one street side to the other, making sudden turns, lurking down side streets, looking over his shoulder and making detours like a mentally deranged man. Or like a killer. Yes, he had time to kill.

Finally, worried and weary, his eyes caught sight of a shelter.

The alehouse, which he had already passed twice, was an old, ramshackle structure in want of an extensive facelift. True to its name, it looked and smelled like a negligent and neglected drunk. In search of some shade and a drink in the scorching sun of the forenoon, he decided to give himself a break and sought the company of a beer. Hartapu didn't mind the other company the alehouse promised.

* * *

Suppilamus, the man from Hattusha, was restless. He narrowed his eyes and stared at the guests at the next table in the alehouse as if he cared. He was only concentrating on his own situation.

He was a civil servant in the service of Hattusili, the present king of the Hittite kingdom. He was a secret emissary of the king, now in Egypt, incognito, on a mission.

Known for his practical ways in tidying up a situation or reaching goals, he had never claimed to be a rainmaker. Thanks to his experience as an organizer and thoroughness, he had been assigned the task of building a network of agents in Egypt while disguised as a Hittite merchant. The previous Hittite kings had built and established a big network of spies in this city. Years of espionage of the past had developed a flourishing relationship with contacts among the Egyptians. Those contacts had to be won over to his side, to the side of the new king. Also, the potential contacts of the Hittite diaspora who were not bound by any loyalty to this or that king but were only spies for hire had to be talked into working for him. All this needed time. As expected, it was a slow process, with most of the expatriates either indifferent and uninterested or already working for the other side.

The man had served kings, beginning with Muwatalli, and followed by his son Mursili. Then, after the latter was overthrown, Hattusili became the third king in his career. The secret of his long duration at the office was his loyalty to the crown, not to individual monarchs who came and went. In his opinion, if a king was replaced, the personnel had to transfer allegiance to the newcomer and continue to serve the throne and remain loyal to the crown. They served "his majesty," whatever the name. This maxim ought to be the sole principle for the whole royal apparatus, not only the army.

The new assignment was to find and bring the fugitive Mursili back to Hattusha. For a man used to quick and concrete results, this additional job was progressing at a snail's pace. He stamped his feet, sighed, and turned his head away as if he could banish the thoughts with one jerk.

In his judgment, for now, both Mursili and his uncle Hattusili had their fears for different reasons. It was plain that the former would resist extradition lest he should face a mock trial, be convicted for his "misdeeds," and be served a death sentence. Hattusili, on the other hand, was afraid the fugitives might find support from the pharaoh. The greater scare was that the nephew might regroup his friends, now partly at home and partly abroad, and attempt to recapture the throne. Therefore, this additional assignment to search for the fugitives was to be fast and efficient. It was a race against time.

The simple solution would have been to eliminate Mursili from the world, a plain search-and-destroy mission. This brutal thought of having Mursili killed in Egypt did not appeal to Hatthusili. He did not want any complication with the mighty pharaoh by staging an assassination on his soil. He wanted the nephew back home, hale and alive, to face a trial. He wanted the man brought in chains before the gods, his deeds to be exposed as crimes, and due judgment and punishment meted out. The supporters of the victim ought to be shown justice had been done and any possible rebellion would be nipped in the bud. The condition was no death to the fugitives in Egypt. In other words, Suppilamus had to protect them, too.

Along with Mursili and the crown prince, a large number of supporters of the old regime had left the Hittite kingdom at least a year ago and literally gotten lost in the foreign land. But this news that the men in question were somewhere in Egypt had reached and been confirmed in Hattusha only after a year. Now Suppilamus had to search for the two celebrities incognito in the two kingdoms of Kemet. He would easily recognize the deposed king, but he had never seen the prince in his life.

His first guess was that they were hiding somewhere in the Lower Kingdom, in the Nile delta, which was abuzz with foreigners from the north, like refugees and expatriates from the ruined kingdom of Mitanni and descendants of the *hekau-khasut* or *hyksos* for short, mixed up with "the sea people." This was the region for foreigners to hide and get support from compatriots, no different from what he was doing.

The Hittite stirred in his small chair. Conspicuous with his stature, too tall and hefty for an Egyptian, the middle-aged man hunched over the low table was no proper choice for his clandestine mission, not the sort that would merge in a crowd. He tried to make a virtue of his prominent looks. Dressed in heavily plaited robes, fashionable among the nobility back home, he emphasized his individuality as a wealthy man from abroad with a fine lifestyle worthy of the precious products with which he dealt.

The table before him was also the office for his "business," and he was awaiting an assistant to pop up any time and inform him. It was all about collecting information for his purpose, pretty late after months had passed with the prey burrowing in. So far, the few contacts he had were passing on to him some gossip or the other, maybe even cooking up stories when under pressure. They were all products of guesswork and led to false tracks and dead ends. The most recent one was that two of his agents had sighted the crown prince in the city. Now, for days, no one had heard from them. He wished he had better-trained personnel.

The alehouse was a meeting point for daily laborers on the prowl for a job, straying aliens, and the local vagabonds that preyed on them. At this early hour, only such elements were around, not at all to his taste. The room would be filled in an hour with men from other strata of society, merchants, and traders on the move, stopping for a day or two in this city and not knowing where else to spend their time before the next move. Residents who worked all the days of the week had no time for such pastimes. The noble and the elderly stayed home with the comfort of being served the drinks of their choice by their servants and slaves.

The girl with dazzling looks and a matching gait who had ushered him to his seat came swinging her hips with a big mug in her hand. She wore a short blue wraparound skirt. She covered her beauty with a flimsy translucent blouse that posed as a veil to no avail. A necklace of colored glass beads dangled on her chest, flopping to the right and left to the rhythm of her stride. As a receptionist, waitress, and what-not, she had charmed him, indeed, with her mere appearance.

He had ordered the precious wine from the famous vineyards of Inet, cherished especially by foreigners. She carried a mug with a floral design on it. Judging by the casual way she held it in her delicate hand, he could guess it was half empty. She set it gently before him and proved him right.

He cleared his throat, tried a benign smile, and asked, "What is your name, dear?"

She half turned, still looking at him over her shoulder, and said while flapping her eyelids,

"I go by the name Mehetweret."

Then she glided away before he could ask, *What? Once again, please?*

For a while, he fancied hiring this kind of people for his mission. Yes, waiters and dancers were ideal agents, for they had their eyes, noses, and ears all around, and for a modest payment, they would gladly lend them to him. He smiled and shook his head at his own absurd thought. His mission was to locate a king and a prince, not to chase the sundry customers hanging out in an alehouse.

Suppilamus looked around. Here and there, he saw small groups of men playing board games, mostly Senet. It was a game for two, with thirty squares and six pieces to each player. Each move was determined after throwing on the table a pair of marked bones serving as dice. The repetitive rattle of the dice falling on the table was yet to be overwhelmed by the chatter, though the voices grew louder after each round of beer. A young man in one corner caught his eye. He was seated all alone with his back to the wall, fiddling with his mug and staring at the table. One more lost soul like himself, Suppilamus thought.

In the corner, Hartapu pushed his mug on the table from one hand to the other, asking himself: *What next?* The voices near him got louder. Two of the three people standing within his reach had gotten into a yelling match. One of them, a furious man, punched the other in his face. The victim staggered back, struggling to get over the shock and hit back.

At this moment, the waitress who had served Suppilamus came running over and tried to intervene—well meant but dangerous. She was slapped on the cheek and thrust away by the assailant. She reeled but recovered and lurched forward, slapping him in the face. The man had turned his head a bit and got the slap square on the nose. Not expecting such a reaction from a woman, he staggered from the blow. The noise of the slap was loud, indeed. To be out of reach, the girl jumped back, hitting Hartapu's table and collapsing into the empty chair next to it.

Feeling for the knife in his belt, Hartapu jumped up; he had to move around the table and reach for the man, but it was too late. A burly waiter had caught and twisted the man's arm behind his back and circled his neck with his other arm in a chokehold. He shoved the man, who was bent backward and struggling. They headed towards the exit.

A colleague shouted, "Never let him set foot in our house again!"

The girl sat there, gasping. Hartapu did not know what to say. He pushed his mug towards her. She nodded thanks and raised it but did not take a sip. Instead, she pressed the cool mug against her cheek.

Then she said, "A horrible fellow. Getting drunk and picking a quarrel with everyone."

Hartapu nodded. "You managed to give him back the slap. I like that."

Brushing a tress from her forehead, she looked at him and said, "Are you here for the first time?"

"Yes. In fact, I was supposed to —"

She cut him short. "I think you are from the other side of the river."

Hartapu swallowed twice. *The code phrase! The answer?* He gave it a shot. "Every story has two sides, also the river."

She smiled. Her cheek was not less ruddy. Instead, the other one had caught up with a blush. She bent forward, laid her hand on his, and whispered, "All right. Now, pretend I told you a joke and laugh loudly." She bent back. He laughed. She joined him, beginning with a giggle. They rocked with laughter for no reason.

She mumbled, "Let's go. Get up and lead."

Hartapu got up, and she caught his hand and rose, two old friends on the move.

She beckoned to a colleague and said a few words to him. Then she signaled Hartapu to walk in a direction opposite the exit.

She said, "We'll take the rear entrance. There's no point in running into the man again at the front for another round. No time for us to get into a street fight. We have much to do."

On the way, she picked up a small bag and a stole to cover the flimsy blouse.

They left the hall, passed the kitchen, and reached the exit. Outdoors, they turned left and were in the street.

* * *

After sipping his wine and staring at the void, at long last, Suppilamus got company. A tall, broad-chested Hittite with a short beard and bushy eyebrows stomped in. Glancing around, he seated himself after a nod as a greeting. He took a deep breath.

Suppilamus looked around. There was no waiter in sight, nor any guest hovering near his table. He gave the man a few seconds and asked, "Well? What is up, Mashanda?"

"That man we talked about who wanted to switch sides and work for us. Did you get the news?" Mashanda said.

"Yes, it is in the air. Found dead this morning. Fell prey to a burglar, I believe. What about that news?"

"I met him in his shop last evening. He lived and slept there, as he was afraid someone would come for his precious wares and break in at night. After a long discussion, he agreed to work for us, but he set conditions. He wanted to get rich fast and even hinted at selling information to both sides. For a start, he was prepared to share some news of late. A high-placed security official has fled from Hattusha and is holed up somewhere in this city."

"The name of the official?"

The man bent forward to whisper, "Zannash or something like that."

"Oh, no! Not Zananzash! I know the man." Suppilamus raised his eyebrows, puffed his cheeks, and blew out. "So, he has quit. Incredible. He is a nasty fellow but highly efficient in his job. He would have been a valuable asset to our majesty. The royal court is now bleeding."

"Some important meeting involving him was being planned with the prince. This copper trader was to arrange it. It had to be somewhere near Zananzash's place, for he has a leg injury and cannot move much. It is to be somewhere in the vicinity of the Avaris market. When it came to more details about when and where…"

The man paused.

"Then…" The man shifted in his seat. "Then it happened."

"What happened?"

"Well, for more information, he demanded advance payment and began to haggle. His argument was that he had already given me enough for nothing and wanted rewards for more stuff as to when, where, and what. All that would be on offer, only if—"

"All right, all right. Did you get all the lowdown?"

"I am afraid not. The haggling turned into an argument, a yelling match, and he reached for a dagger hidden beneath his table. I was quicker. That's it. I left him dead."

Suppilamus's jaw dropped. He gasped but controlled himself.

The man paused and then went on. "I made the scene look like a burglary by picking up some precious articles and bundling them and my knife in my soiled tunic. Around midnight, I snuck out through the rear door, went straight to the river, dumped all the stuff in the water, and washed myself. Then I returned home for some sleep. I am sure I left no traces."

"Did anybody see you leaving the shop?"

"No, for sure. As I said, it was pitch dark, and the only witnesses were stray cats." He chuckled and threw a nervous look at his boss.

Suppilamus shook his head. He hissed some curses and banged the table with his fist.

"Great job! A story with a great ending! Great worthless information. You idiots do not understand that you cannot go on silencing your own sources. This is not a board game to offer them as pawns."

The man hung his head and stared at the table. To cool himself, Suppilamus called out to a passing waiter and ordered a beer for himself, ignoring his assistant. Now and again, the latter looked at his boss. No reaction.

After a long pause, Suppilamus stirred.

"Did you really hear a meeting was planned for Zananzash and the prince?"

"Yes, for sure. That was the moment the argument began."

"The meeting cannot be arranged now that the contact is dead. Unless he is replaced. That could take time. The prince would have been alarmed, and all movements will be frozen for a while. No contacts, no meetings. And we do not know where Zananzash is. But how do we find out where on earth…" He fell silent.

Generally a slow and methodical thinker after years of bureaucracy, he had one contrasting gift. When under pressure, he could think fast, and usually, the first simple solution that occurred to him was the right one.

"Did you say Zananzash cannot move much because of an injury?"

"Yes. Because he wounded his leg during his escape to Kemet."

"Wounded or hurt?"

The man took a second to reply. "He is wounded. That is what I heard."

"Try this. If he is wounded, he may have reached out for help. Send all our people to look for healers in the area of the Avaris market who may have treated him. One or the other would have visited him, and not the other way, for he is badly hurt. Ask for a wounded alien, a Hittite managing to speak their language. I will give you his description. Our men must be astute without arousing suspicion. They should all pose only as compatriots concerned about their comrade."

He described the age and looks of Zananzash, adding as a special feature his high-pitched voice and minimal language skill.

He closed by barking the command, "Start the search. Right now!"

Chapter 7

THE CONTACT

Hartapu was still recovering from all the fast-paced drama ever since he had reached the copper store. He had to swallow the fact that his contact was dead and he did not know what to do next. He had wandered for a while and then settled down in a quiet corner, hoping for some inspiration. Even there, he had witnessed an alehouse fight and been rewarded with a beautiful girl who spoke magic words. Now he had been asked to lead, but to where, he did not know.

What did he know about her, and what did she know about him?

"My friends call me Harti," he said in a low voice. "I didn't get your name."

"My name is Mehetweret. You can call me Met."

They walked along a paved road and came across an old hawker hunching in the shade of a hut with a basket of sweets, dates, and fruit before him. He was hooded to avoid the hot sun. Hartapu was feeling hungry. He stopped and bargained for some nuts and dates. After the purchase, he offered them to Met, and they walked up to a potter nearby and asked for water. It was the custom never to deny water to any stranger at a household or shop. Besides being a matter of decency and courtesy, this rule was rooted in the ingrained fear all had of thirst in the desert, in *deshret*, the Red Land, which stretched beyond the cultivable Kemet, or Black Land, of the banks of the Nile.

Having quenched their thirst, they settled down for a chat under the shade of the pottery store. The girl caught Hartapu with his mouth full and said, "Harti. Is that right?"

Hartapu nodded. She said, "I noticed before that you speak our language pretty well. You can even bargain like a native. But I was told you are only a scribe."

Hartapu smiled. "In our business, we have to know many trades and tactics. Only on the surface am I a scribe, and you are…"

Met shrugged and chuckled. "They call me a waitress. I call myself a receptionist. Often, I am a soul priestess. I can handle sorrowful souls, men on the loose like rudderless boats, sometimes driven away from home but more often alone for their own fault. For my service, I get food and shelter from the boss of the alehouse." She giggled and shrugged.

Hartapu smiled with a frown and looked at her.

"I have to laugh," she said. "Just imagine the name of my boss is Anpu."

She added after a brief pause, "Oh, you wouldn't know. Let me explain. Anpu is the name of our god who leads our souls after death to the ultimate judgment by Lord Osiris. We could say Anpu is the lord of lost souls seeking redemption. My boss Anpu gives shelter to lost souls even in their lifetime, right here on earth, in his alehouse."

Hartapu laughed. After a few steps, he asked, "What do you know about me, Met?"

"About you? All I know is you are a Hittite scribe sent from my boss Tenemun to lead you to a man called Zananzash. That is all."

"You are well informed. In fact, I was first supposed to meet a man at the…" He hesitated.

"That is tragic. They got him. Until then, I did not know it was such a dangerous mission."

"Who are *they*?"

"The others. Hittites loyal to the present king, whatever his name. We call them Red Hoods. We are the Black Hoods."

"Like the two regions or lands of this kingdom. But aren't you from here?"

"Yes. I am a native. I get paid for my job. Maybe there are not enough Hittites around here to support the fugitive king. I also heard the crown prince of the Hittites is in Kemet," she added as they got up,

"If they got our man at the copper shop, they must know he was a contact and was trying to help us find Zananzash. Or there was some other reason. Maybe the shopkeeper refused to cooperate with the Red Hoods. Anyway, we have to be doubly careful and hurry up. Let us move."

To Hartapu's surprise, she left him standing and dashed in the other direction, back to the vendor. She made some remarks to him and gave him the rest of the dates she had in her hand. Hartapu joined her in time to hear her tell the man, "Don't look now. There is a man lingering near the tree wearing a blue and white striped headscarf. He may come to you. Give him these dates, a present from me. Tell him he should stop chasing me. I have a boyfriend already." She threw him a broad smile.

The old man nodded and grinned, flashing white teeth that contrasted with the swarm of creases beneath his crow's feet.

Hartapu stood in wonder. She hooked her arm in his, and they walked off.

After quite a distance, as they turned a corner, Hartapu cast a glance over his shoulder and said, "That man is talking to the vendor. Your real boyfriend?"

"Of course not. A stalker I have never seen before. He must be one of those Red Hoods. I don't know why or how he picked us up. He won't trail us anymore—out of professional pride, if he has any." She jumped a few steps and laughed.

As they took a turn onto a broad street, she pointed to two oxen drawing a cart coming towards them. She charmed the driver with some words in the local Gizem dialect. He called out and pointed to the rear with his thumb. After the cart passed them, she ran up and hopped onto it from behind and tossed her head towards Hartapu. The prince sprinted, jumped on the wagon, and settled beside her. Met smiled, put her index finger to her mouth, and pointed at the driver behind the goods heaped on the cart. Hartapu nodded, and they kept quiet for the rest of their ride, merrily dangling their legs. The stalker was nowhere to be seen.

Hartapu the tourist enjoyed sightseeing the new city while moving backward. The ride offered an interesting view of Per-Ramesses. The name meant "the House of Ramesses." The pharaoh had made it the new capital of Egypt.

Apart from the fact that Ramses had grown up in this area, his purpose for founding the new capital was its proximity to Sinai and the Asian vassal states. It was located on the eastern shore of the easternmost branch of the Nile in the delta region. Its city center was well protected, as it lay on an island in the river. Besides serving as the new capital, it was also the major military headquarters of the north, with a large permanent army that could be mobilized with speed to guard the entry and prevent Asian aliens from invading Egypt.

The grand city of Per-Rameses had its own attraction as the most modern city in ancient times. On its own, it was also developing as a commercial capital, thriving on trade with the neighbors. Riverine, like all other major cities, and with 30,000 inhabitants in an area four miles by two miles, it was one of the largest cities of Egypt, built to guard against foreign invaders but at the same time tolerant of alien merchants and traders. It hosted a floating population buzzing with people of all nations and tongues, including sinister elements, like any other international metropolis.

The palace and a temple complex devoted to Amun were situated in a large area in the center of the city. To their west, the layout of the posh region facing the river had a grid pattern of streets. The town planners had taken the measures to ensure the majesty and beauty of the city in the boroughs to the west. The locality was orderly, studded with noble mansions and villas. In contrast, the eastern part had ceded to the will of the inhabitants and developed haphazardly, with the usual winding roads, cul-de-sacs, and big and small houses popping up in free-for-all chaos, as in any other city. This was the region Hartapu had known so far, except for his visit to the palace.

This long ride gave Hartapu time to think of his situation. The contact had turned out to be an enticing girl, but he reminded himself he was here on a mission and not out to play hero and win a heart. He had yet to beware of the girl; he was still treading on insecure ground. Teremun was her boss, but to whom did the two owe their allegiance? Should he trust her just because…because what? She was not even a Hittite. As a native, she could have easily switched allegiance. How did she know about the dead man? Of course, such news would spread fast, reaching the ears in an alehouse in minutes. But yet…where was she leading him? Maybe Teremun was on his side, asking her to lead him to the fugitive officer. Yet she might be leading him elsewhere. She might be delivering him to the door of the devil's den. It was an abnormal situation. He felt like a child marching on, holding the hand of his mother, trusting her like none other.

At her hint, Hartapu followed her and jumped off the cart. She ran up to the driver and thanked him for his help.

"What kind of locality is this?" Hartapu asked. He was not the least impressed by the decrepit look of the place. It was the remnant of an old city, with narrow, winding lanes. There were more crisscrossing tracks with hurdles and gutters to jump over than roads, no easy passage, not simple even for nimble limbs. The dwellings were so close to the path or road that a passer-by could hear family dramas behind the thin walls.

"It is the safest place in town, at least for me, and I will tell you why," Met said, "but first let me know something about you."

Hartapus related the limited story he had rehearsed, about his mother being a Hittite healer from the north, his knowledge of both languages, and his profession. He confessed, rather, lied, that he had nothing spectacular or impressive to add. They turned into a lane with old mud houses interspersed with small shops.

"Do you want to hear about me?" Met smiled and looked up at him.

"Yes, of course. I am more than curious, but only if—"

"No cause to fear." She giggled. "As you may expect, it is a sad story. But with a happy ending."

She stopped before one of the shops, glanced at him over her shoulder, and said, "Wait here."

She walked in. Perplexed, Hartapu hung around, watching the few people around. He found her getting ever more mysterious with her words and moves.

After a few minutes, a boy of about ten came running out of the shop and ran down the lane. Met emerged from the shop with a smile.

They proceeded the way the boy had gone.

"All right, we are doubly safe here," Met said. "That boy is going to spread the word."

"That we are here?"

"Yes. This is our district, my district. I grew up here. We keep a close watch on all strangers who turn up. We do not want any disturbance, anyone stalking and lurking. We protect ourselves. We do not have the luxury of protection by the city guard. We have our own guards, all volunteers, keeping an eye on queer behavior in the community and suspicious intruders. The boy who ran ahead is spreading the message of our visit, and for the next few hours, several shopkeepers will keep an eye on strangers pursuing us."

"But customers are strangers." Hartapu did not see the logic in her explanation.

"Of course. By 'strangers,' I mean those who loiter and prowl here for no apparent reason. We have our own vigilance. The boy is going to announce our presence—"

"My presence, you mean."

"Yes, of course. I am from here. I don't need an announcement. The point is that if anyone follows us, like that fellow before, they will block him with all kinds of distracting offers and delay him until he gets exasperated and gives up."

Hartapu was impressed but did not know how to react. He said in a low voice, "Is it not a dangerous life you lead? What did you tell these people? What are we supposed to be doing here?"

"They know that I am taking you to my parents for business. That is all. My parents know you are coming. Teremun was here yesterday in the morning and hoped you would turn up yesterday or in the following days."

"Whew! I seem to be receiving more protection and care here than the gods would ever grant me. Did you tell the shopkeeper what it is all about and where we are ultimately heading?"

"Of course not. They know me, and they trust me. That is it."

Hartapu felt more honored than protected. In a way, his visit had been announced and appreciated. He belonged to a rare kind of nobility, thanks to Met. Now he, a foreigner on a sinister errand, belonged here in this community.

After a long silence, Met said, "Now for my story. Most such stories begin sadly, with child abuse and the like. In my case, it was not that bad. I was neither born a slave nor sold into slavery." She paused for a deep breath, slowing her pace. Hartapu adjusted his pace. He would have rather stopped to listen.

Her face turned grave. He noticed her lips droop, and she cleared her throat.

"My bad luck was I got orphaned when I was five, with my parents both falling ill and dying within weeks. Only the gods know why they took them away from me. I grew up at my aunt's. That woman was a beast. She had no children, and maybe that was the reason she hated children. She treated me like a slave, even worse."

After a few paces in silence, she said with her eyes fixed on the ground, "When I was about twelve, I overheard her talking to a merchant. Just imagine. They were discussing *my* future. From my neighbors, I found out who the merchant was. He was a procurer of girls for his customers in the nobility who wanted a service far more than what the maidservants would give. They wanted very young girls for hire to pamper and pounce on. I ran away from home. In fact, that was the best decision of my life.

"I ran up to a couple, both friends of my father who proved to be benevolent parent-like figures. Adopted by them, I grew up in their household with their children in a grand family atmosphere. They say I have a talent for making social contacts everywhere. No wonder everyone knows me in this community. I may even boast they all like and respect me. Working in an alehouse as a waitress or even an entertainer is not disdained in this community of simple people. None of us can afford to live a so-called respectable life of pretend normality and affluence but with all kinds of secrets behind thick walls and closed doors. That is the way of the genteel."

Hartapu absorbed the details in silence. Hearing the down-to-earth report of real life, he felt empathy but also embarrassed that he did not know how to react. He marched on, moved but helpless. Allowing some respectable lapse, he changed the subject,

"Is Zananzash holed up in this locality?"

"Yes, in a safe house, but a bit far off, almost at the end, near the main road leading to town. But first, we will meet my foster parents."

She looked up at the sky and laughed, her way of breaking the tension. "On time for dinner. They know our mission and where the man is kept. They work for Teremun, too, so do not worry."

* * *

They had passed the street full of shops and entered a residential area with small one-story houses. The surroundings offered a sight no different than elsewhere. It was the same landscape of the flat delta region, swampy, with reeds, tall grass, and low bushes between the houses. Some of the dwellings even had gardens in front. This could have been the dreamworld of the commoner but for a major defect. Without exception, the houses were all very old and dilapidated, needing repairs, if not demolition.

As he glanced around, Met said, "This is the ancient part of the city. This is near the region of Avaris, which was the capital long, long ago under the Hyksos. Have you heard of them?"

"I know that word only as a derisive term." Hartapu had often heard this word used as a curse by customers while shopping if a Hittite hawker would not budge in a bargain. He did not want to go into an explanation.

"Oh, they were people who came to power and took over the whole of our land."

"The whole of Kemet?"

"Yes. That was hundreds of years ago. All that I know of them is that they were brutal people who came from somewhere outside, from the north, with no culture, all aliens… Oh, I am sorry, Harti." She bit her lip.

Hartapu laughed. "Now I know even your tongue can slip. I don't mind that. I assure you, Met, I am a foreigner but not one of the Hyksos."

"I did not mean it that way. To be honest, you are no alien to me." She touched his shoulder with her fingertips.

"Nor are you an alien to me, dear." He playfully stroked her arm.

"Anyway, we have different origins and occupations, but we do have something in common, maybe much in common." She cocked her head and threw him a sideward glance.

After a pause, she asked, "Married?"

Hartapu shook his head. She said, "Sure, you have a girl somewhere."

Hartapu let that statement pass; anyway, it was a statement and not a question. He was in no mood to spill out his story.

"All right. I get it." Met gave up. "Maybe it was too personal. But I ought to know why you are doing all this. What for? As for me, in addition to my work in the alehouse, I do chores and get support and protection from the Hittite Teremun. How about you?"

"Same here. There is no difference. But we have yet to reach our goal."

Met fell quiet. Hartapu had to risk her being offended. He was too tired to keep on spinning tales about his life. At any rate, polite inquiry would come up once again when he met her parents.

The roads seemed not to have been constructed but to have appeared on their own accord, evolving with the trampling and persistence of mortals over the ages. Past a recess opening to a side street, there was a corner house conspicuous by its decoration: it presented in its front all kinds of wares made of reed and hemp. Amid a forest of baskets, bags, and furniture, from chairs and tables to chests stacked high, interspersed with smaller items, like handbags and sunshades, and with ropes of varying thickness dangling between them, Met led him to the entrance. While following her, he had to duck now and then beneath the baskets.

To their great comfort, they reached refuge from the glaring sunlight and its heat when they passed through an open door and entered a pitch-dark interior.

As his pupils were adjusting to the environment, Hartapu heard a woman call out, "Most welcome dear," followed by a rustle he interpreted as an embrace between the women, for it was followed by sounds of kissing.

Gradually, he saw Met standing before an elderly woman resting her short arms on Met's shoulders. Met introduced the woman as her mother, Tiaa, and mentioned that he was the visitor on the assignment.

Tiaa nodded. "We expected both of you. Teremun was here yesterday morning to announce your arrival on one of the coming days."

"Mom, where is Dad? Is he away?"

Tiaa said, "He has gone to deliver some medicine to a patient. He will be back soon. First, I propose both of you sit down and relax. After Ankhef comes, we will have dinner together."

After a pause, she asked, "What would our guest like to drink? Besides water, of course." She waved towards the jug and the mugs in the corner and smiled at Hartapu. "A beer? I can also offer you wine."

Hartapu nodded his thanks and asked for a beer.

As she walked away towards the kitchen, Met offered Harti a chair in the corner and curled up on a reed mat next to him.

"She is a healer," she said, tossing her head towards the kitchen. "She takes care of the sick and the injured in the neighborhood and is known for her talent in healing."

Hartapu began the chat after Tiaa handed over to him the beer mug. "You have an interesting vocation, I hear."

"Well…" Tiaa shrugged. "If I am of help, I am glad. I cannot call it my trade, but in a way, it amounts to that, without any bargaining, as you do before deals. They thank me with some presents of value in return; I would not call that a fee. I am not a *heka* priestess. In the present case, my husband has gone to the patient only because the patient believes more in my medicine than I do." She broke out in merry laughter.

"What do you mean by that, milady?" Hartapu asked with some hesitation. A healer not convinced of her own medication?

"The problem is this." She tapped her cheek. "That patient had a lockjaw. You know, when a person cannot open their mouth or close it. The jaw gets stuck. It happens when the cord connecting or hooking the claw-like end of the jawbone to the cheekbone gets contracted. I helped with warm and cold massages at different times and asked the patient to eat plenty of nuts after recovery. I also gave him a vial of chamomile for better sleep. After a week, he recovered, but he still insists on a second vial. He is convinced the chamomile was the cure, so I let him have it. Ankhef did me the favor of delivering it to the patient."

"How is Dad getting on? Tell me now whatever he would not want to hear."

Hartapu found this discreet approach by the daughter to discuss her father remarkable. His father would call it "kitchen talk." He, for one, felt honored to be present and treated as a family member this way.

"What shall I say?" Tiaa said, slapping her lap and rolling her eyes. "He is managing what he can. He loves his work and has now begun training youngsters in his trade. Formerly, they were only kids weaving for fun."

Met turned to Harti. "My dad is a basket maker. It is his trade, passion, and—"

"His life," Tiaa added, seating herself beside Met on the mat. She turned towards Hartapu. "The problem he has is his failing eyesight. I cannot help him with my art and magic, and no healer I know offers a remedy. It is his old age. With the grace of the gods, his fingers are as nimble as ever, and he has enough customers. Life goes on."

After a pause, she added that they sold the wares at their door and did not go out to hawk in the streets. Once a month, they borrowed a cart from one of their neighbors to offer an assortment of items at the Avaris market.

The room got dark all of a sudden. The light from the entrance was eclipsed by a silhouette of a man at the door. He strode in and went straight to a corner to put away his walking stick. It was Met's father, Ankhef. He turned around slowly, noticing the presence of his visitors. He greeted his daughter with glee and turned to Hartapu with the same mood, as if he were meeting an old friend.

"Nice to be seeing you here, young man," he said with a broad smile. "Only yesterday, Teremun was in all praise of you. You seem to have impressed him a great deal. Have you been working for him?"

Hartapu had jumped up on Ankhef's entry. He waited for the old man to take his chair and remove his shoes. Then he squatted next to him. Met came up with a glass of water for her father, a gesture of respect and love.

"Not exactly," Hartapu said. He was ready for these casual questions. "I happen to know him from a previous encounter, like the man I will be meeting soon."

"Of course. That poor devil. I believe he got hurt during his escape from Hatti." Ankhef looked at his wife.

She nodded and added, "I asked Teremun to get the man a new bandage from Kem.

"Kem?" Met asked.

"Yes, she has a stall not far from the house, on the corner of the main road. Besides her usual wares, she also sells some articles from here."

"It is good you reminded me of her, Mom. I need some kohl paste for my eyes. I wonder if you can spare me some, or should I go to her?"

"Ask her, dear. You know I rarely use makeup for the eyes. Kem deals with cosmetics and scents as ever. Now medical stuff is a new line for her."

"Zananzash is quartered in a house Teremun has arranged," Akhnef said and smiled at Met. "It is very near the stall. In the 'ghost house,' as Met would call it."

"Oh, that one." Met turned to Hartapu. "It is not far from here. When I was a child, it stood empty for ages. We children gave it the name 'ghost house,' spreading the gossip that spirits of the dead visit it at night. Later, an old woman lived in it. She left, and once again, it stood empty for months. It was not even locked up. Now Teremun says he uses it as a guest house or safe house for the refugees. I do not know whatever arrangements he has with the owner, if there is one."

The dinner was vegetarian. They were not affluent enough to serve meat. The menu consisted of fresh as well as baked vegetables, from radishes and lettuce to beans and onions, spiced with garlic. Hartapu enjoyed the delicacy of the cuisine, noticing variety even in the bread rolls stuffed with peas or fruit. All this was served along with a pot of sauce for the bread. In addition, there was a plate of melon, grapes, and dates. On a separate plate, sweets based on honey and carob had been spread.

It was, indeed, a festive dinner, considering the simple social status of the family. Hartapu wondered if he was being honored or Met was being pampered. He thanked the family for the grand dinner. Tiaa acknowledged the complement without any further comment.

When it came to after-dinner chat, Hartapu tried his best to block any talk about his past. He turned the topic to his present occupation and discussed the problems of importing wares from Hatti, the reason his boss had gone all the way to Ugarit. Ankhef was a good listener, and on his turn, he went into his problems with his customers and his new venture of teaching novices in basket-weaving.

After exhausting the subject, he asked, "When do you propose to meet Zananzash? He is in a house not far from here if we use the shortcut through the bushes."

"Yet it would be too late to make it today," Tiaa said. "Soon it will get dark, and you have a long way home. We suggest both of you stay here for the night. Accommodations are no problem. We have two rooms upstairs. Met and I can arrange to make enough space in each room for a bed. You can visit him tomorrow unless he is expecting you today."

Hartapu looked at Ankhef, who nodded with a smile. Met leaned towards him and said in a low voice, "By the time you have spoken to Zananzash, it will be dark, Harti. I suggest we stay here tonight, walk through the bushes in daylight tomorrow, and return to the city."

It was, indeed, very gracious of the family to put him up—one more surprise for the day, this time, a cordial one.

Hartapu nodded. "You are right. It is, indeed, a long way home. I thank you for the offer. I can look him up tomorrow morning and proceed from there." He noticed Met lean back and smile.

Hartapu was, indeed, feeling tired. It had been a day that felt longer than usual, one full of strange events. It had begun with his contact getting killed, his aimless stroll, and an incarnation of a wonderful girl—in an alehouse, of all places. Now he was secure in the fortress of a family offering undue hospitality. All this was a whirlwind of occurrences with his job yet undone. He needed to be prepared for any more surprises in the coming days. Still, he could not just jump up and run to bed. Politeness demanded more conversation after this matter of staying overnight was settled.

His host was quicker to continue the chat. "I hear, like Teremun, you are also a Hittite. Yet we all have the same interest. We support you."

"How come?" Hartapu asked.

"First of all, we are doing a favor for the compatriots of Teremun. We have known him for a long time, and we do not want to refuse him help nor let his people down. It is not a crime to help others in dire need. Not in this country, not under our pharaoh."

That remark could be taken as a careful reproach of the Hittites and their tumult, but Hartapu took no offense. Had Ankhef used it as a taunt? As if to soothe the matter, Ankhef added, "Anyway, we are always on the side of those who seek protection from persecution."

"Let it be," Tiaa said. "Our guest may not be interested in our views. He is only a scribe seeing an old friend."

That remark got the better of Hartapu. He stepped into the trap and released his opinion, yet he just managed to control his emotion as he spoke.

"It is all the fault of the present king of Hatti grabbing the throne and causing misery to one and all."

"Precisely," Tiaa said. "That is one more reason for us to take care of the stream of refugees crossing over, risking their lives. Look at that officer Zananzash, who has lost everything, even his family, and is sitting forlorn and insecure in a foreign land. Whatever is going on in Hatti, all we know is Mursili is the dynastic heir and rightful king. His uncle has usurped the throne."

"You are well informed about the goings-on in my land," Hartapu said.

Tiaa laughed. "All this we know from Teremun. His version."

Ankhef sat with his lips pressed together. He stretched his arm out to hand the empty mug to Met.

He shrugged said, "Quite. There is also another version of the story that I heard from others. Some of my Hittite customers say it is the fault of King Mursili, who attacked his uncle and lost the bet. Do you want to know that story?" He looked around, not sure if he should go into that.

"Tell us, Dad," Met prompted, looking up to him with her eyes wide open like a child wanting to hear a bedtime story.

"Having ruled in peace for seven years as king of Hatti, Mursili attacked his uncle, who was governing two small regions in the Hittite empire. It was without any provocation. In retaliation, Hattusili drove out his nephew from Hattusha. So, the story goes."

"Whatever happened," Tiaa said, "Mursili is the dynastic heir and has to be respected, even by his uncle."

"You are right, dear. Most Hittites think that way. There is a rebellion in the offing," Ankhef said.

Hartapu was quiet, trying to be nobody. How could he defend his father without exposing himself? As they did not know his identity, his opinion was not called for. But he did, indeed, feel the call for some comment on his part, some kind of engagement. He reminded himself he was a simple scribe with no political opinion. From the others, there had been no provocation, no offense meant. Maybe Ankhef was also testing him, having heard some hints on his identity from Teremun. He attempted to get out of the mess without sounding harsh.

He stretched his back to show some indifference and said, "Well, who knows which version is right and which one is true? It is a matter of interpretation. The matters in Hatti will get settled one way or the other."

All along, he noticed Met had been giving him a steady stare, scrutinizing his reaction.

Abruptly, he turned to her. "You are looking tired, Met."

She winced as if awakened from a dream. She shook her head, and her locks swung over her shoulders. She paused and then said, "Oh, no. I was just thinking of Nonjmet. I had expected to see her today, Mom."

Ankhef smiled and said to Hartapu, "Nonjmet is my daughter. Met has a sister and two brothers."

"Oh, really?" Hartapu was relieved with the change of subject. "Have they all moved out? None are living here with you?"

Tiaa beamed and said, "Tell him, dear. In the meantime, Met and I will clear the table." They picked up the plates and mugs and moved away to the kitchen. As the women walked away, Hartapu heard Tiaa say, "My other daughter will be coming the day after tomorrow."

Ankhef took a deep breath. "You know Met's story, about her childhood?"

"Yes, I do."

"She came to us when she was twelve. A gem of a child. She is more often here than the other kids. Anyway, Tiaa and I have been blessed with wonderful children."

On entering the kitchen, mother Tiaa was free to talk about the family, as the men had gone back to serious discussion about the rest of the world as if they had influence and mattered. The kitchen was the place for the real themes that affected the family directly and conversations were not meant for the ears of others. Moreover, there was much "female stuff," as she used to call it: talk about the marital lives of the children, for which only her daughter would have an open mind. She gave a brief report about the sons, Anen and Khety, away in Iunu and working as stonemasons. Then she turned to the daughter, Nodjmet, living with her family in Per-Ramesses, and delved into the state of the girl's pregnancy.

"It is a pity you will not be here when your sister comes," Tiaa said in conclusion. "We are expecting her only the day after tomorrow, and I hoped you would offer her some company."

"I don't know, Mom. Of course, I would love to see her. It has been a long while."

As they turned to return to the living room, Tiaa grabbed Met's arm and stopped her. She tossed her head towards the room. "Are you friends?"

Met frowned and turned to the door. "I don't know, Mom. I think Dad called us," she said.

Tiaa shook Met's arm. "Dad can wait. But tell me first, are you friends only or…"

Met puckered her lips and shrugged. Tiaa knew that gesture. She was only avoiding the question.

"As I told you, Mom, it is too early for me to say. Now, let us go."

Tiaa could bet she was lying.

Chapter 8

COMRADES IN ARMS

In the morning, after breakfast, Met and Hartapu set out for a stroll along the short passage to the "ghost house." The shortcut meant they had to walk through the vegetation, but as both had footwear, thorns and insects were no problem. However, they had to watch out for small snakes and scorpions.

While Hartapu concentrated on the ground, Met spoke of her adventures in this region during her childhood, running around these spots and playing hide and seek in this wilderness. Sometimes it was even serious hiding from her parents after some mischief with her siblings. Once, they had discovered in the kitchen a jar resting far above on the shelf. It was stuffed with sweets with nuts and honey their mother had prepared for some guests coming the following week. They had plundered it and gobbled half the contents. On hearing their mother's scream, they had bolted and hidden here in the undergrowth for hours, waiting for her to cool down.

Hartapu listened to her memories, reflecting on his own childhood but suppressing the urge to respond. Always behind her, he signaled his interest, reacting with chuckles, laughs, and brief comments.

After they had stamped through quite a few thorny bushes and fallen branches trampled by others, Hartapu saw the house from its side, standing a bit aloof from the bushes. The clearing was only a reminder of a formerly maintained garden; it was now under the slow attack of wild nature reclaiming its possession. The house looked no better or worse than the others he had seen so far, though more languid, tired, and lonesome.

After climbing the three steps in front, he knocked on the door. He heard, "Come in." He pushed it open; it reacted with a reluctant moan. He turned back to Met, and she followed. On entry, they stood in a hall with a man seated on a heavy-looking chair with armrests. He was in his forties, with a receding hairline and a scraggly beard. One leg was stretched and bandaged.

He said, "I presume you have been sent by—" He stopped. "By whom?"

"Teremun. It is about some information you would like to pass on to me," Hartapu answered, wondering if the man also wanted to hear the code words.

"They call me Harti," he added.

"Right." Zananzash grinned and nodded. "I am Zananzash. I hope you remember."

"Of course, I do."

"I remember meeting you with your parents at the *Purulli* festival," the man said. The autumn festival lasted for weeks, together with the procession featuring the Hattian storm god Telipinu and the goddess of Arinna, which began in Hattusha and proceeded to various other cities. Zananzash had been the official in charge of the organization and had met the members of the royal family, who were the hosts of the occasion. After a due greeting, the royal pair had taken over the responsibility, and Zananzash had attended to the royal children.

But Hartapu mentioned one more occasion.

"I recall more clearly the boar hunt to which you took me. I could accompany the seasoned hunters, who told me so many stories. Some were tall tales, but I am sure some were true." He had been so excited as a lad to join a group led by Zananzash, a passionate hunter. In anticipation, Hartapu had spent a sleepless night in excitement.

"Oh, yes, I remember that. I bet you were impressed by the company. Maybe we will make it together again and go after some other beast the next time," Zananzash added and laughed.

He threw a quick glance at Met and turned back to Hartapu. "Do forgive me if I do not address you in the customary way. You will understand. But I do know you and recognized you right away. My self-introduction to you was also a formality."

He turned to Met and said, "You are the daughter of—"

She completed his sentence with, "Tiaa and Akhnef. My name is Met."

"Fine." Zananzash nodded. "Your parents were of great help to me. You have noticed I can speak your language a bit, but when it comes to business, forgive me if I carry on in our language with Har—Harti. As a friendly gesture, I propose you call me Zan for short."

Met nodded with a smile. Hartapu ignored this offer. He had known the officer since childhood, and out of respect, he would never call by name an officer who had worked under his father.

He cast a wary look at the surroundings.

Zananzash chuckled. "Are you admiring my residence?"

Hartapu smiled and asked him, "Are you really safe here? I see you are alone and have no guards."

"Teremun brought me here only two days ago. He has trouble finding guards, mainly for the night. Anyway, he said there would be guards from tomorrow evening onward, day and night. As of now, I cannot imagine some devil coming after me all the way from Hattusha."

Hartapu did not react. Was Zananzash being modest, downright ignorant, or only naïve, taking shelter in simplistic logic? He also refrained from asking why the man had left Hatti. Instead, he asked about Zan's health.

He heard the account of the injury incurred during Zan's flight from Hatti by sea. He had been hidden in a cargo boat after it had been loaded.

When the voyage began, a barrel had freed itself and rolled towards him. He had tried to jump away, but his leg had been caught up. His ankle had gotten jammed, and the injury had begun to bleed.

As if to break the chat, Zan picked up the walking stick lying beside him on the floor and got up slowly, declining any help.

"Drinks and water are over there in the corner. Please help yourself. I will be back in a minute." He hobbled off with his stick to another room, which would be the kitchen if the house had the customary layout.

Met squatted in a corner, bearing silent witness to the chat between Harti and their host. Hartapu seated himself on a small chair in front of the empty one. Zan returned with a bag hung over a shoulder while the stick guided him to his chair. After seating himself with a loud sigh, he retrieved from the bag a bundle wrapped in linen and opened it. It contained several clay tablets. Hartapu recognized the standard size, typical of the official ones used in Hattusha.

Zan held out one of them and said, switching to Nesite, "I have nine tablets in all. Here is one of them. I have another bunch stored elsewhere for my safety. Take a look at these. They are official messages from the present king. You will have no problem with the officious language used."

Hartapu frowned as he looked at the piece. He leaned back when he noticed it was an internal communication with the royal seal. The text was in the direct style of an authority, not a rigmarole with redundant passages in the style of diplomatic texts. There were no elaborate greetings and salutations.

One of them was a note by Hattusili in response to a query from his envoy to Ugarit, a major port and protectorate of the Hittite kingdom. The emissary had been apparently sent there to convince the local ruler to continue the military alliance with the Hatti kingdom, an accord that had been established along with nearly twenty states over a decade ago. Hattusili had cleared the doubts of his envoy and affirmed the need for a continuation of the agreement.

When Hartapu stretched himself without any comment, Zan handed out the next tablet.

Hartapu took his time to read all the nine documents, one by one, and mull over their meaning and significance for the pharaoh.

"Well, what do you make of them?" Zan asked.

"Very interesting." Hartapu was impressed, but on impulse, he felt he should not show much enthusiasm. "I do not know how much the pharaoh is already informed about the situation in Hatti and the intentions of Hattusili, but these documents are authentic, and if they are recent—"

"They are two to four months old. I left Hatti only some two weeks ago." Zan was leaning forward, his eyes alert. His face remained calm, but he could hardly hide the anxiety in his voice.

"Why are you bringing these documents to the attention of the pharaoh?" Hartapu bored further.

"You can imagine I brought them along for my own security. I hope this valuable service will be of help in seeking refuge and protection here now that I had to flee from the regime. I am sure the pharaoh would appreciate my authentic help."

"How the pharaoh judges or values this information will depend on his state of knowledge. I cannot comment on that."

"I have more such correspondence, not here but hidden somewhere else."

Hartapu had to take his word for that. He did not want to belittle the poor man's hope. He conceded, "Your position as the chief of information of the previous king will be a great asset if you are willing to cooperate with this kingdom. It is beyond any question. But as far as the value of this information is concerned, I cannot say much."

"I know. But you will appreciate my interest in this matter. This information ought to be part of a bargain."

"Yes, of course. It concerns your safety and your future here. But I am not coming as an emissary of the pharaoh. Right now, I am only a messenger you can trust, and I can assure you the tablets will reach the eyes of the pharaoh and his vizier. But I cannot make any commitments

nor give you hope on behalf of the pharaoh. The best way would be—"
Hartapu paused on purpose.

Zan leaned forward and raised his eyebrows. "What do you suggest?"

"You come along with us. I could accompany you to the palace
as your escort and let you explain the messages personally. I am sure
the royalty will not turn a blind eye to your documents, nor to your
present situation. Only, do not expect to haggle over this subject with
the pharaoh. He did not solicit help from you. You have come to him on
your own and have a plea, not the other way around."

"It would be a great opportunity if you could open the door for an
audience. I am prepared to go with you." Zan stared at his leg.

"Do not worry about your wound. We can arrange for a cart and drive
the hour or so it takes to get to the palace. I will try to accommodate you
somewhere nearby and in safety until you get the audience."

Hartapu turned to Met. "Would that be possible?"

"I don't understand you," Met replied.

Hartapu apologized and put the question in her language: "Would it
be possible to get a cart for us to take Zananzash away from here today
to a place near the palace?"

"Do you mean to get a cart right now?"

"Yes, I propose we move right away."

"I do not think we can get hold of a cart and a driver today at all. It is
too late. All are engaged bringing wares to the market; my parents could
try to get one tomorrow for half the day."

Zan took the tablets from Hartappu and began wrapping them up
again.

"Let us hurry. Maybe we will be lucky and get a cart, at least, for
tomorrow," Hartapu said. "Any cart will do."

He would have preferred to move away with the documents without
dragging Zan along: mission accomplished. But he understood Zan
would not sacrifice his one chance of securing his position as a fugitive,
which was hardly better than that of Hartapu and his father. Moreover,

Zan's personal appearance would give more gravitas to the documents. Now his concern was the total absence of guards, let alone other aids like servants, for the prominent fugitive Zananzash. One more night alone with the documents? He wondered why Teremun had ignored this minimal precaution in protecting Zan.

* * *

When Met and Hartapu reached Met's home, it was getting cold and dark. After a quick dinner and a chat with her parents, Met announced she would go to bed early. When Akhnef nodded with a yawn, Hartapu got the hint. The beds had been made, and sleep needed no preparation.

Bidding her good night, Hartapu went into his room and stared at his bed, spread out on the floor. It had been a leisurely day for him, quite a break from the monotony of his daily life as a scribe. He had met the man and read the documents. He would be completing his task the next day. With the tedium disrupted and pepped up by youthful vigor for adventure and action, he felt no weariness. He could have spent another hour chatting or alone on a long walk in the moonlight, just dreaming. Instead, he gazed at the bed with reluctance.

"Do you need anything, Harti?" he heard Met call out through the door behind him. Her voice sounded so clear and dear.

"No. I am fine." Then he heard the door close. He turned and squatted on the bed. When he looked up, he was surprised. Met was in the room with her back to the door. He jumped up.

She said with a bewitching smile, "My parents have retired for the night."

Most of the time, he had seen Met in profile. Now, with a frontal view, he had the joy of perceiving her total beauty. There she stood in simple splendor, her head slightly tilted, her arms dangling. He was dazzled by the allure of her posture, grace, large brown eyes, and warm smile with pearl-like teeth, whose radiance would disarm a warrior.

Hartapu stood motionless. The partners stared at each other in silence.

Suddenly she stepped towards him; she had never been so close to him. He felt her breath and sensed her smell and warmth. His hand took the initiative. It touched the long curls in her hair and stroked them. His breath quickened. His heart throbbed. She raised her hand to his. Would she push his away? She did not but grabbed it and kissed it.

She swallowed, bent forward, and said in a low voice, "Let us be more than just friends, Harti."

Her whisper and words broke down the last bastion. His mind sought the void, and his reason faded out. He felt his lips quiver. She put her finger on them for silence. Her lips followed the finger as she slid into his arms.

During the long kiss, his chest seemed to expand with a sensation of liberation. Then, as it collapsed again, he felt gratitude. Hartapu watched his instinct, his other self, take over. It was *Harti*, the free man within, one possessed only by passion, without a need to struggle, survive, and hide, one no more chained by thoughts about decorum, duty, and destiny. *Harti*, a vagabond without shackles, let loose to roam the world, free of commitment. *Harti* had met his match.

He gave in, secure in a space of privacy to celebrate the intimacy, secure in a time, by centuries removed from the age of forbidden sensuality.

* * *

Soon after dawn the next day, Hartapu felt relaxed, having slept well in the shelter of a family where he was somehow welcome, although he was not even a relative. As he rubbed his eyes, he felt honored to be the only one Zananzash trusted. Hartapu had again found someone for whom he was not a nobody. He was the prince. On the other hand, even without knowing his identity, Met had made him her lover. For Anat, he was a hero. What was he really? A scribe, a courier, a spy on a mission, a hero in an epic, or a prince of his own dreams? What really mattered ought not to be what he thought of himself, nor what he felt. In the eyes of the others, he would be known and recognized for his deeds, not his inherited status. He must prove his worth to himself first and then to others.

After a simple breakfast of bread and goat's milk, he stayed back with Ankhef while the ladies left to pick up a cart from a neighbor. Ankhef spoke to him about the plans he had to move into a place near the market and set up his shop there instead of transporting the articles all the way to the marketplace once a week. As Hartapu listened, he noticed how he was learning more and more about the daily worries, struggles, and little joys of the commoners. They were glad to maintain their health and existential status and hardly had the energy, time, or resources to defend and cultivate their ego. They shared what little they possessed. That was real life.

It took quite a while before the women walked in through the door.

"We had to wait so long. The cart had been lent to someone else," Tiaa said. Sweat pearls on her forehead spoke of the heat the sun had picked up in the meantime.

"They have to find another one, this time a cart drawn by an old horse. But there is no driver."

Met was drinking water and said after a sip, "There will be no problem. I suggest we proceed with the cart even without the driver for this short distance."

"It is a good idea, Met. Zananzash will be waiting for us, and I want him to come along before he changes his mind. We will bring him here first. But can you drive the horse?" Hartapu asked.

Met said, putting on her shoes, "Sure."

"Don't worry," Akhnef said. "The women know how to handle an old horse." The joke caught on when he laughed. Tiaa smirked and shook her head.

Met said, "This time, we have to drive around to reach the main road and proceed from there. No shortcut."

Tiaa said, "On the way, you will come across Kem. She will have her stall open by now."

"Ah, yes. Thank you, Mom. We will stop at her stall first. After that, we will pick up Zan."

She threw a quick glance again at Hartapu. "Oh, Mother asked me to stay on for one more day to see my sister Nonjet. I will stay here after we return with Zan."

They hopped onto the cart before the house. It was spacious and empty but still smelled of the previous cargo. The vegetables, which could have been fresh on delivery, had left the ghost of putrid refuse.

Hartapu sat next to Met, who drove the horse. She made a clicking noise with her mouth, and the horse obeyed and moved. She steered it towards the main road. On reaching it, they turned left, and after quite a while on the road, Hartapu saw the corner stall where a narrow road turned to the left off the main road. After turning onto this road, she stopped the cart and jumped off. Hartapu followed.

The stall was a shelter of reeds with some wooden support guarding against the sunshine and occasional wind and rain.

"Do you know that woman Kem?" Hartapu asked.

"I have seen her once or twice visiting my mother. She would not recognize me. Nor do I want to introduce myself to her."

"Why not?"

"She would think I am trying to take advantage of her acquaintance with my mother. Moreover, remember, I am on a secret mission." She laughed.

On Met's call, a woman on the floor popped up from her squat. Kem looked old, with wrinkles all over her face, and was chewing some stuff, some kind of leaves popular among the natives. Hartapu had yet to find out what it was. He stood at a distance, half listening to the discussion about kohl and other items concerning makeup.

After the matter was settled, Met peered at a corner in the stall and said, "I see you also sell herbs and even tinctures for healing wounds."

"Yes, all things, including medicine. If you want— "

"Oh, you have bandages. Can I have one?"

Kem moved to the corner, looked over her shoulder, and asked, "For that man in that house?" She tossed her head at the rear.

"I don't know what you mean."

"Only an hour ago, some men came here and asked me if I knew any of their countrymen who were wounded and looking for help. They could hardly express themselves properly. I told them I had helped the man living alone in that house over there around the corner." She pointed to the rear with her thumb. "It is strange. Only two days ago, I was asked by another friend to go along with him and dress the wound. But this time, these new friends were not interested in the bandage I offered. They just walked away."

Hartapu stepped nearer to listen carefully.

Kem pointed at him and asked Met, "Another friend of that man?" Met said, "Yes."

Kem looked down and muttered half to herself, "All foreigners."

Hartapu could read her face. He shrugged off how that word was meant. But his thoughts raced ahead.

"Did you hear that?" Hartapu asked Met as they proceeded toward the cart. "There is something wrong. When did Teremun visit your parents?"

"They said that was two days ago, in the morning."

"If the first one was Teremun, who were the other 'friends' today, two days after Teremun, asking for a wounded compatriot?"

She shrugged. "How would anyone know about the wounded man besides Teremun? If they were the guards, they would not be posing such questions. Teremun would not be sending anyone like that to look him up. In fact, it is top secret."

Hartapu said, "I thought even Teremun did not know where Zananzash was being hidden. I had to look for contacts to get the information. All right, he did not want to tell me."

Hartapu stopped and turned. Then he hesitated.

"There is no point in asking that woman more questions. She would only get suspicious and spread the word. As it is, she gives a damn for foreigners and would only make some gossip out of it. I noticed you did not introduce yourself. Could she have recognized you?"

"No. I saw her only once or twice when she visited mother. That was years ago."

As they approached the cart, Hartapu said, "Let us leave the cart where it is and go on foot. First, I would like to take a view of the house from a distance."

On turning to the right to enter the narrow road, they saw the front of the lonely "ghost house" occupied by Zananzash. The narrow road was apparently rarely frequented, for it led to only a few houses situated at a distance. The surroundings consisted of wild vegetation, the low bushes and small me-too plants yearning to be called trees. There were no cultivated fields or gardens in view. After they turned towards the house, they noticed a chariot parked to one side in the front, in the shade and quite some distance away from the entrance.

After a few steps, Hartapu grabbed Met's hand. Pulling her, he rushed to the right and crouched in a recess among the bushes. He had heard a sound and seen the front door open a crack. As they watched, it flung wide open, and a wiry young man stepped out. He strode towards the chariot, fumbled around in it with his back to them, and turned. Another man, tall and broad-chested, filled the gap of the door. The young man had picked up a coil of rope. Hartapu and Met were near enough to recognize the coarsely woven hemp rope, the sort used by fishermen. He held it up to the man at the door, who nodded. The rope was brought in, and the young man closed the door behind him.

"Two visitors," Hartapu whispered.

"At the least." Met nodded. "Who could that be?"

She tried to say something, but he raised his hand, and she fell silent. Hartapu had a hunch. He was right.

* * *

That morning, Zananzash had been surprised by an unwelcome guest.

Suppilamus was seated on a small chair directly facing his erstwhile colleague. He had been quite senior to him, and their career paths had never crossed. Suppilamus was in charge of internal affairs pertaining only to the Hittite kingdom and reported to the vizier. Zananzash had overseen internal security, which also included the vassal states and protectorates, which depended on the safety offered to them by the king. Accordingly, he reported directly to the king.

Staring at this erstwhile senior and deserter of today, Suppilamus took a deep breath with his impatience still under check and said, "I have to remind you again, dear colleague, that this is not a chat between old chums, nor do I have any past grudge against you, for we never had any clash or grudge with each other in our profession. I do not know, nor do I care to know, what made you a deserter of your cause, a traitor to the crown, whatever personal allegiance you might have had for the previous king. I can imagine you got scared after the turn of events. You had cause to fear that once the previous king was toppled, you would lose your position and protection. Then your victims waiting outdoors would pounce on you, seeking revenge. Anyway, it is your decision and your problem."

There was no reaction to the taunt. Zananzash sat blinking without having uttered a word.

"Your problem now is you do not understand the gravity of the situation you are in," Suppilamus said. "Right now, I have taken plenty of time to solicit your cooperation in my official work. Your silence is no encouragement. Once again, I am not raising any absurd demands. If you assist us in finding the fugitive king, our erstwhile majesty that fled the kingdom, you will be free to go wherever you like."

He licked his lips and added as an afterthought in a soothing tone, "It will be an easy matter for me to put a word to our king that you cooperated and were even instrumental in my finding Mursili. He may even pardon you and re-install you as his spymaster, stationed here as my successor to lead the informants serving his majesty. There will be enough work to track all the other fugitives. You may even be united with your family here or back in Hattusha if you choose. We can work it out, and I can beseech a royal pardon and approval."

Zananzash made no signs of response. Suppilamus would not let up. "I do not know whatever you have been promised from the other side. What for? You were the master of information for Hatti. You were also involved in various operations against Kemet, in fact, against all the military adventures of Kemet. If it is a matter of your loyalty to Hatti, do you really want to prove your loyalty to an erstwhile king, losing your home, family, and whoever your friends were, roaming in a strange land as a vagabond? All that for a king and prince who are doomed? Or has someone put you under pressure? Is that the reason you are speechless, acting deaf and dumb?" Suppilamus shrugged, shook his head, and slapped his thighs.

He paused again and looked around, throwing a fleeting glance at the two men standing beside him. One of them was his subordinate, Mashanda, the tall man with a beard from the alehouse. The other one was a restless figure shifting his weight from one leg to the other and pressing his lips. A third man stood at the door, clasping his hands and awaiting orders.

Mashanda butted in. "Your life does not count. Not even that of your king Mursili." He looked at Suppilamus. "Tell him."

Suppilamus sighed. "As it stands, either Mursili agrees to come with us and face justice in Hattusha or we show him another door straight to the underworld. In this context, do you think your life counts at all?"

After a long silence, Suppilamus shook his head. "All right. I notice you do not get it. I repeat: all I want is for you to cooperate with me and find a way through your contacts to lead us to Mursili. I want to have a word with him. His response will decide his fate, not what you say nor what I say."

He raised his voice. "You are staring at me without a reaction like a donkey in the desert. We are both professional in these matters and get things done. In fact, we have much in common. You were known not only for your quick work but also for the brutal methods you used. I know all your tricks to bend one's will, all your inventions in intimidation to extract information. I would say most of them are your own creations, improvisations, and are standard professional methods by now."

Another pause followed.

"Remember, we can apply your own methods to arrive at a conciliatory situation. You know well what I mean. I am sure you do not want to know how it is to be on the wrong side of the tormentor's tongs." He grinned and pointed at Zan's leg.

"We can start from there."

Mashanda cleared his throat. Suppilamus turned to him and raised his hand. He looked back to Zananzash.

"Mashanda is eager for action. But not here and not now. I have found a remote place for you where you can take more time to sit and think and we can have another kind of talk. If you do not find your voice even then, Mashanda would see to it, shall we say, he will be of help. It is up to you whether that new seclusion will turn out to be your new home or a prison; it depends on how you conduct yourself and what you experience in that damned dungeon. It could be a prelude to your encounter with the goddess Lelwani in the netherworld. Your choice. As for now, I will be off to make the arrangements for your reception and will return soon. In the meantime, you can enjoy the company of Mashanda. Maybe your mouth will open in my absence."

He slapped his thighs and rose, raking away the chair, which wobbled.

"Once again." Suppilamus glared down upon his captive and pointed his finger at him. "I demand to know where we can find Mursili and his son. If you really do not know, swear to work with us and find their burrow with the help of your local friends. Don't ever tell us you do not know how to go about it. You know ways and means. You have enough contacts who have helped you so far. We will keep you under observation and make sure you do not flip back and forth. This is not your spy game. Make a decision and give us your plan at the latest by when I return. Your future is in your hands." He laughed and patted Zan's shoulder. "And your body is in *our* hands."

He turned to Mashanda. "See what you can do. But be careful."

He swaggered towards the door.

* * *

Hartapu and Met were about to get up from behind the bush when they saw the door open again. A young man, not the one they had seen first with the rope in hand, was followed by a burly, tall man of middle age. The men walked up to the chariot. The youth helped the other heavy man climb up and seat himself. Then he went around to the other side and jumped onto the vehicle.

The first man turned to the door and called out to the tall man standing there, "Mashanda, once again, be careful with him. Don't mess up this time."

Hartapu watched the two drive past and managed to get a close look at both of them. They drove up to the end of the road and turned left, the way Hartapu and Met had come, presumably to get to the main road heading back to the city. Hartapu heard Met gasp.

"I know the man, the older one," she said. "He is a regular customer of the alehouse. Only yesterday… Oh, look there." She pointed at the turn. Two men came around the bend from the other side and stopped. They were having an animated conversation. One of them was conspicuous, wearing the blue-white scarf. That stalker again. On closer look, Hartapu recognized the other man as Teremun. His head was bent, and his face was grave with a deep frown.

Hartapu asked Met, "Do you recognize them?"

"Sure, one of them is Teremun," she said. "But the other one is the fellow—"

It was too much for Hartapu. "Come," he said, cutting her short. He ran across the road and stopped before the two men. Met was quick to join him.

"Hi, I am glad to see you. What is going on?" Teremun asked once he'd recovered from his surprise.

Hartapu controlled his breath and lowered his head. He pointed his finger straight at the other man with the scarf and asked in a deep voice, "That is what I want to ask you. First, tell me, who is this fellow?"

"Oh, this is Bak. He works for me."

"I ask because he was tracking Met the other day."

Hartapu could have lashed out at them. Teremun frowned and looked at the man.

Bak said, "I am sorry about that. I was to follow you until you met the contact in the copper shop to protect you. After you missed your contact there, I was curious when you came out of the alehouse with a girl, so I followed. I did not know she was your contact."

"Even then," Hartapu hit back, "do you think I need protection when I am with a girl? I don't need a guardian."

Bak stared at the ground. Teremun shook his head and stared at Bak.

"But Met was quick to notice you were being followed," Hartapu said.

Teremun tried to take the steam off the discussion. "You are very attentive, Met. My compliments." Teremun bowed to her with a broad grin.

Taking the hint, Met changed the subject.

"Did you see the men in the chariot? One of them is a regular customer at the alehouse."

"Sure," Teremun said. "That is why we are worried. The elder one is Suppilamus, the chief Red Hood, the major spy of Hattusili. The other one must be his aid or driver. They were coming from Zananzash. How did they find out where he is? What is going on? On whose side is Zananzash?"

Hartapu told them of his visit the day before and how they had returned to pick him up and the documents and get back in a cart. Met added that there were at least two men left in the house.

Hartapu had to act fast. There was no time for planning, let alone look for more help. He said, "We know now there are at least two more men beside Zananzash. Maybe there are even more men hanging around. We must take our chances and find out. We will all walk in as friends of Zananzash and assess the situation. Let us see how they react and how Zan introduces us to them. If there is any resistance, hindrance, or even a sign of malevolence, we must overpower them without a trace of hesitation, no holds barred."

Bak looked up. "And if Zananzash resists?"

"No matter. There is no time for discussion. He will be carried away by us, gagged and bound, if need be." Hartapu remembered the rope they had indoors. He looked at Met and said. "You can stay back."

Teremun said, "Alone here, she won't be safe, either."

Met said, "I want to be with you. If I am with you, it will give a better semblance of a group of friends visiting Zananzash. I can fight if need be. Give me one of your weapons, Teremun. I know you have one more knife tucked in your belt at the back." She stretched out her palm. Teremun grinned but made no move.

Hartapu gave in. "All right, come with us. When indoors, keep an eye through the front window to watch for the arrival of more strangers. You never know."

He turned to the others. "Any questions?"

Barely allowing time for a discussion, he tossed his head and said, "Let us move."

It was an unusual attack team, neither running up, shrieking and swinging swords in self-induced frenzy and courage, nor sneaking up to the house, hooded and huddled, crouching and crawling. On the contrary, it was a casual group of three swaggering men accompanied by a woman swinging her hips, all in a leisurely gait. Teremun was the most conspicuous member, taking the lead with merry behavior, making jokes, and goading one or the other to grin despite the suspense. In appearance, all were in a good mood and acting as though on a social call, visiting a friend. This act was over when the height of the tension was reached at the door. Teremun knocked on it.

There was no reaction. After several seconds, Teremun clenched his fist and grimaced, ready to bang on the door. The door opened a crack, revealing the tall man with a beard and bushy eyebrows.

"Is Zananzash here?" Teremun asked. "We are his friends."

The door was shut. After a few seconds, it was opened again, and the man growled, "Come in." He let them pass, closed the door, and stood blocking it.

They moved in to find Zan slouching on a rickety chair, biting his lip, with his knees spread and his fists on his thighs. He was tense from head to foot. He seemed ready to jump up despite his wounded leg. Behind him stood the other man they had seen bringing in the rope. The coil lay in a corner.

Hartapu strode towards Zan, with Met a step behind him.

"*Assu!*" Hartapu said, greeting Zan with "Hail" in the Hittite tongue. "I wish you a good morning. Are these your friends?" He neared Zan. The latter neither uttered a word nor made a move.

Teremun and Bak approached the man and stood behind the chair.

Met strode to the window next to the door and cast her gaze outdoors. A misstep.

In the silence, the tension was about to explode.

"Who are you?" the man behind Zananzash asked. The question was a challenge, the tone aggressive, yet the crack in the voice exposed anxiety. On impulse, Hartapu reached for the grip of his dagger as he turned his head to the right to look at the man.

At that moment, he heard Met scream. He turned and saw at the window the tall man with the beard standing behind her. He appeared to have twisted her arm behind her back and was using her body as cover. He held a dagger to her side, close to her throat.

"Drop your weapons and raise your hands," he barked, a killer's command.

No one moved.

After a dreadful second, Hartapu drew his knife and raised his hand to waist level. By force of habit, its grip lay on his palm with his forefinger stretched across its spine and his thumb on the side. The ring finger pressed the grip to the palm. One foot was put forward, and his knees were slightly bent. He heard behind him and to the right metal falling to the ground, clang, clang—twice.

Met attacked. She drew back her head, jerked it past the weapon, and dug into the man's wrist with her teeth, ever deeper. The man jerked to the left, trying to wrench his wrist free. The move was enough to expose his chest. Hartapu bent backward, swung his hand up to eye level and, in one move, flung his weapon, throwing his weight forward. The knife flew as trained and met its target, and its narrow blade passed through the man's rib cage. The man released his grip on Met, staggered back, and collapsed. Met jumped away. Bak sprinted towards the fallen man.

Hartapu ran up to her and held her in a tight embrace. When he turned towards Zan, he saw the result of the scuffle he had heard earlier. With his second knife, Teremun had taken down the other man from the rear. It was all over in seconds.

Zananzash was a silent witness in his chair. Now he stirred and said, "That was hard."

Teremun was kneeling beside his victim. He rose slowly and cracked his knuckles. Putting on a sneer, he said, "Sir, in this business, we take no prisoners."

* * *

The ensuing silence for a recovery could not last long. While the immediate danger was over, the victors had to realize the next wave they faced. Zananzash, the person who had contributed to the operation the least but benefited from it the most, had the only knowledge to warn the others. In his brief and breathless account, he went into what was going on when they had entered his home and explained the danger he was still facing despite their timely appearance. Suppilamus would be returning at any moment, possibly with more of his men. They all had to get away immediately. There was no time to attend to the dead.

Hartapu nodded and gave orders to get out of the house posthaste. Met proceeded to pick up the cart she had parked. She was accompanied by Teremun lest any associate of Suppilamus pop up in advance. Zananzash showed his few belongings to Bak, who picked them up to bring to the front door. Hartapu reminded Zan of the documents, the precious baggage he had come to pick up.

The latter smiled, said, "Of course," and hopped towards the kitchen. Hartapu stayed back out of respect for him to fetch his goods from whatever secret spot he had found in his small kitchen.

Zananzash called out from the kitchen, "Only those I showed you. The others are all elsewhere in safe custody."

They had to wait at the door for only a few moments before the cart came up with Met driving. They got into it and dove off, with Bak relieving Met. She sat to his side. Teremun sat with Hartapu at the rear of the covered cart, with their view to the rear, while Zananzash sat behind them, sideward, stretching his legs. The goal was to reach Met's home, drop her off, and proceed. All were relieved but only to an extent, for their minds were still under tension. Suppilamus could turn up at any moment. In addition, they were also exhausted and in no jubilant mood for a talk. It was a silent ride.

Just before they turned to the right at the second corner to leave the high road, Teremun and Hartapu sighted a chariot coming up towards them, followed by a horse-drawn cart with four or five men. The heavy figure of Suppilamus could be easily spotted seated in the front, next to his driver. Teremun and Hartapu exchanged glances.

After watching that group drive straight on without heeding them, Hartapu heard a sigh of relief from Teremnun. Still in suspense, he explained in a low voice why he had turned up with Bak to look for Hartapu. He was concerned after hearing that the man in the copper shop had been killed. That shopkeeper had been one of his best men, a faithful local man from the south.

On reaching Met's home, Teremun and Hartapu hopped off. Hartapu helped Met to alight. It had to be a quick valediction, and there was no time for Zananzash to get out and climb in again.

Hartapu accompanied Met to the door, where her mom was waiting. Tiaa said, "I hope you had no trouble with the horse, Met."

"Not at all. All went well," Met lied with a smile. This was not the time for the whole story. She was in no mood for it. Hartapu nodded.

"All right, I will see how our guest is getting on. He may be needing a new bandage." Tiaa walked up to the cart.

Teremun went to the shop at the front to look for Ankhef.

Hartapu steered towards the front door, following Met. He was also steering towards a farewell, at least for now.

They had not been away from the others ever since that dramatic moment when her life was at stake. In the confusion, he had hardly thought of congratulating her for her brave move when in danger. He reached for her arm. After entering the home, she turned back to him.

He cleared his throat and said in an awkward way, "Whew! That was close, Met. While we were all at a loss, you saved the situation. "

Met raised her eyebrows and shrugged. "My teeth did it. They were my only weapon." She scoffed. "With three armed men around."

She added after a break, "At least you chose to act. Your knife and the throw saved the situation, and you saved me. Are you a warrior?"

"I am only a scribe." Hartapu lowered his head modestly.

"Really?" She threw him a slanted gaze and a mischievous smile. "At first, I only wondered, my prince. I almost saw through the veil, but that was only much later." She paused to lick her lips.

"I noticed how you took charge of the situation with Teremun, who became so subservient to you. First, I wondered; then I thought you ought to be a Black Hood supremo. Later, I had a word with Teremun when I went with him to fetch the cart. He had to divulge your secret, your identity."

"Teremun?"

"Yes, but mind you, that was *after* our night together. *After* the night of the impostors: you a charming scribe in my eyes, me a wayward waitress in yours, just a contact but wanting more. Your body was with mine, but your heart was elsewhere. A woman notices such things, dear. Life is a masquerade, Harti, but there was one truth in this drama: my love was and is real, and I am with you, even if..."

She lowered her gaze. "It remains only a romance for you, a flirtation." She pressed her lips together.

Hartapu opened his mouth, but his voice failed him. His throat was dry. His mind got foggy and seemed to fade out. In the dreadful silence, he spread his arms, speechless.

She swallowed and stared at the floor. "I guess you have been promised a princess. Give her my best wishes, wherever she is, whoever she is."

His mind searched for an answer. He could only clear his throat. She nodded as her lips drooped. Then she squared her shoulders, raised her chin, and tossed her head. "I will be waiting for you where we met, Harti. I will be there, remembering the first kiss you gave me, with this." She grabbed a mug from the table, gently pressed it against her cheek, and forced a smile. "Remembering your first words, *every story has two sides*."

Did she chuckle? No. Her drooping lips and fluttering eyelids spoke otherwise. She turned her head to the side, dumped the mug, and hustled away towards the kitchen.

Chapter 9

DREAMS AND PLANS

They were on their way back, with Bak driving the cart, Zananzash stretched out in the middle, and Teremun and Hartapu at the rear, all quiet, collecting their thoughts.

For Hartapu, Met's words were still ringing in his ears: "*I will be remembering the first kiss you gave me, with this.*"

He felt caught up in a series of events tossing him from one emotion to the other, love, fear, triumph, relief, and loss. He dangled between two women, his heart lost to Anat, his mind lost to Met. Did he deserve this strange luxury? Was he worth their attention? Values like honor, commitment, duty, and love could not be traded nor compromised, and of course, neither could the blossoming friendship with a person he had met only two days ago and with whom he had shared, in that short period, not just an event. It was a short story of love, peril, and rebirth.

Met had called it a masquerade. She had been right. Even his life was such. He was on the run. Both women, Anat and Met, had been upset because he had not confided his identity early on. But they could not blame him for not showing off. The fact was that these developments had arisen even to his own surprise. What then? Why was this disconcerting? Were they holding up a mirror to point out he was wearing a mask? Even before himself, before his own image?

The mission on hand was to secure his father's position, first and foremost. He was doing all he could to save his father. And next, how about his own lot? Was he true to himself? His past was a secret, his presence a mess, and his future…was there a future? Was he not hiding from a duty to himself and instead involving others, innocent girls and their innocent hearts? He was provoking feelings of others, too confused and inept at managing even his own emotions. Was all this commotion his own fault? Was he the source of his misery?

Whatever. He only knew he was an accursed prince and not a commoner—no, not even a commoner, just a pauper. He was a destitute dupe, despised because he was a coward hiding behind a façade.

He gritted his teeth and closed his eyes.

They reached Teremun's home, not far from his own. It was a hut big enough for a single person. Hartapu was led by Teremun to a room with a table, a few chairs, and a bed at an end. Bak helped Zananzash follow them. After a short break and some refreshments, Bak left to drive the cart back to Met's home.

Hartapu said to Teremun, "Bak may be your right-hand man, but I don't like the fellow. Watch out. There is something wrong with him."

Teremun defended his assistant. "Do not worry. He has excellent credentials. He worked as a herald for the military of Kemet."

He offered his guests another round of beer and said, "Sometime soon, we will have a visitor here who will be glad to hear the documents have been secured. He is the head of information to the royalty, the official in charge of collecting and assessing news pertaining to the safety of the kingdom."

He waited for the announcement to sink in and then proceeded. "He happens to also be the royal shaman advising the pharaoh on spiritual matters. He goes by the name of Sennefer. The procurement of the documents was supported, in fact, assigned, by Queen Nefertari, and we are glad to have succeeded in the royal mission."

Hartapu raised his eyebrows.

Teremun looked out of the window. His face brightened. "There he is."

The shaman entered the room after removing his slippers. He knew no one except for Teremun and needed to be introduced to others. In this close-knit circle, Hartapu had the honor of being properly introduced as the prince of Hatti. The shaman responded with a broad smile, bow, and nod.

Zananzash related what had happened before his rescuers had reached him. Now and then, he stopped to choose his words, possibly wanting to sound free of feelings. He went into Suppilamus's secret mission of finding the ousted king and abducting him, even sending him to the netherworld. He made no secret of the threat to his person and thanked the men for rescuing him at the right moment. He pointed out how determined Suppilamus was in following his royal orders, true to a faithful civil servant. He would go to any lengths with his methodical mentality and career ambition. In addition, with his family back home, even as a senior officer, Suppilamus would fear for their safety if he should fail.

As an afterthought, Zan added, "Suppilamus has lost two men, and I have escaped from his claws." He turned to Hartapu. "He demanded that I lead him to your venerable father. In my opinion, now he would try other means to get back at me through his friends. The girl is in danger. I hear she works at the alehouse, which is frequented by this man, and if he should put two and two together—"

Teremun butted in. "No way. She was always with us, and none of us were seen by Suppilamus and his cohorts..." He added with a grin, "Except for two of them, and both are now dead."

Hartapu's memory flashed to Met and him meeting the vendor Kem at the street corner. The Hittites could reach out to her again. Luckily, Met had not announced herself to the woman, so there would be no reference to Met's parents. Yet Zananzash was right. There was a danger. She must be protected.

Zananzash brought the shaman's attention to the prize. "How do you value the documents I have produced?"

Sennefer said, "I browsed over some of them. I am impressed by the content. Luckily, the messages are confidential and, therefore, explicit. There will be no cause for a debate over the context, meaning, and interpretation. They make quite a few questions clear. Nevertheless, you will understand I must have the scripts verified by a scribe we have found who is conversant with your language and can confirm the authenticity. After that, we will present the documents to our queen, who initiated and supported this venture. She will be delighted. I am sure the vizier and the pharaoh will be impressed, too."

Teremun asked, "What next?"

Hartapu looked at Sennefer. "As for our next step, I have a proposal."

* * *

For Met, it should have been a day like any other in the alehouse. But her mind was elsewhere. Much had come to pass in the short holiday of two days she had had. After the adventure with Harti and the misadventure with a knife at her throat, she had occasion to push away all the events as if they were in a dream-turned-nightmare.

She wanted to divert herself with a merry day in the company of her sister. They had a lot to talk about, not having seen each other for nearly a year. Refreshing memories of their childhood was also a relief. Nodjmet had her own family and was well settled. The news was that she was planning her second child. Curious yet considerate, she was the typical sister, wanting to inquire about Met's male acquaintances, but when Met changed the subject for the second time, she let it go. She would have noticed, Met was in no mood to tell her about her beau, or was it a flirtation?

Although it was pretty early in the pub, there was quite a crowd this time, two different groups of loud men occupying several tables. But most conspicuous on this day were two new customers, sullen and silent, at a corner table. They hardly spoke to each other but for a few words muttered, drank little, and ogled Met and watched her movements all the time. She ignored them. She had customers at other tables to serve. One of these was a single soul growing animated by the groups singing and joking beside him.

Suppilamus had found a seat at a table not far off. Today he was seated without his companion, whose final moments Met had had the pleasure to witness. If only he knew.

She caught him bending his head all the way back for a final swig, catching the last drop in the mug, and then putting it down. On this day, he had not been there long, and she wondered why he had drunk up the precious Inet wine so fast.

She glided to him with feline majesty and asked, "Would you like to have one more of the same, sir?"

"No, thanks, dear. I have to go." He plastered a forced grin on his face. He was definitely in no pleasant mood for a chat.

Met picked up the empty mug, walked straight to the two men watching her, and put it on their table. One of the men turned to his comrade. He muttered something and pushed his mug towards the empty one she had put down. She picked up both, swiveled, and hurried away towards the kitchen. Over her shoulder, she stole a glance to get a glimpse of Suppilamus maneuvering his heavy figure towards the exit and the two men following him at a discreet distance. Their clothes hardly concealed their knives at waist level.

* * *

Suppilamus was deep in thought. Everything was going wrong. His men had cleaned up the mess in the house and removed the two corpses in a hurry to load them onto their cart, hopefully with no onlookers. As they had driven back to his quarters, Suppilamus had digested the setback in which his right-hand man, Mashanda, had lost his life. He had to regroup and hit back but shadowboxing and throwing punches in the air would be of no help.

The news from Hatti was getting more urgent and severe. The king was getting nervous that the pharaoh might grant Mattusili asylum and formally make him a protégé. Hattusili's new order was to find the foe and, at the slightest resistance or attempt at escape, forward him to the place of no return. He would be better off in the underworld than abroad, better dead than alive.

The driver helped him onto the chariot.

"Are you the merchant Suppilamus from Hatti?" he heard. Two armed men had appeared from behind. One of them flashed a palm-sized bronze medal with the insignia of Kemet's central authority. "We are from the royal guard. The governor of this district would like to have a word with you. It is in connection with a house near the Avaris market with two dead men."

"And" the other man added, "before that, the death of a copper merchant over there." He pointed in the direction of the shop. "You have been brought to our attention in both matters. Please accompany us without resistance."

They signaled the driver to get off the chariot. One of the men climbed in and picked up the reins. The other slipped beside Suppilamus. They drove off, leaving the driver stranded. Not for long. Two more guards appeared behind him.

* * *

After seeing off Suppilamus, Met was sure he would be taken care of by the guards, as assured by Teremun and the other master from the palace. Now she turned to her daily affair of keeping customers happy and busy ordering their drinks.

A group of guests was in a party mood, with shouts, cheers, and intermittent loud songs in a strange language. In their last song, the men sang each refrain ever fiercer and hoarser, followed by a guffaw. Two waiters were taking charge of the crowd, watching them rather than waiting on them.

Previously, Met had spotted a solitary man seated in a corner, beaming all the time at the drunks. This newcomer was in his thirties and obviously looking around for company. He had ordered a beer and appeared to be in a great mood for a chat. She thought, when he finished his drink, it would be time to charm him into another and then another; that was her job.

He seemed to have read her mind and took a final swig from his mug. She approached him and raised the usual question, making her voice sound as personal as possible: "Wouldn't you like to have another drink?". Her plea would work its way to his heart, and he would accept her invitation to stay for longer. In exchange, he could expect to have a chat.

"Yes, indeed," he said with a grin and gave her his empty mug.

She picked it up, half turned, and looked back. "You are new here, aren't you?"

"Yes, indeed. I am a traveler. I am on the move."

"I thought so. You speak our language quite well."

"Oh, thanks. I come from the north."

She threw her routine welcome smile and tossed her head towards the loud group, who were too loud for her to continue. When they turned their volume down a bit, she asked the young man, "Why don't you join them?"

"They are Hittites."

"And you?"

"Also a Hittite, but they must be from Hattusha or even farther north, far from where I come. I don't know their dialect or songs."

When she brought him his mug, the group had begun playing the usual board game, and their noise had subsided.

The young man nodded his thanks after discovering the mug had been liberally filled almost to the brim and then looked up at her. He licked his lips and hesitated.

"Did you say you are on a visit?" Met asked.

"I am a construction worker. I am looking for a place to work. Like many others, I am also looking for a job," he said, looking away with a quaint smile.

A glimpse at his hands told her he was lying. They were not those of a manual laborer, much less someone used to handle coarse materials like bricks and stones. One more sinister individual from the north. *It is best to keep away from him*, she thought. She had had enough adventure. At any rate, he was not the sad and solitary soul needing solace. He was only seeking company.

"Tell me," he almost shouted lest she end the conversation. "I am looking for a man called Teremun. Can you help me?"

"A customer?"

"Yes."

"Maybe, maybe not. I do not know the names of the customers here. Nor do I know your name."

"Oh, I am sorry. My name is Demos, short for Tarkondemos, and I come from Tarhuntashsha. And yours?"

Met laughed and said, "You are not a construction worker. Don't tell me, either, that you are the prince of that place."

"What?" His voice was earnest. "How come you—"

"Never mind. I was just teasing. All right. I can ask if any of my colleagues knows a person with that name. What was it? Tere- what?"

"Teremun."

"Can you describe him?"

"No. I have never met him."

"Great. A man from somewhere wants to meet another whom he does not know. How can I help him? Once again, what is your name, and what is the other man's?"

The man from Tarhuntassa patiently repeated where he was from and both names, Teremun and Tarkondemos.

She murmured a few times and said, "I will ask my boss. I must hurry, or I will have forgotten the strange names."

She walked away. In the kitchen, she memorized the name of this guest and where he came from, repeating both several times. She returned after a respectable amount of time had passed.

"I hear my boss knows a man called Teremun who is an occasional guest. He comes once or twice a week at about this time. Your only choice is to keep coming every day, and I will put you in touch with him when the boss sees him."

"Thank you so much. I have an important message for that man. Can I see your boss to thank him?"

"No. He prefers to keep his distance. He does not want to be involved with customers and their stories. It is gracious of him that he gave you this tip."

The man got up, bowed, and said, "I thank you all the same. It was very nice of you."

Met smiled and nodded. That was not a gesture she encountered every day.

* * *

After all the hustle and bustle of the previous days, Hartapu had wanted to have a rendezvous with Anat to relax with her in a secluded place and report to her all that he had gone through of late. He had chosen the same spot under the sycamore tree near the palace gate, which seemed to offer him peace, solace, love, and even some success in his life.

Anat listened to the detailed story of the assignment he had received indirectly from the queen. He explained the importance of the objects he was to procure. He also went into the initial worry he had of proving his own identity to a man whom he had met years ago. The contact he was to approach was found dead on arrival. At a loss, he had wandered around before finally resting in an alehouse.

When he spoke of Met, Anat looked up for the first time to ask, "How old was she?"

A funny question.

149 |

"About your age. Why?"

"How did she look?"

What the hell?

"She was okay. Do you know her?"

"Oh, no. I just wanted to know if she was a beautiful dream girl."

Hartapu felt like he'd been punched in the stomach. *Female instinct?*

"I don't understand. She happened to be my only contact. I had no choice."

"Never mind. I was just curious. We women are like that." She laughed.

He swallowed and moved on to the rescue operation and return of the victors.

"Pretty soon, I will be meeting Teremun. If you like, I will introduce him to you. He is my best friend and would also like to meet you."

Once he had finished the story of how he had secured the documents, Anat was jubilant. She jumped up, clenched her fists, and called out, "You did it, Harti! It is great1" She bent forward and kissed him on the cheek.

After a while, she looked up at the sky as if in prayer and looked back at him. "Here we are again to celebrate. Remember? This is where it all started, right here under the sycamore tree we call 'the tree of love.'"

She spoke as if they hadn't been there for ages since their audience with the queen.

"Yes, I do. It appears to be only yesterday. Time passes fast, doesn't it?"

"That is the past, Harti. But I do often think about our future. Or should I say I dream? Somewhere far, far away, just the two of us, not long from now…"

Hartapu read dreams, hope, and optimism in her eyes.

He was relieved to note she had touched the topic he wanted to broach. She was not catching him off guard. On the contrary, she had given him the prompt: the future, their future. He had to search for the right words. Exhausted, he lay down, rested his head on her lap, and looked up at her from the new angle with the foliage of the tree in the background. For him, she was a beauty from any angle, but the leaves in the background seemed to offer a special significance to the mood of hope and happiness she reflected.

"Next week, I am going to the temple," he began.

"To which temple?"

"The Amun temple near the palace. Precisely, to Hathor's temple in the complex."

"Oh, I thought you worshipped other gods. Do you pray to Hathor?"

"God is everywhere. I could pray there for the gods' blessing for my future, *our* future. But I am going for other reasons."

"Is there any other reason to go to a temple? I do not get it. Is there a festival?"

"I have been asked to meet the queen there. I guess she wants to greet me after my service to her. "

"To thank you."

"No. That would be too much of an honor. A queen has no need to thank anyone. After all, she is trying to secure asylum for *my* father. I only assisted her in her endeavor to do us a favor."

"If she is happy about your success, she may offer you asylum, too."

"If she does, with all politeness, I will decline, Anat. You well know why." He sat up and rested his elbows on his knees. He sighed and shook his head. "I cannot hang on here as an alien, laboring as a scribe for a merchant all my life. I have been born and trained for some other role. But as of now, instead of swinging a sword like a valiant prince, I throw knives like a scoundrel, a killer."

Anat said, "You have to adjust yourself in life, Harti."

"Listen, Anat. I do not know about my father. He lost his luck and maybe even risked too much and lost his kingdom to his uncle. He has no choice but to seek asylum and protection from the pharaoh. If it is granted, he will live in some luxury yet in protective custody lest our opponents should get him. He will have no functions and will be a guest by profession, vegetating for the rest of his life. Do you want me to lead a similar life? As a prince in exile, achieving nothing in life: no experience, no accomplishments, and no reminiscence? As an egg that never hatched?" He scoffed.

Anat said, "If you look at it that way, I would say no. But look at me. What prospects do I have? But for you, I would be wedded to a nobody and drudging all my life, bound to household chores and rearing children. With you as a prince under protection, I need not worry about your life or our future. I will be staying in my homeland, near my parents, and leading a comfortable life."

"Would you like to share your life with a husband languishing in custody, a man who hates himself for his fate, a lion that roars and rules over its cage? We must put in the effort. If things work out well for us, it would be an outcome that you will have earned, too."

There was a long silence.

Hartapu picked up a stick on the ground and began drawing designs in the mud.

Anat said, "Do not hate yourself for your situation. We all have a right to live, but foremost, we have to struggle to survive. I can understand you. You will have to fight for your right, even if it is your birthright. After all is said and done, after all the appeals to others and to the gods, ultimately, it is up to us to solve our puzzles. Now you do not want any protection from the royalty here, you do not have any other prospect becoming of your upbringing, nor do you want to live as a mere scribe. What do you really want? Have you thought of a third way?"

Hartapu pounded his knee with a fist. "Yes, indeed. I will be a king someday."

Anat raised her eyebrows. "Where? Back in Hatti?"

He said, "I don't know. Maybe elsewhere. If I cannot find a kingdom, I will found one. Yes. All I need is some support and the help of the gods."

"Now you are dreaming too, dear." She chuckled.

He ignored her remark and turned to her. He placed his arm around her shoulders and said in a soft tone, "Above all, I need your support."

"Of course. But remember, darling. For me, you are a king wherever you are. I will go where you go. Wherever you settle down, that will be my kingdom. I shall always be in your kingdom."

"And you will be my queen wherever I may be."

Anat shrugged and smiled. Then her lips drooped. "But seriously— "

Hartapu bent forward. "I am not just dreaming, dear. I have my plans. Let us see how things work out."

* * *

Tarkondemos, the man from Tarhuntassa, had been visiting the alehouse daily, and at long last, on the fifth day, the angel serving the drinks glided up to him to say, "It is a lucky day for you, Demos. The man you wanted to meet, Terman or Termun, is waiting outside for you. You just go out and stand at the door. He will come up to you."

He got up. The girl swept the mug away and scooted towards the rear.

Demos did not have to wait for long. A lanky man with a square jaw and athletic build crossed the road and walked up to him.

"*Assu!* I am Teremun. Are you Tarkondemos?"

Demos nodded.

"I hear you want to see me," the man said.

"Yes, indeed."

Demos introduced himself and explained the reason he was approaching him. He had been sent as a royal messenger from Tarhuntassa, a vassal state situated to the south of Hatti, to meet Hartapu, the prince of the Hatti kingdom. He had been instructed to reach out to the Hittites in Per-Ramesses who called themselves the Black Hoods. One of the names suggested to him was Teremun.

"I am glad to meet you," Teremun said, sensing no harm in revealing his identity. "May I say, I was a bit amused to hear your accent, the special southern twang."

Demos laughed. "I can't help it. It is Luwian, although my parents are from Azawa, to the west of Hatti."

They walked away from the alehouse.

"Where are we going?" Demos asked.

"I do not want to go into the alehouse for a chat. Let us sit down in the open with only passers-by and no eavesdroppers. You must realize it is not easy to meet the prince or the king, even if they are free men in this host land. The supporters of the present king are hunting for them."

"Do you mean the so-called Red Hoods?"

After a short break, Teremun said, "Quite. Tell me about your voyage from your place all the way to this city."

Demos did not like this chat, which sounded like a cross-examination. The man was testing the authenticity of Demos's background instead of telling him where he was leading him. Anyway, to keep the chat flowing, he obliged.

"Was it not the capital of Hatti long ago?" Teremun asked after the brief report.

"Yes, but that was some seventy years ago when the prince's grandfather provisionally shifted the capital from Hattusha for a few years. Now Tarhuntassa is an independent kingdom. The present king is Kurunta, the younger brother of the prince's father. There is no animosity between the brothers Urhi-Teshub and Kurunta, nor between Kurunta and King Hattusili. Our king holds a neutral position in the quarrel in Hattusha."

They had reached an open space or square with chairs and tables beneath a huge tree spreading its generous shade. The chairs were mostly empty. Farther away, people were streaming down a lane branching off from the square. They were of all ages but mostly families with kids.

"We can sit down here," Teremun suggested. "Perhaps you have heard that from tomorrow onward, a big festival will begin here in honor of one of their gods. Don't ask me which one." They chuckled and seated themselves. "The festival will go on for five days, yet the celebration has begun today. There is a fair down there around the corner, with all kinds of entertainment, attracting the folks ever ready for fun. When it closes by dusk, this place will be filled with people, and drinks will be served. But right now, it is quiet here."

A water carrier's donkey, now off-duty, began braying from somewhere behind them. It was the usual long, drawn-out wail ending with a staccato.

After the last of the three hiccups of the bray had subsided, Demos said, "I hear someone who disagrees with your comment on this place being quiet."

They laughed.

"Do you mean we are waiting to meet the prince—here?" Demos asked with a frown and a smile.

"Not so fast, my friend. I will be introducing you to a contact. As you do not have any password or means to identify yourself, I will personally introduce you to that man—on trust. After checking up on your identity and mission, the contact will take you to the prince. It is a precaution. As I said before, there are supporters of the present king afoot who want to lay their hands on the prominent fugitives."

On the one hand, Demos was impressed with all these measures they were taking to protect the king and the prince. On the other, he had not expected it would be so difficult to deliver a simple message and be done with the assignment. So much of a fuss. Anyway, he had to get used to the situation.

He looked around. All the seats were vacant except for a family of four. The children were quarreling over something they were seizing from one another. The father was trying to maintain order, while the wife relaxed and smiled. She appeared to be saying, "It is your turn, dear. Manage the kids. Now you know what I go through all day long." The father snatched the sweet the kids were fighting over and threatened to put it into his own mouth. The litigants froze. An outburst of tears was in the offing. He laughed, broke it into two pieces, and stretched his arms wide, each with a piece in the fist. After the kids tapped his hands, he gave them one each.

"It is a good lesson for the kids," Demos said after the happy ending—half happy for each kid. "Do you remember the proverb, 'If two quarrel over a booty, the third one snatches it'?"

"That reminds me," Teremun said in a low voice. "I admit I am curious. What do they say in Tarhuntassa about this family quarrel in the royal house of Hattusha?"

"Do you mean the ousting of King Urhi-Teshub Mursili?"

"Precisely. On which side are the subjects and the royal house?"

"Like our king, we, the subjects, have a neutral position. You should know the difficulty we all face—I mean we in Tarhuntassa."

"No, I don't."

"The quarrel seems to be a highly personal matter between two blockheads, if I may say so."

Demos laughed. "Yes. The fact is, Mursili intimidated his uncle. He forgot Hattusili's support by the military."

Demos did not know how well this man Teremun was informed. For good measure, he went into details about the achievements of Hattusili as commander. One of them was the re-conquest of the holy city of Nerik in the north, which had been captured by the Kaskans two hundred years ago. All his life, he had been very close to his elder brother, King Muwatalli. As his right-hand man and commander, he had had the backing of the military.

He finished, stating, "At any rate, King Kurunta assumes a neutral position in the family quarrel."

"For now," Teremun said.

Demos nodded and laughed. "I know what you mean." He added after a thoughtful pause, "Also, the kingdoms of Kemet and Hatti are in a long, intermittent struggle for no grand reason. Right now, there is a respite, and we are welcome here."

The chat turned to the two cultures. Demos was visiting for the first time and, therefore, was full of observations and surprises of all kinds.

Finally, he conceded that Egypt did have some tradition and culture. The people were not as bad as he had heard.

Teremun said, "You are right. We speak so much about the difference in our cultures, the Hittite and the Kemet, but at the core, people are the same, the values, the hopes, the fears, and of course, the greed and self-assertion. But we are also modeled by the different surroundings. I come from Hattusa, and this is how I see the difference to this land, from my point of view. This is a flat country. All year round, they have the sun god to hover in the sky and scorch the earth. They depend on one river and the mercy of the gods granting a rich harvest and then floods and deluge; ours is a land depending on rain, fearing fire outbreak, and at the mercy of the storm god."

"Anyway," Demos said, "it is the rule of the gods. Our concern is now the rule of the kings. Who knows which king is favored by the gods and for how long?"

He saw a pair walking up to them. At first, he spotted the attractive girl, a dark beauty with a merry gait, who would elicit more than a second look. The young man accompanying her had fixed his stare on Termun and greeted him from afar, waving his hand. The other hand held his girl. After reaching their table, the man threw a cursory glance at Demos and nodded.

"How was the performance?" Teremun asked.

"Oh, great. I was spellbound, watching the acrobats," the girl replied

"The two jugglers were great, too. But I was more interested in the archers' contest," the man added. He looked around and sat next to Demos while the girl sat opposite him.

The chat went on about the fair until Teremun interrupted, saying, "Well, this is our guest from Tarhuntassa I was telling you about. He is a royal messenger. His name is Tarkondemos, and he wants to meet the prince."

The man graced Demos with a glance for the second time. "Yes, you told me. That would be difficult. I hear he has gone to see his father."

"Can you take me to him all the same?" Demos asked. "I have a message for him from our king. I have come all the way only for that purpose."

Demos found this man unbearable. He had the air of a lord deciding over the fate of his mission. This was the arrogance of a "contact," a sundry gatekeeper acting like a palace guard, possessing all the secrets of access plus the golden key to the door. He wanted to impress his girl and show off his might. Next, he would be asking for some suitable present for the favor, some kind of an admission fee to enter the den where the prince was hidden. No way.

The man ignored Demos and addressed Teremun, tossing his head. "Did you tell him about the Red Hoods?"

"Yes, I did," Teremun answered.

He looked at Demos for quite a while and then asked, "Can you identify yourself as the emissary of Kurunta, the king of Tarhuntassa?"

Demos took his shoulder bag and produced a bronze disk with an emblem on it. He held it out for all to see and said, "Can you recognize the insignia?"

The fellow nodded and asked, "And the message?"

Enough interrogation, Demos thought. "The message is on a clay tablet, and I will produce it only when I meet the prince."

"No."

"What do you mean?"

"Either you have it right now and show it to me or you do not have it when you meet the prince."

Demos was infuriated. He felt like getting up and leaving the company. Then he saw that all three were grinning. He had not reached his goal, but he would have no more of this nonsense if it turned out they were only playing a prank at his expense.

He got up. The man reached out to him and gently pulled him down.

"Do you understand, dear friend? I am the prince." He looked at the girl and laughed.

Yes, of course. Dressed to impress and claiming royalty. Enough.

"Are you joking?"

The man's expression became stern again.

Teremun grinned and said, "No. It is true."

The man stared at Demos with narrowed eyes. "How should I prove it? Can you describe the emblem I am about to show you? What would you like to see on it? Mention some details."

Demos opened his mouth but did not know the answer.

The fellow laughed and said to the girl, "Show him."

She pulled out her necklace and displayed the signet ring. It had an image identical to that Demos held in his hand: two crossing swords and, above them, an eagle spreading its wings.

He said, "What else? It is from the same house, the same dynasty. This ring was presented to my mother by my father on the occasion of their marriage, and now my bride is carrying it. Got it?"

Demos's face brightened, and his eyes widened. He laughed loudly and said, "Of course!"

"I was only acting a bit funny until I was assured you were not one of those from the other side, my friend. No hard feelings." Hartapu clapped Demos's shoulder.

A bit confused, Demos muttered, "It is all right, my prince." He rose again, this time for a bow.

The prince pulled him down again. He bent forward and whispered with a smile, "Don't call me prince here. In this land, I am only a traveler, alien, or a guest like you."

He looked around to drive home the point.

"For your peace of mind, I will tell you this much about my contact with your king," Hartapu said. "After reaching this place nearly a year ago, I wrote to my uncle and sent the message with a trader in whom I had confidence. I did not receive any response to the address I had given. Anyway, this could be the answer after all."

Demos now believed this man. He had nothing more to hide. Now it was his turn. "With both our identities established, allow me, sir, to introduce myself in detail and my mission. I am not just a courier to deliver some goods and be done with it."

He sat erect, raising his chin and his voice. "You may know my position and the gravity of my mission when I state I am the son of the *hazannu,* or the lord mayor of the city of Tarhuntassa, one of the table-men and the palace staff *panku* in the service of his majesty Kurunta, may the storm god Tarhunt bless him with a long life. This is an important message from his majesty, your uncle, the younger brother of Urhi-Teshub Mursili. I am here to answer questions and give any details not clearly explained or that might ensue from the message."

He removed a sealed clay envelope from his bag and solemnly held it out with both hands. Hartapu received it with his right hand in solemnity and retrieved from it a clay tablet. He turned away to hold it up for better light with the sun about to set and scrutinized it with a deep frown. All fell silent.

He took his time, reading it twice.

"Hmmm," he said. "Good news."

THE QUEEN

Chapter 10

THE VIZIER

Nefertari had received a request for an audience by Paser. She was curious about his approach. It could be a signal for some news he wanted to pass on to her.

She had known Paser all her life as the most respected man in the court. Ramses was blessed with a wise and experienced vizier of noble descent from Memphis. He had also served in various high offices under Ramses' father, Menmaatre, also known as Seti. In the final days of Seti's reign, he had served as city governor and vizier, receiving a multitude of titles in the course of his career. Paser had also supervised the construction of the tomb of Seti. Ramses had accompanied his father on his expedition to the north in the last years of the latter's reign, and on this occasion, he had gotten to know this man of experience as a faithful and intelligent assistant to the pharaoh.

It was a welcome occasion for Nefertari to confide her fears and doubts and seek his support. After all, she had no one to talk to about such matters. It was all politics concerning another power, where she had no experience, but now she was encountering the genius in these matters.

He was approaching her on his own for some given reason. What could it be? What did this move portend? Maybe he had something on his mind that he wanted to share with her while the pharaoh was away. It could also be a way for him to hear what progress she had been making since the last conference to be well informed when the pharaoh returned. Of course, she would proudly reveal to him how far she had come and seek his counsel.

Then her mood swayed from one of elation to one of caution. For a moment, she lent her ears to the rebel girl in her. She was not sure if she should divulge all the information and her interpretation of the situation. Shishi had wanted her to work only with the shaman, not as a team with the eternal vizier in the lead. Why? He had wanted two lines of experts. She was to dig out information with her own methods and contacts her own way, while the vizier would do his due diligence in the conventional manner with the help of his subordinates. With her, Ramses had sought a layman's approach to this matter, and maybe her female intuition. Or was she flattering herself?

At any rate, she realized, she ought to be careful about giving Paser too many details and sharing her conjectures with him. He could turn the tables on her and use all the information, however incomplete, to support his own contrary argument in the conference. She decided to hear him out and then decide on the spot how to react.

In the late afternoon, when Paser entered her chambers, she fondly greeted him and offered him a raised chair. After initial hospitality and small talk, she waited for Bennu to recede and broached the subject for the audience.

Paser was his usual self, sitting composed, his knees and hands together. His eyes stared at the ground from beneath heavy eyebrows. With this appearance of total concentration while searching for words, he could instantly create an atmosphere of grave concern.

"Your majesty, I do not know what progress you have made with the inquiry about the military state of affairs in Hatti and the strategy of the present king there. I have come only to share with you what I have on my chest." He looked up at her.

"Do you have a problem, my vizier?" Nefertari asked calmly so as not to sound curious.

"Not exactly. But the situation is turning bad for peace. We have information that Hattusili is, indeed, preparing for war against Kemet. He is not just brandishing his sword. The matter is serious." He had a sad smile on his lips.

"Any news as a basis for this observation?"

"Yes. We have been receiving corresponding messages from our agents." Paser waited. Maybe he wanted some reaction.

Nefertari lowered her gaze, absorbing this remark. Then she asked, "Who are they? Where are they? Are they really reliable? Are they authentic? I remember the false report by the spies at Qadesh that led my spouse astray and into great peril, almost destroying his troops."

Paser laid one palm over the other in his lap and seemed to be engrossed in the creases of his palms. Then the creases on his forehead faded as he said, "They are reliable sources, your majesty. They are our military agents and experts, and this is the official information from them..." His voice trailed off.

"Yes, go ahead." She wondered why he had paused.

"That is what I heard from the commander. I found no need to ask questions about authenticity and the like concerning our own military experts. This being the truth, we can only surmise we have been exaggerating the turmoil in Hatti. The king seems to have regained control over the situation by now and to be shifting his attention to reacting to our previous campaign. He is, indeed, preparing to attack Kemet. Besides retaliation, it could also be the typical ruse of an insecure monarch: to silence local unrest that could escalate to a rebellion by pointing out a common enemy abroad and even carrying out an attack. This tactic is commonly applied by a ruler to enforce unity within a kingdom."

"Let us assume the news is confirmed and corresponds to reality. What next?" she asked, closely watching him.

"You know my position, your majesty," Paser said with a frown. "If you will allow me to elaborate a bit, I will explain my stance."

Nefertari said, "Do go ahead. I am always grateful for a frank conversation."

Paser said, retaining his frown, "I am not a seer, prophet, or religious guide. I am an adviser, vizier to the pharaoh, as I was to his father, may the gods bless his soul. I cannot afford to impose my views of war and peace on the world. My duty is to act in the interest of our kingdom. On occasions like this one, my fundamental reluctance towards war and aggression may not play a role. It is not for me to alter the rules set by the powers. I have to deal with belligerent warlords and get equal to their means and measures, even if deception should be one of them.

"Whether we like it or not, war is a means to hold power and rule. As for reasons or aims, I would mention the need to impress other powers, ward off untoward attempts by others, and settle disputes among others. It is easy to declare that war should not be waged for its own sake, for bravado, or to keep the soldiers engaged. But there are many occasions for war, some at the monarch's choice, some not. War is another means of self-assertion and commanding respect from other powers, as well as a demonstration of valor."

"Will mankind ever learn?" the queen asked.

"I am afraid the answer is never. However powerful a land or kingdom, others will always try to tip the balance. This is the law of nature, to level and equalize any difference in power or energy. For a prosperous and peaceful kingdom, constant vigilance is needed, and even offense at chosen times to prolong the peace with the enemy by means of fear and respect. It sounds like a paradox: war is needed to ensure peace for the near future. Even if it should sound absurd, war is, indeed, a means to conquer peace.

"We are always at a disadvantage if war is imposed on us and becomes inevitable for the sake of self-defense. It is better to be on the offensive, initiating war. The best way is after due preparation and choosing the moment of attack, when the enemy is at its weakest or at least caught off guard. To sum up, if we had a choice, we ought to go to war on our initiative.

"Our campaigns to the north, all on our own initiative, have been of no value ever since the time of the previous pharaoh. Although we celebrate them as victories, in effect, there was no lasting result in our favor, and they did not change the situation to our advantage. We failed to that extent, in contrast to Thutmose of the previous dynasty. The failure was not due to a lack of determination or valor on our part. We had not prepared ourselves for a long assault, including sieges lasting for months or securing the chain of provision, communication, and the like.

"Again, also in the present situation, we should not be maneuvered into a defensive position by the enemy. We must take the initiative before the enemy does, choosing an earlier moment for an all-out attack and not limit the offensive to a single campaign. We can settle the matter once and for all only with conquest of terrain on a permanent basis."

Nefertari tried to stop the vizier in his jingoism. But he raised his hand, smiled, and went on. "Do not fear, your majesty. I am indeed for peace—for now. That is for tactical reasons. We are not ready for an offensive, and I doubt we are even prepared for a serious assault by the enemy, even if our commander assures us, as he did last time, that we are. I see no way but to surrender the fugitive to avoid war. That measure could momentarily thwart the aggressive plans of the Hittites. For the time being, at least, Hattusili will feel appeased and have no basis to call out for an attack. The alternative of retaining Mursili as a threat and offering a cause for war would have been appropriate had we been ready for war, too, making the first move and beginning an invasion up north. Nevertheless, we can do so at a later appropriate moment with Mursili out of the way."

His voice broke off. His face showed no enthusiasm for his proposal nor contentment. He sat with a stoop, his lips drooping.

"To surrender, you mean," Nefertari said. Paser looked up, alarmed. She added, "I mean, to surrender the hapless fugitive to the devil."

He mulled over this remark, straightened his back, and said, "Believe me, your majesty. I am not at all in favor of inaction. After all, it is a man's world. One man understands only the language of another man. Only action is the language, only action is assertion, not words and arguments. But we are not ready to act, to attack, nor, I fear, are we prepared to defend against an all-out assault from the other side. For this reason, I have to fall back on what is possible and not what is noble. In the forthcoming meeting, I will advise our pharaoh to concede and surrender the fugitive and stall a move from the enemy." He threw a close look at her and added, "Unless, of course…"

The queen waited.

"Unless your majesty has any evidence to the contrary."

She sensed the trap and played dumb.

"I do not understand you, my vizier. What do you mean by that?"

"I mean, if you have evidence stating Hattusili is definitely neither in a position nor willing to wage war against us and it is all just a bluff, only the grimace of a baboon. In other words, the evidence has to *prove* our experts wrong."

He sighed and looked up at her.

She sensed he was only acting forlorn but challenging and putting pressure on her, *the cunning panther.*

Boldly, she chose to tell him the truth—but not the whole truth. She gave a report of the source of Zananzash and his documents, which had been secured personally by none other than the fugitive prince of Hatti. Zananzash, himself a fugitive, was within reach and prepared to swear to their authenticity and explain how they had come into his hands. Moreover, there was no doubt about the identity of the officer, nor suspicion about his being a spy posing as a refugee and feeding misinformation.

Turning to the content of the documents, she was careful and refrained from giving any details or the impression she'd gotten after her first perusal of them. She only said she could not go any further now, for the documents were now in the hands of experts, who were verifying and translating them in their meticulous way.

"As of now," she concluded, "we are also awaiting more information. Only after a few days will I be able to answer the question on your mind."

Paser appeared to be impressed but not satisfied. He rose and said, "Anyway, your majesty, as it stands, you can go by the imminent decision of the pharaoh on his arrival in favor of war, even as a preemptive strike. My advice will be to maintain peace and stall belligerence by offering the fugitive. If I fail, I will plead for a partial invasion to unsettle the foe and bring its war preparation into disarray. In either case, I deplore that your majesty and my modest self may have to agree to disagree."

After he left, Nefertari sighed and sat gazing out the window. She had to swallow this bad news and absorb this jolt from the vizier. His subjective opinion apart, he was well versed in these matters of the kingdom and had a better nose for handling them. She was new to this business of geopolitics. She was a novice adhering to principles: shelter for a fugitive and preserving peace. In the conference, his word would weigh far more than hers. Shishi would have to decide between the two, again on his instinct and divine guidance. Did she have to lay down her efforts and give up? No. She should not underestimate nor overestimate Paser's words.

Nevertheless, dejected and in despair, she tried to put away the thoughts, just banish them, as if the issues would solve themselves or dissolve into thin air. She drummed her fingers for a while. Then she got up and went out into the garden for a long walk, daring all those mocking faces in her imagination to glare at her.

In the late afternoon, with the sun getting tired and milder. The birds were becoming active, leaving the shade, and merrily calling out to one another in their own language of cries, cheers, and chirps. While strolling along her favorite path, in the distance, she saw the pomegranate tree the gardener had been so proud of. As she passed an acacia tree waving its thin branches, she felt on her arms the evening breeze getting cut off by the tree.

Breathing the fresh air with her gaze on the peaceful landscape made her mind still and relaxed. Her thoughts receded from all worries about war and peace, and she let them stray, demanding no search for a solution, not even a prompt to handle the problem. Just as she let the weather take its course around her, so, too, should she let this affair with the Hittites take its course. She was for the moment only an onlooker, a distant spectator, not responsible, not an agitator nor a contestant.

She stopped at the first of the five ponds. This spot offered a place to rest one's gaze on, also resting the mind, even cooling it. She sat down on the grass and watched the fish in the clear water in the basin. The red and gold creatures in the pool were moving in their silent world in all elegance with no concern for the din and dust in the world beyond.

She briefly smelled the fragrance of jasmine. But when she looked around, there were no flowers in sight. They blossomed in some hidden corner in the garden yet announced themselves in a modest way. A question popped up. Should her life follow that of those jasmine flowers? Would her peace effort persist and prevail with the author out of sight—its source unknown?

After the long walk, the distance she had covered mentally from her first dejection to her present reflection seemed to have an effect. She was now positioned to look at the situation with optimism. After all, the vizier had chosen to inform her beforehand what to expect unless—well, unless something happened, something turned up to support her, to prove she was on the right path. That thought alone gave her a hope of saving peace.

True, the Hittites were preparing for war with great fervor. She could confirm this opinion with what she had found on her first reading of the tablets. But something was amiss. Even if it was not just a grimace and a threat, even if it was all serious war preparation, something was lacking. In all the correspondence in the documents, she did not remember any mention or even a hint of preparation of war against Kemet, nor of a call for retaliation for Kemet's previous campaign. Moreover, Paser had not gone into the basis for the assertion by the agents that the preparation was not for defense but an assault on Kemet. Was that just conjecture? Was there no evidence?

On her part, as Paser had pointed out, she needed evidence to the contrary: that Hatti was *not* preparing an assault on Kemet. Proof was needed, not an interpretation. A mere absence of the mention of an assault on Kemet as the purpose for the war preparation could not serve as proof.

The documents were, of course, still in her possession, for they had been verified. She spent the next hour carefully rereading all the documents. There was a clear indication of war preparation for whatever reason. The conscription might have been to support the rule and resist the rebels, but the procurement of new weapons and backing of the vassals seemed exaggerated to suppress their own subjects. It would be appropriate if a civil war were brewing. However, there was no evidence or even anything inviting an interpretation that the war preparation was a prelude to an assault on another land.

Finally, she was left with the last message, written not in Akkadian but in Nesite, the official language of the Hittites. She searched for its translation and went through its text again. There was a term and an allusion she could not understand. She set that tablet aside for a further review.

* * *

Hartapu had been asked to meet the shaman in the Hathor temple. This time, he would also be meeting with the queen to hear her opinion of the documents after due verification by the shaman's experts. For the sake of secrecy, this meeting was not to take place in the palace as an official audience. Nefertari had to be on guard against Paser, who would be on the prowl for any new development in her venture. She had duly warned Sennefer, who had to set aside his loyalty to the vizier despite being highly indebted to him. It was a long story.

A century ago, the pharaoh Amenophis IV had founded and propagated the concept of the sun as the only god to be worshiped. He had introduced the name Aton for the sun god, replacing the name Amun. Amenophis had even changed his own name to Akhnaton.

From then onward, Aton was the one who nurtured nature, and in the pharaoh's opinion, there was no need to worship other gods than the sun. He went to extremes, forbidding the earlier name Amun and any mention of divinity in the plural. He even had all other portrayals of gods defaced and their names erased. After his reign of seventeen years, the belief he propagated died with him.

His son Tutankhaten changed his name to Tutanchamun and restored the worship of Amun. The revisionists went so far as to forbid even the mention of the pharaoh Akhnaton by name. Although the Egyptians reverted to their old ways after the pharaoh's demise, the idea persisted that the sun was the first God, emerging as the first being from a primordial sea called Nun. This was almost a compromise re-establishing the prominence of the sun god. This view was now quite popular among the priests.

Like all others, Sennefer was opposed to the heliocentric concept of Aknhnaton. Sennefer's argument went a bit further. He had his own point of view regarding the position of the sun god in the pantheon. For one, he opposed the belief that the lonesome sun god reproduced the divine siblings, brother Shu, associated with air, and sister Tefnut, associated with fire, by way of a union with his own shadow. He pointed out that the sun possessed no shadow. Shadows were cast by objects like clouds, trees, and houses interfering with the sun's rays. Secondly, gods were not directly perceptible to mankind. The sun, perceived as a disk with radiance and heat, could be only a manifestation of the sun god, not the god himself.

He fell out with the local priests on this theological issue. The priests were also annoyed at the name he had made in the community as a healer. Sennefer had a reputation as a prescient and insightful character conforming to his occult vocation. The secret of his success was beyond their grasp, even if they would not admit it. It was a matter of divine power bestowed upon a few, as well as honed by the practice of shamanism for years after the right kind of initiation.

The vizier, Paser, knew of Sennefer's qualities as a shrewd thinker and deducer of information, worldly or otherwise. He appreciated the shaman's interpretation of portending chances and risks, even in politics. To bring peace among the priests and honor his worth to the kingdom, Paser had brought Sennefer to the shaman's hometown near ancient Avaris, now part of the newly founded Per-Ramesses. The statesman had appointed him as the royal shaman and healer, attending to the health and well-being of the royals while serving the common man. Sennefer functioned as a priest in the Amun temple, approaching the gods on a spiritual track for these duties.

The prince arrived early to have a chat with Sennefer before the queen joined them. In the age of syncretism, entering a shrine of any god or goddess was no problem for anyone. A divinity with special attributes could be found in any belief of any region. There was no clash of cultures and their gods. Worship of any deity by any devotee was current and not blasphemy or a crime. The beliefs differed mainly in their customs and rituals. Terms like "pagan" and "infidel" were yet to be coined.

The goddess Hathor, in particular, was no stranger to the culture in which Haratpu had been raised. She was a deity who was also known beyond the borders of Egypt. In the Sinai and in the north, several temples had been erected for Hathor, and her worship was popular. She had become synonymous with Ba'alat, the special protective deity of the miners of turquoise, and was even known as "the Lady of Turquoise." Hartapu could imagine he was visiting the temple of Hepat the local version of Wurusema, the sun goddess of Arinna to whom his great-grandfather Mursili II had been highly devoted.

This was the first time he had approached the temple complex on foot and barefoot. Until now, he had passed this way often in one cart or the other, never daring to stop for a stroll. He had been told one did not loiter before the temples. But even for the passer-by, the huge gateway or pylon and the whole front were meant to be seen and to impress, with the enormity belittling any human being however important he or she might be in society. On entry, the mortal was to feel the superiority of the almighty and subdued to modesty. The individual was to be induced to walk past, lowering their head. Only on festival occasions was entry allowed. On such occasions, people were free to move around at ease with their kith and kin, yet in conformity with the expected solemn behavior.

In Hatti, a prince was educated in his military, administrative, and religious tasks. One day, as king, he would have to perform, not just participate in, religious ceremonies in temples and elsewhere in the name of his subjects. Therefore, Hartapu had a thorough religious knowledge of his culture, including the mythology. But for him, it was his first time visiting a temple in Kemet. In fact, he was coming here for prayer like a devout indigent, striding in somnolent solemnity. Yet, as an alien, he was deeply interested in the different culture he was encountering. He felt he could dare to stroll as a visitor, absorbing the greatness of the architecture. He thought of approaching one of the obelisks for a closer look.

As he set foot in that direction, he was startled by a gruff voice: "Entry is not allowed today. Move on." A temple guard appeared from out of nowhere. With his hefty figure, tall but no taller than Hartapu, he had raised his chin to look down upon Hartapu from head to foot, appraising him with disdainful eyes shrouded by a frown. Hartapu could imagine that this posturing of authority for the earthling before him was a practiced routine, more instinctive than intentional.

Hartapu mirrored his posture, gesture, and voice. "I have an appointment here at the Hathor temple."

"Don't waste my time. Who are you?"

"My name is Hartapu. I have been asked by none other than the priest Sennefer to come here and meet him. The priest is awaiting me in the Hathor temple. There need be no cause for delay. *You* are wasting *my* time. But if you object and obstruct…" He left the rest lingering and unsaid.

The clouds cleared in an instant. Wide-eyed, the guard stepped back as if he feared a blow. He bowed. What a transformation to his act.

"Yes, of course. I have been asked to help you, sir. I am sorry for my first reaction, but you understand. You are most welcome. This way, please."

The obsequious servant ushered Hartapu to the arch in haste, with little consideration of the guest's interest in the colossal structure or a worthy and solemn pace. There would be no delay. After they passed through the gate, the guard stopped and gave directions to reach the temple.

"Sir, keep walking straight on through the open courtyard and then through the sheltered hall. Straight on until you reach the main temple and then turn left and keep going. Hathor temple is adjacent to the main temple. Please do not meander and get lost."

The mention of the name Sennefer must have worked the wonder. Hartapu obeyed with a small feeling of satisfaction that the guard had not set any conditions, like a time limit. He was glad the man did not accompany him all the way. He was spared this additional honor.

After entering the open court featuring huge colonnades, he looked back to be sure the guard was out of sight. Hartapu promised himself to come someday with Anat on a festive occasion and snoop around to his heart's content.

He marched on, surrounded by enormous pillars of huge girth and as tall as a three-story house. He could easily get lost amid this man-made army of silent giants. He walked around the first pillar. Impressed by its thickness, he walked around it again, measuring the steps he needed to complete the circle: fourteen. Returning to the starting point, he understood what the guard had meant. If he did not keep his walk straight on and strayed from the path, he could easily get lost amid the silent sentries, the guard's colleagues.

The open-air hall led to a semi-sheltered hall. The central colonnades were covered to block the sunshine, but with a few skylights. As a result, the hall was dimly lit. Beyond this hall, the individual shrines could be entered, with a further reduction in sunlight. The devotee progressively turned his attention from the outside world towards an inner world, inviting self-awareness, contemplation, and a devotional mood.

He walked on, and his mind became subdued. Was this his present state of mind or even a reflection of the state of his life? He was in a strange land, guarded by the pillars, friends granting him support and safety. Or did they stand for obstacles, with foes that could be lurking behind each? Was he astray in an open desert with only imagined hurdles, a wanderer with dreams and no deeds? He thought of the goal in life he had set. He had, indeed, received a divine call beckoning him to act. He was to proceed in the direction that was right, to follow the kindly light.

He smelled the incense, which he was not used to from the temples back home. Was it myrrh? No, it must be something he had never come across. On reaching the main shrine of Amun, he turned left and walked on. The fragrance got stronger. The next shrine ought to be that of Hathor. He saw the kindly light. It was from a waist-high oil lamp of bronze set outside the entry door to the shrine. As he advanced towards it, he noticed his brief passage to the shrine was nearing its end, but his life's journey had just begun.

He saw Sennefer appear at the entrance door.

"Welcome, most welcome to be blessed by our goddess Hathor," the shaman greeted. "I finished my morning prayer thanking the gods for your well-being and success in your mission. This is our concerted effort, with Amun's and Hathor's help, to assure the security of you and your father. The documents you have procured will be of great help."

"Oh, thank you. I hope there is nothing amiss with the scripts. Did your experts approve of the authenticity?"

"Yes, they did. We passed them on to the queen. She will be here to thank you for your achievement."

Sennefer leaned on the doorframe and smiled.

Entering the shrine, Hartapu followed Sennerfer and stopped before the beautiful idol of Hathor. It was a majestic figure with a tall crown on which was balanced an orange disk depicting the sun, cradled between two cow horns, the symbol of her motherly care to the world. He closed his eyes and thought of his mother and prayed to her soul and the goddess before him, both invisible but able to be visualized with the eyes closed.

After a long time lost in thanking Hathor for the grace she had shown him, an alien child on a lost trail, he prayed for guidance. He opened his eyes and stepped back to turn to Sennefer.

The shaman broke the silence. "With your mind cleared by prayer, young man, may I greet you with some more good news. This time, it comes from the war front in the alehouse. Your idea."

The shaman recounted the arrest of Suppilamus, the operation that the prince had initiated. Delving into the matter of his men picking up the right man in the alehouse, he said, "Before that, I met Mehetweret in that house. She is, indeed, a charming and smart girl. As they say, she has eyes in the back of her head. She is a great asset. On hearing Suppilamus was after your father's throat, and also yours, she got really upset and did a great job of tipping off my men discreetly."

Hartapu shook his head. "She was in greater danger than I ever was. If only she knew."

Sennefer nodded. "She knows and is immensely thankful to you. Be assured." He winked.

Hartapu maintained a serious expression.

Sennefer goaded, "Is there anything serious between you?"

"No. I am in love with someone else."

"Oh, back home?"

"No. Here."

"A princess from Kemet?"

"No. But an angel." Hartapu smiled.

Sennefer nodded. Gradually, his playful expression changed to a scowl. He bent forward and said in a low voice, "Now, dear prince, please listen carefully. I am going to let you in on the whole background, which is highly confidential. I have permission to tell you so you will understand the contribution you have made for our queen's cause. It is a closely guarded secret, for she knows the ways of the palace, with its ears and eyes everywhere. Any effort on her part could be sabotaged by someone just to throw muck in her face. That is the reason we are meeting here and not in the palace. Do you understand?"

"Yes, I do," Hartapu said.

Taking a deep breath, Sennefer told him what the queen's effort was all about. It was not just offering resistance to extradition on principle. It was, indeed, also self-assertion of the land without sacrificing a peace effort, which had to be approved by the court. Hartapu had to see the broad picture, where the fugitives were not to be offered as a sacrifice in the name of peace. It ought to be an absolute peace for all souls on both sides.

Hartapu sat attentively, staring at the floor with his elbows resting on his knees, hands clasped, and head hanging. He absorbed the propensity of the situation and his contribution. When Sennefer finished, Hartapu raised his head with a smile.

Sennefer followed him with his eyes and said, "Well, what is on your mind?"

Hartapu said, "In a flash, I realized there is a resemblance to the divine stories I have heard in my childhood. Do you want to hear?"

Sennefer, who had no knowledge of the Hittite culture, much less their myths and mythology, was shocked.

"Sure, please go ahead." He was curious and, as always, ready to broaden his horizon. "I am not the wise man who knows everything."

"All right, first, let me say we are raised with stories dealing with our gods and illustrating the ideals for us to follow. This is also a part of our training in applying our faith. We believe morals are just one purpose for these stories. The other is to know that the gods are our friends, too. Now, listen. The first story I will tell you is called 'The Slaying of the Snake.'"

He told the story in the same dramatic way he had heard it from his mother and from storytellers during the New Year festival of Hattusha, when rituals were conducted for ensuring prosperity for the land.

The story was about a python, Illuyanka, who represented evil. It fought against Tarhunt, the god of thunder. Lo! The snake defeated the god. Tarhunt had a son, Telipinu, and a daughter, Inara. Goddess Inara of the wild animals thought up a plan and reached out to a mortal called Hupashiya and asked him to help her. They invited the new lord of the world, the python Illuyanka, to celebrate its victory. During the festive occasion, the mortal Hupushiya got the snake drunk, and it fell into a morbid stupor. Then he shackled the drunk in heavy chains. The storm god Tarhunt returned and slew the evil creature.

In the second story, the god Telipinu, mentioned above, neglected his duties and absconded, leaving the agriculture unguarded. All plants and animals begin to perish. In deep despair, the gods searched for this god who had failed in his duties, but in vain. The Hurrian mother goddess, Hanna-hannah, sent a bee to search for him. It found and stung him. That made the god even more furious, and he caused floods and more devastation. Kamrushepa, the goddess of magic, tried to pacify Telipinu. A mortal, namely a priest, prayed for the alleviation of the god's fury and succeeded in sending all Telipinu's anger to bronze containers in the underworld, from which nothing can ever escape. The god returned to his duties.

Hartapu enjoyed telling these stories, at times even enacting them, to such an attentive listener. The wise man's face was lit up like a child's. Giddy from his performance—could he become a storyteller? —Hartapu topped it off with a question: "What do you make of the two stories? Do you see some parallels?"

The shaman lowered his head.

In triumph, Hartapu prodded, "Not just between the two stories but also with our present situation."

The shaman raised and shook his head.

Hartapu explained, "Gods are not infallible. There are moments when even they would reach out to us mortals for help. Likewise, on earth, the kings are the mightiest among mortals but have their faults. My father had to turn his back on his folk and flee, with the following commotion even spilling onto your land. The chaos has to be resolved in the name of peace in the world.

"This is what the queen is attempting, assigned by the goddess. But both can claim assistance from mortals like us, like you and me, to reset order in the world, to seek and secure peace for all mortals. We cannot lean back and leave everything in the hands of the royalty or the divinity while offering them no support. It has to be a joint effort of one and all. This one is, again, a Hittite myth, like the other two I related, this time enacted in this land—by us. Am I right?"

Sennefer nodded. In the silence that followed, Hartapu could bet Sennefer had begun scouring the myths of his own land in search of a similar story.

Hartapu interrupted Sennefer's thoughts with a comment: "Earlier, while praying, I imagined hearing a voice that said, *Hartapu, as a mortal, you must help gods help you.*"

They heard heavy steps at the entrance. A palace guard arrived at the door. After a bow, he announced the queen.

Queen Nefertari walked in with her majestic gait, but a frown hovered over her brow. Hartapu thought this look could have nothing to do with the reverence to the holy room in the temple she had chosen for a conference. But again, this was in contrast to the mood in which she ought to be after he had brought her the documents. Could it be a sign of vexation?

After a cursory nod to greet the two men, she remained formal.

"First of all, let me congratulate you, Prince Hartapu, for your accomplishment in procuring the documents."

Hartapu drew in a breath. She raised her hand to block any modest protest from him. "I hear it was, indeed, not an easy affair. I do not know the details. Now I can thank goddess Hathor for her answer to my prayers. The contents have been verified and are, indeed, valuable for the decision ahead, awarding asylum to your venerable father."

After a break, she added, "Well done, young man." Her smile spoke more than her words. His ears heard: *Bravo!*

Hartapu smiled and bowed.

"I have more news, your majesty." The shaman bowed and beamed. He threw a glance at Hartapu. "At the wise suggestion of the prince, we have pursued and detained a high-ranking civil servant by the name of Suppilamus who was sent from Hattusha by the present king to search for King Mursili."

Her eyes glared. "Well done. Under what charges are you holding him?"

Sennefer began with the previous incident at the copper shop, most likely related to the agent from Hattusha. He had no choice but to go into the grisly details about the two people dead in the house, one of them at the hands of the prince in an armed scuffle. When he reported what their informant Zananzash was facing at the hands of Suppilamus and how timely his rescue was, the queen was quite upset.

"Do you mean to say this person… What is his name…Suppilamus is a royal civil servant sent for the sole purpose of hunting down Hattusili's opponent? Has he been pretending to be a Hittite merchant?"

"That is right, your majesty."

Her lips quivered. She raised her voice. "If he were on a peaceful mission to contact an erstwhile monarch of his land in a foreign land, it would be an internal affair. This was not just a messenger from Hatti trying to reach the erstwhile king. The subject dealing with King Mursili is now officially in our hands now that we have received a formal request for asylum. If people are getting killed, the matter looks grave, indeed. A foreigner, much less an officer, cannot carry on clandestine operations leading to death on our soil and get away with it. We cannot allow such mischief."

"Your majesty, those are the charges against him. But I will personally interrogate him and find out if there is more to it. Besides the details of his mission, I will also find out the real state of affairs in Hatti, especially its military objectives and preparation. Of course, I will make sure he does not lie one way or the other. As a reference, we have Zananzash on our side. Perhaps I can even turn Suppilamus into an informant at our service after the extraction of truth."

"At least you have blocked him from stalking King Mursili. We cannot tolerate such schemes and watch our guest get abducted. You have foiled their attempt."

Hartapu said, "May I make a remark, your majesty? You can hold Suppilamus as a pawn."

"A pawn?" The queen shook her head.

"I mean as evidence for the improper methods my grand uncle is employing. On the one hand, he is making a formal request to the pharaoh for extradition, and on the other, he is ordering a secret operation to abduct my father, even sending a senior civil servant disguised as a trader for the purpose."

Nefetari nodded and turned to Sennefer. "If he defends himself by stating he was only following his royal orders like an obedient civil servant, remind him what punishment awaits a spy in our kingdom. I am interested to know whether the Hittites are planning an attack on our land. Interrogate him and get the whole picture, and by all means, suggest to him clemency and freedom in exchange. We can compare his version of the state of affairs in Hatti with the version of Zananzash."

She turned to Hartapu. Then, as an afterthought, she swiveled back to Sennefer. "But do not use violence for the 'truth extraction,' as you call it. No violence in the name of peace."

The shaman smiled. "My methods do not need corporeal violence on a defenseless man, nor mental terror. The method of persuasion could be laborious and take time, but…"

"I know. But you do not have much time. You have about ten days. That is all."

"Yes, of course." Sennefer squirmed with his head hanging and arms folded, squeezing his biceps with his fingers.

Nefertari turned her attention to Hartapu once again. "You will have noticed one of the documents has been written in your language. I am not sure whether the scribe we found for the translation has done it properly. I would like you to translate it once more for me to have a second opinion."

The tablet she handed to him was, like the others, an internal communication. This time, it was from the *auriyas ishas*, or lord of the watchtower, the officer from Qadesh of viceregal status, to the king in Hattusha. The topic was whether Ramses was preparing for yet another campaign by amassing his troops in Per-Ramesses.

The officer referred to Hattusili's conjecture that the city had been promoted from a military outpost to the capital of Kemet primarily to be the center for aggression to the north to conquer the protectorates of Hatti. To this comment, the officer replied curtly that as they had discussed before he had left Hattusha, there was a danger from elsewhere, especially after Hanikalbat.

Nefertari asked, "What is 'Hanikalbat'? It was not translated in the version I got."

"It is a region to the east. The Assyrians call it Hanilgabat. We call it Hankalbat, and you call it Naharin. I have met quite a few refugees from there."

After a brief pause, Hartapu continued with a frown: "In a way, it is unusual. We use in our language the name Mitanni for that kingdom. *Hanikalbat* is used only for the region bereft of the kingdom. Only the Assyrians use their word 'Hanilgabat' consistently, which is what the region was called before the kingdom came into existence."

The queen asked him to read the content once again slowly, stopping him often. After he finished, he raised his eyes and saw that her face had lit up.

She swung towards Sennefer. "In your interrogation of Suppilamus, broach the topic of the most recent preparation of Hattusili for war. With pointed but not misleading questions, find out if such a war preparation is now meant for an attack on Kemet, and if not, against whom. You can also ask Zananzash, although his views may be outdated. This point is very important."

There was a long pause.

Then she said to Hartapu, "Now, I would like to ask you a personal question. It is about your stance and your plans."

"Yes, your majesty," Hartapu said.

"If the pharaoh grants your father the audience he seeks, of course, you could be granted the same, too. But foremost, you will have to ask for an audience to petition for asylum. Are you prepared?"

Hartapu was not ready to reply to this direct question. He sought his words. Avoiding eye contact, he kept biting his lip and staring at the ground.

Then he said, "Your majesty, it is an honor for me that you show concern for my future and have raised this question. With my greatest gratitude for any support, I may receive from you in this matter, I am afraid I must clarify a doubt in my mind."

"Yes, I am listening."

"If an asylum is granted, then just like my father, I would remain in your land with ample protection from any surreptitious attack from home."

"Yes, of course. It is guaranteed. It will be protective custody, to put it in a dire way, but by your own choice."

"I do not know about my father, your majesty, but as for me, I see no future in leading a hunted life without an aim. I would rather return to my land when my time comes or find another place where I will be on my own and not live as a guest forever. Please do not take this to be an impolite rebuff to your kind query or offer of hospitality. I have to form my own future."

Nefertari smiled.

"I had expected this position of yours. I respect and accept your view. We will see how we can help you in your venture. *Nefer sedjmek.* May you hear only good news."

Chapter 11

TRACKING DOWN THE TRUTH

Truth extraction by way of interrogation of foreign spies was not a daily affair for Sennefer. His work only involved collecting voluntary information from known informants or strangers. He was a priest and a healer, and violence was not his nature.

He had considered his options. At first, he had thought of sending Zananzash as the interrogator to demonstrate to Suppilamus the new situation. Zananzash would have enjoyed the exchange of roles in their chat and the implied threat, but he was not sure if Zananzash was not a double spy. He could not guess what that man would tell Suppilamus. Even in Sennefer's presence, their talk in the Hittite language would remain unintelligible to him.

The queen had clearly set the condition that there be no violence in the process. In effect, if he should go by the demand of the queen, he could apply no pressure, not even threats: "No violence in the name of peace." Even means like starvation and sleep deprivation would be out of the question. He had to limit himself to a polite chat without mental terror.

The method of suggestion he applied on patients was to subject them to a voluntary sleep-like state and inquire about their life and habits. Often, they would reveal certain details they would not easily speak of when fully conscious. This method was accepted, even welcomed, by his ailing patients seeking relief from pain or hoping for therapy. Of course, this differed from subjects of interrogation, leading them to trade a confession for relief, if not freedom. Here he had to deal with a prisoner, one who would resist any release of information in mere talk devoid of threats and intimidation. This was a senior official, an envoy of a foreign king. A civil servant under oath would not budge to any enticement. At best, he would cooperate, knowing what would await him otherwise. An offer of clemency would be the best he could offer the man, but only as a last resort.

He decided on another approach. Suppilamus would have discovered when he entered the house of Zananzash again that the latter had absconded, most likely rescued by some Black Hoods. In this case, he would assume Zananzash had reported what treatment awaited him at the hands of Suppilamus, maybe even exaggerating Suppilamus's intention to evict Mursili from the world altogether. He would use this probable assumption of Suippilamus as leverage.

After his arrest, the Hittite had been taken to a secluded spot, a safe house in the neighborhood, where one of Sennefer's men was waiting. The man announced himself as a deputy of the local mayor and inquired about the identity of the captive. These questions found no answers. The captive was at a loss to prove that he was a merchant. He could neither convincingly describe the goods he was trading, nor show where he stored his wares, nor name the people he was dealing with. He had been sent to prison to await formal charges, treated as a sundry felon caught red-handed. He had spent the days and nights in chains and in solitude, with little nourishment besides bread and water.

Only a few days ago, he had been brought back to the safe house, a better environment, as ordered by Sennefer. The shaman had thought up a peaceful means of preparing his candidate for interrogation. His practice of healing was based on prophylactic measures and medical therapy with practical results. They employed several herbs and drugs, some of them even affecting the mind. As a shaman and healer, he had a thorough knowledge of the combination of ingredients needed for a particular purpose.

He improved the man's diet in steps to get him back to his normal nourishment. But with a difference. He used herbal extracts from mandrake, henbane, Nile lily, and acacia (which contains a hallucinogen). He had them macerated and added to the meals, which would make Suppilamus's mind and will less resistant and more malleable.

In addition, the man was now being served his favorite drink, the wine from the vineyards of Inet. It was original and not adulterated, retaining its flavor and taste. Combined with the diet, the wine would loosen the man's tongue so that he uttered the truth.

Sennefer entered a room at the rear of the house. It could be seen as a luxurious chamber compared to the dark and dank dungeon the captive had come from, but it was otherwise a dire enclosure with blank stone walls and small windows near the ceiling. He saw Suppilamus seated on a small stool, his shoulders hunched and his elbows resting on the table before him.

On hearing steps, the man slowly raised his head. As he was meeting the man for the first time, Sennefer could make no comparison with his previous appearance, but he noticed the dark rings around his eyes. He imagined the Hittite had been stouter before, the cheeks not hollowed and the neck without the wrinkles. The man had been isolated all these days with no human contact except a silent servant providing food and water and a guard standing behind. He had gone through enough anguish under constant silence, isolation, and uncertainty.

Sennefer introduced himself as the royal authority in charge of special affairs, not bothering to mention his name. He added that the chat would decide whether Suppilamus would be returned to the prison or stay in this house to await formal charges and a decision by the pharaoh on his future. The mention of a looming sentence was enough for a start. He made no mention of clemency. It was too early for that.

"Well, as I hear from my colleague, we have an alien impostor posing as a prosperous merchant who is, in reality, a secret envoy of our enemy, a royal envoy." He chuckled. "It may not be a crime to call oneself a merchant with no wares to store or customers or contacts to show, but if the envoy is out to abduct or do harm to a guest of our land…what shall we say?"

He paused and raised his hand.

"Before you begin any explanation, I ought to point out your erstwhile colleague Zananzash has reached out to us, and we have his version of the story and your identity. Whom shall we believe? The one who is cooperative with information, the one we can trust, or the one who would only offer more lies?"

"What do you mean by that?" Suppilamus said. He cleared his throat. He had hardly spoken to anyone all these days, except for a few words to the deaf and dumb servant and the guard twice a day. His voice was weak. "What does that man say?"

"Not for your ears. Now, we have also heard from other sources that the lives of Mursili and the prince are in danger. Even here in our land. Can you confirm this?"

"They pose a threat to our king."

"*Do* they? Hiding in a foreign land with no means for an assault." Sennefer laughed. Then he tried his luck with insinuation, a bluff. "Does that mean King Mursili and the prince are to be found and slain?"

"Not the prince."

"Urhi-Teshub Mursili, the previous monarch of your kingdom, is to be found and slain. Is that right?"

"I did not say it."

"No, you did not. But you meant it. You left it unsaid. Did you have the order personally to search for him and destroy the possibility of his ever raising his head? Just chop it off?"

Suppilamus winced and froze, his face as still as if it had been cut from stone.

"Sure," Sennefer went on. "There is some oath of confidence not to concede any details about the orders from your king. Gory orders. All the same, from other sources, we know it is true." He bluffed again to provoke Suppilamus. "Do you realize such testimony points to your being an agent of death in search of a guest in our land, a civil servant at the royal service of Hatti with a license to kill? A killer? When we add to that the testimony of threats to Zananzash and your behavior, stamping around on our soil and spilling blood, what should we make of the whole picture? Do you know what punishment awaits you?"

Suppilamus took a sip of his wine. The shaman noticed his hand trembling slightly. He could tell the sip did not indicate nonchalance but a desire to release stress. Hopefully, the herbs had begun to take effect, with the wine following them.

Sennefer broke off the interrogation and left the room without a word, leaving the man alone— yet in the best company. There was a full jug of wine on a table in the corner.

He let plenty of time pass for his captive to nurse his wine and ponder his options. He returned after a long break of an hour or longer.

He began, "No one knows you have been apprehended, neither your friends here, your king, nor your family back home. My men took care of your driver. If you perish here, that is it. You know well that you have dug yourself into a hole. The only way you can get out is to come up with some news to show cooperation. Are you ready? I cannot wait another day. You have to make up your mind now, right NOW!" the shaman banged his fist on the table.

"What kind of news? What do you want to hear?" Suppilamus's voice was now plaintive. Sennefer had brought him down to the mat, as a wrestler would say.

"Tell me all you know about the military preparation and strategy of your king to attack our land."

Suppilamus looked up with surprise and raised his eyebrows. "What preparation?"

"You heard me. The war preparation to attack Kemet."

"What? Our king has too many worries at home to even think of attacks on other lands. This is no state secret. If you do not hear this from me, you will hear it from others. Or is this nonsense about attacking your land coming from Zananzash's gossip kitchen?"

He took a deep breath.

"All right. First of all, remember this." He raised a hand and pointed at Sennefer. "I owe my allegiance to our king and our king alone. I was, am, and will be a loyal and trustworthy servant of the Hittite crown all my life, come what may. I served under Mursili when he was my king. As my loyalty is to the crown, now it is to Hattusili, who wears it. I am not going to say something untrue to save my skin, neither stuff you want to hear or try to feed into my mouth nor facts you imagine or have only heard. Unlike the defector and traitor Zananzash, I am not a master of rumor and hearsay, which he would call information. I am a civil servant presently in charge of the internal security of our land, Hatti. I am not led by spies and goons."

After a pause, sitting bolt upright, he resumed his talk, raising his voice.

"Mursili absconded without a word, plainly giving up his throne and crown once he realized he had lost his hold on the kingdom. It was a voluntary departure, in effect, a flight, an abdication. The main concern of our king now is the turmoil that has been raised by Mursili's corrupt officers, who fear reprisal. Their resistance is taking a martial turn, suggesting a war within our land. This opposition of rabble-rousers and muckrakers is being perceived by the vassals as a sign of weakness of the new reign. Also, they are raising their heads to sing along and destabilize the kingdom. Our king is trying to put down any budding rebellion and recruiting forces for this purpose. Even this may be interpreted as war preparation by your dumb sleuths and scouts snooping around in our land."

There was a break after this breathless prelude. Relishing the attention of his adversary, otherwise in command of the interrogation, Suppilamus took a sip from the mug and followed it with an emphatic gulp.

"Of course, our king is not ignoring the defense against any assault from without. The recent attempt to seize our protectorates to the south by your pharaoh is the cause for this concern. But the major adversary and enemy is someone else."

He cleared his throat again and bent forward to proceed. He stared with a deep frown.

"Remember the fall of Mitanni. Years ago, Mursili's father, Muwatalli, defended Qadesh against your pharaoh, but this engagement diverted his attention and military power from Mitanni. Once, it had been a great empire, but at this time, it was our protectorate; its people spoke our language. Muwatalli let the protectorate Mitanni fall into the hands of Adad-nerari, the ambitious Assyrian emperor. Two years later, Muwatalli's son Urhi-Teshub Mursili ascended the throne. In the seventh year of his reign, to show off his prowess, he attacked his own uncle Hattusili and seized Hakpissa and Nerik from him. The uncle hit back and won.

"Now the Assyrian Adad-nerari's successor, Shalmanazzar, is even more aggressive. He is busy devastating what is left of Mitanni. It is now a wasteland. You may not like to hear what he did to that land and its subjects, the defenseless men, women, and children—especially the women."

He paused and nodded, tapping his fingers on the table.

"Shalmanazzar's next move will be westward towards our vassals. The Assyrians tasted blood after Mitanni, with no retaliation from Hatti, and Shalmanazzar believes we would easily give up other vassals, too. He is on the march. Our major worry right now is the advance of the Assyrians, not Kemet's campaigns, which were only pinpricks. This concern with the Assyrians is paramount.

"No wonder we have cause for worry and a good reason to prepare ourselves and our vassals for defense. In this background, it cannot be a surprise that our king wants to block Mursili from returning with the pharaoh's support and opening an additional front. He would have that threat eliminated once and for all.

"Get this plain truth as to whom we fear most. They are the Assyrians. Get it into your head whether you like it or not, whether it suits you or not."

He sat back, raised his head, and stared with contempt at Sennefer. He released the shaman from his stare only with a big swig from the mug.

"Can you prove it?" Sennefer demanded in the brief silence.

"No!" Suppilamus yelled. "Take it or leave it. Wait until Shalmanazzar bangs on your door to offer you your proof. If this truth is not to your taste, behead me. I am prepared to die for my king and his kingdom."

Was it the truth?

* * *

Could truth have a twin? Even a doppelgänger?

Sennefer chose to seek Zananzash's counsel. He did not want to lay out the views of Suppilamus. There was no point in prejudicing him, nor in suggesting an option to confirm. Sennefer needed an original opinion from a new angle, one of an erstwhile spymaster. He must take into account, however, that Zananazash worked under the previous regime and his views might be a bit outdated, as the queen pointed out. He would have to compare the statements of the two men and work out a common factor, if any, especially when it came to the strategy the kings had been pursuing.

Zananzash was still quartered in Teremun's residence, with two guards in civilian clothes standing on the other side of the road. Two more were posted in the rear of the house. Zan was again a prisoner, only one who needed no special measures for an interrogation.

Sennefer used to visit him off and on and to attend to his healing leg. As he approached the house, he was seen and recognized by the men across the road. They discreetly looked away, letting him pass. Teremun greeted him indoors with the usual news of ever more refugees arriving from Hatti.

When Sennefer sat down with Zananzash for a chat, Teremun joined them, curious as ever. But that was not a problem, for Sennefer was not going to mention Suppilamus at all.

He began a casual chat and gradually broached his subject as a matter of interest in the general topic of the new king's antics in Hattusha. Zananzash answered his question with aplomb.

"Of course, I can comment on the strategy of the present king," he said. "In fact, he is hardly well versed in foreign politics. Right now, he is ruled by fear and advised by equally inexperienced and scared men of questionable wisdom. He will be sticking only to the policy of the past monarchs, namely a defensive one, this time ruled more by fear than mere caution."

"You could have gone into these details before." Sennefer could not control his reproach.

"You never asked." Zan looked surprised. "It was all about granting asylum to Mursili."

"Never mind. What I want to know is, could Hattusili be preparing for an outright war or assault on our land?"

"What? Where did you get that idea? It is your pharaoh who has been sending forays into our vassals in our south, hankering for Amurru, Qadesh, and other protected territories of ours. Such incursions from mere pinpricks to regular campaigns began even before his time, under the pharaoh Seti. Of course, our king, whoever it is, would like to settle the matter once and for all. But by force? No, not now."

Those last words sounded too bland, begging an explanation.

"Not now?"

"Listen, my friend." Zan took a deep breath. "I spoke of the Hittite policy, which is ruled by fear, not cowardice. The reason for such a defensive policy is this: ten years ago, your pharaoh marched up the Orantes River with his eyes on Qadesh and the surrounding provinces.

Muwatalli, our king at the time, was in a dilemma, as the Assyrians were attacking Mitanni at the same time. He chose to face down your pharaoh. As a consequence, he had to sacrifice that whole region of Mitanni, which was also our protectorate. Ever since, we wondered if there was, and still is, a collusion of forces, an alliance between Kemet and Assur.

"I was in charge of the office of information and had to leave the question open, for I had no answer to that. All these years, we have dreaded such an alliance, a simultaneous and concerted attack on two fronts from both powers to conquer our protectorates. Once they possess our foreign territories, Kemet will have free passage for a march to join forces with Assur and invade Hatti."

This was not a new angle but a total confirmation of Suppilamus's words. The men might be on different sides, but the truth had to be the same. It was not a matter of perspective, nor could it be a ploy to influence Kemet. Sennefer took care not to reveal any reaction.

"I spoke about my reserve clay tablets I have stored somewhere," Zan said, turning the conversation to his personal interest. "They deal mostly with reactions and suggestions from vassals on strengthening their positions, as well as demands for security against foreign aggression. There are concrete facts of the aggressive plans of the Assyrians, even speculation about them counting on Kemet in the long run for their purpose.

"As I said, I had no reason to go into this subject, as it does not refer to the fugitives and their extradition. Moreover, I wanted to see how much the first batch of documents was of interest to your authorities, how your seniors reacted to their content before I could hope for protection from your side."

He paused again and bent forward.

"Now is the time I would like to have some assurance of my shelter and protection here and uniting with my family, which is in exile elsewhere. Only then would I gladly surrender all the security I have left."

Sennefer nodded and made a split-second decision. He let out the agenda ahead.

"There will be a final conference soon where our queen will make a case for non-belligerence. That means no war with your kingdom. She needs all evidence to support her. It is only after that event that one would think of rewarding you as one of the sources supporting the cause. You can keep your documents as reserve anywhere you choose, but I must have a look and verify to be convinced they are, indeed, valuable enough to even be mentioned in the conference. The queen will then have at least my word for it. If you like, I will accompany you, along with two guards, to look up the documents, let us say, two days from now?"

Zan nodded. "And I must have your word that you will not confiscate them and leave me helpless. Mind you"—he threw a quick glance at Teremun— "if they fall into the wrong hands, I can easily be charged with treason by the Hatti kingdom."

Sennefer nodded. "Neither I nor anyone under my direction will take possession of the documents without your consent, ever. You have my word and my oath, right here with Teremun as the witness."

Zananzash absorbed the statement. He paused, tilted his head, and patted Sennefer's back, looking closely into his eyes. He added, "I trust you. You are a priest, so there is no need to swear. Anyway, I am happy at least and at last that you understand the situation. The Assyrian Shalamanazzar is our real foe, of Hatti and of Kemet."

He paused and bit his lip as if to resist, but then he added, "May the gods forbid! I cannot believe the pharaoh or his vizier never fancied this possibility, which is a reality."

Teremun grinned.

* * *

In the early morning, as usual, the sun beamed benignly, though it would get serious very soon. Anat could still feel the sun god caressing her cheeks; soon he would be reminding her to find shelter for her own good, the received wisdom of every child: stay out of sight when dad is angry. But on this day, she was too excited to care. She had met Hartapu for a special appointment with another man close to her heart: her uncle.

She had decided to surprise the elderly man by presenting her hero to him. She was sure both the men would get along well. Uncle was a tolerant man and would hardly care where Hartapu came from.

Nevertheless, she had not wanted to tell the uncle in advance. The surprise was not meant as a prank; she just wanted to overwhelm him with the man of her choice, her prince. She had avoided a due announcement on purpose. Otherwise, her uncle, like all old people, would make a big fuss of the occasion. She had wanted the introduction to be informal, not a festive occasion with an elaborate ceremony for a welcome. It had to be casual, without lofty words and a raised forefinger.

Hartapu had no objection to this encounter. She loved the way he pretended nonchalance to hide his curiosity and excitement at meeting a grand seigneur. Of course, Anat had not failed to notice how Hartapu had dressed up for the occasion. He was clean-shaven and wearing a new long shirt with half-sleeves and a brocade border held up with two strips tied at the neck, a garment she had never seen before. He had not forgotten to put on his sandals. As for her, she was dressed like usual. She was only visiting her uncle. This was not a formal occasion. She should have warned Harti. Too late.

When they reached the steps to her uncle's residence, she whispered, "Wait here." Leaving him around the corner, she ran up the few steps to the front door.

On her knock, her uncle opened the door.

He had hardly let her in and greeted her when she interrupted, saying, "Uncle, I have a surprise for you. Would you like to meet my boyfriend right now?"

He was taken aback. "Did I hear you right? Your groom?"

"Yes, you can call him so." She was gasping. Annoyed, she tried to check her breath.

He cocked his head and smiled. "Really?"

"Yes, he is here. I will ask him to step in, and you may ask him yourself if you like." She followed this with a merry laugh. She could never be so open with her parents and speak so freely. At any rate, she could hardly check her excitement.

With no time for a formal preparation of a visit, she was sure she had confused him. She waited for his protest and fuss. *Nothing on impulse, please, not for such a serious matter as presenting a groom!*

On the contrary, his smile spread out to a grin. There was a strange twinkle in his eyes. Curiosity?

Anyway, no objections. Uncle was always a sport. Anat turned to the street and called out to Hartapu.

Hartapu came running up the steps and entered her uncle's home with gusto. But when he stood before the uncle, he froze.

Time came to a halt.

Then the uncle began to laugh. He laughed and laughed, rocking back and forth. At first, Hartapu stood wide-eyed and with an open mouth. After a full second, he burst into laughter, too. They almost laughed their guts out. Poor Anat stood motionless, feeling left out, wondering if the joke was on her.

The uncle said to Hartapu, "Yes, dear prince, I am the shaman, the spymaster, and also her uncle, all in one."

Anat was still too confused to smile. She looked at Hartapu, then her uncle, and back at Hartapu and asked him in an urgent tone, "Did you hide this fact from me, Harti?"

"Oh, no," Harti said, laughing again and putting his arm around her shoulders. "This is a revelation for me, too."

He turned to Sennefer. "She always praised her uncle, and today she wanted me to get to know him in person, more on impulse. I couldn't imagine... She never told me what her uncle did."

197 |

Anat said, feeling relieved, "I was glad you never asked. I thought you would be scared if I said he is a priest. You would have thought he is more prejudiced than Dad."

"It is, indeed, a great, pleasant surprise for me," Hartapu said. "So, it is all in the family."

"Where you will also belong." Sennefer smiled, but his voice was low, making his words sound like a foregone decision rather than a declaration. That was his brief welcome address. "Now, I want you to know I have had a personal interest in your well-being and success all along. Had you guessed it?"

"No," Hrtapu said. "I only knew you had this assignment from the queen and wanted to support the Black Hoods and Teremun where you can. At first, I had even wondered why a royal official like you supports my father, whom even all the gods appear to have deserted."

"Besides the royal order, there was always a special reason for me." The shaman patted Hartapu on his shoulder. "I had heard about you even before we met."

"Really? Only good things, I hope."

Sennefer nodded. "Yes. All along, I knew who you were."

Hartapu threw a glance at Anat and frowned.

Her uncle shook his head. "Not from Anat."

"From Teremun?"

"No," the old man said. "I only asked Teremun to get in touch with you to procure the documents. I knew about you beforehand." The shaman smiled.

Hartapu shook his head. "How come?"

"I heard about you from my sister Bennu." He smiled.

The young man's eyebrows shot up.

Sennefer led the guest into his small living room. Anat followed. After they sat down on a mat near the window, Sennefer said, "Bennu could not keep the secret about your identity after your audience with the queen. She had to share it with someone, if not with her husband. No harm done. On the contrary, as I said, I had a personal interest in this case."

There was a pause as both young people digested the development, so far full of surprises. Sennefer got up and gestured for the others to remain seated. He moved away with youthful steps, returned with beer and three mugs, and placed them all in the middle of the mat.

As he sat down again, Anat watched his face getting grave. He poured the drink into two mugs and handed them over to the guests.

Then he said to Hartapu, "I met Bennu's husband and laid out the secret about your identity."

There was a hush. Only the sound of Anat's uncle pouring beer into his own mug could be heard.

Dad knows? Anat could not bear it any longer and asked, "How did he take it?"

Sennefer sipped his drink and swallowed with vehemence. Then he said, staring ahead, "At first, he was alarmed on hearing your groom is someone from the other side, the enemy he had fought."

He turned to Hartapu. "It was not easy for him to learn you are the grandson of the king of the Hittites at the battle for Qadesh. After quite a while, I would say after the reality slowly sank in, he sought some solace in the thought that he had experienced the Hittites as honorable warriors. I did not enter into a discussion on the matter. I let him sort it out for himself. Finally, he took it in stride. On the next occasion, he even muttered something about how he was impressed by your person, that you are someone with intelligence and character. Gradually, he even got excited at the thought of his daughter becoming the bride of... You can imagine the rest."

"I am relieved." Hartapu leaned back and looked at Anat. "I had heard his war cry in the smithy during a chat about that battle. It was full of passion, even scary."

They laughed—all three this time.

The following break invited them to change the topic for the moment. Anat got fidgety and looked at Hartapu. She said, "Tell him."

Sennefer sat erect and frowned. He raised his hand and slowly reached for his belly. Stroking it and looking alarmed, he whispered, "Come on, Anat. Do you want to say—"

"No, Uncle. Good news, all right, but not what you fear."

Hartapu joined in her merry laughter.

Hartapu explained, "It is about our future, all right, but not what you thought. This is even more serious."

He went into the encounter with the man who had come all the way from Tarhuntassa, located near the coast far to the south of Hatti. It was a port and a minor kingdom, of which Kurunta, the younger brother of Mursili, was the king.

"The message this man brought to me is from my uncle Kurunta. The news is that Hattusili and my uncle have reached an agreement of mutual defense. This is a typical preventive measure taken by Hatti for generations with many of the neighboring minor kingdoms, ostensibly for the protection of the latter by aggressors but also for Hatti to rest securely behind a defensive barrier."

"It is good news, indeed. But how would this affect you?"

"I wrote to my uncle after reaching Kemet, giving him the address of my employer. I entrusted it to a reliable trader on his way to that port. However, I never received an answer. Now this message that the man from Tarhuntassa brought happens to be the response. It says that in the course of the year after his ascension to the throne, Hattusili offered to Kurunta a mutual defense agreement on an eye-to-eye basis. The treaty also includes a safe haven for my person in Tarhuntassa, provided I lay no claim to the throne in Hattusha. Hattusili is only after my father."

"It is, indeed, great news for you, but—"

"Wait. There is more in the message. My uncle offers me a high office in his court so that I can be of use to his reign, applying my knowledge in governance. I have been asked to come at the earliest opportunity unless I choose to seek asylum here and stay away."

"Hmmm." Sennefer's forehead creased.

"What is the matter?" Anat poked. She had expected an outbreak of joy at the news.

"Dear prince," Sennefer said, "with all due respect to the magnanimous offer by your family member, your own uncle, are you sure of the authenticity of the message?"

"Yes. I checked it. I won't be throwing my lot with—"

"Even then, even if the message is really from the king of Tarhuntassa... please do not feel I am offending your uncle Kurunta, but are you sure which side he is on? Let us assume he has been intimidated by the desperate Hattusili and is now forced to make this offer to get you to his realm, only to turn you in to—"

"It is a difficult question. You have to trust someone sometime. The only trust I have in this matter is my aunt Puduhepa in Hattusha."

"What do you mean by that?"

"Hattusili's spouse, the queen Puduhepa, has a big say in all matters of state, thanks to the fact that she nursed her husband in his difficult days during the recurrence of his childhood ailment. It is said he was healed after her constant prayers to the goddess Lalvani, queen of the infernal world.

"Puduhepa is, or was, the favorite cousin of my mother. After my mother passed away, she looked after me for years. She practically brought me up. I had, or have, a good relationship with her. Even then, there is always a hazard. I am taking a chance, for sure. I propose to set foot on Tarhuntassa unannounced and incognito and find a way to get to the truth before I expose myself. I sent back my uncle's messenger with a response stating only that I would come as soon as I could and would report to him on arrival. No details."

"Does that mean," Sennefer asked after a quick glance at Anat, "you plan to leave at once?"

"No." Hartapu laughed. "Not at all. When I set foot on Tarhuntassa, I must be sure there is no chance of Hattusili trying to get his hands on my father through me. First, I will await my father's audience at the pharaoh's court in about two weeks to offer him asylum. On that occasion, I will meet him in the palace, seek his counsel and blessings, and take my leave."

Sennefer smiled and said, "Now I understand. You have thought over the proposal very well. You have to take chances at some point and cannot waste your life letting opportunities pass."

Anat sighed with relief.

When it was time to leave, as they neared the door, Sennefer said, "By the way, do you remember our last chat in the temple before the queen arrived? You mentioned that we mortals have to help the gods help us. You are in that position now. Be careful, but do not let fortune speed away. Moreover, we can also learn from our queen, who acted on a prompt by the gods to begin her peace efforts. When given a prompt and a chance by the gods, never say no."

Hartapu nodded.

Sennefer asked, "Does king Kurunta have an heir?"

"No, they have no offspring," Hartapu replied, bending down to adjust his footwear.

Before he looked up, Anat exchanged glances with Sennefer.

* * *

Sennefer had wanted to keep the trip to fetch the documents secret. He had arranged for a cart for Zananzash to be taken for treatment in some remote place. The driver arrived on time and helped the shaman get Zan onto the cart. They drove off via a detour to Met's parents. Sennefer watched the rear, making sure there was no other vehicle following them.

He began a chat, comforting the lonesome colleague from Hattusha, also a spymaster but now on the run and without any formal protection,

"Is your family at home in safety?" Sennefer asked.

"I would say they are beyond the reach of Hattusili. Before I quit, I sent them away to a place outside his realm."

"Any news from them?"

"How? They do not know where I am. All that they know is that I am somewhere in Kemet. I am playing hide and seek with my own family. What a life!"

"Do you have a large family?" Sennefer wanted to let the poor man air his feelings.

"With my dear wife, Shena, I have two daughters, both grown up, followed by a son, a latecomer. For him, I am an old father, but I cannot help it." He shrugged and smiled. "I love them all, but I should admit I miss Mahhuzzi most."

"Your son?" Sennefer was at a loss to make out the gender in Hittite names. They all sounded strange to his ears.

"Yes, that is my son. We had plans to go for hunting and what-not. You know, at that age, boys cherish and follow their fathers." He smiled and added, "Later, the sons begin rebelling and challenging them."

"Were we any different?" Sennefer asked.

They laughed.

All of a sudden, Zan's face turned serious. "First of all, I must thank you people for your hospitality and protection so far. In fact, I was rescued from that Suppilamus…"

"You were rescued by your own people, Zan. We only offered the stage for the drama." Sennefer tried to keep the chat lighthearted.

"Sure. But the whole affair will be of no use to me if I am returned to Hatti. I will have a lot of explaining to do there to save my skin. How could I ever unite with my family and live in safety?"

After musing for a while, he added, "Do you see any chances of my seeking protection here for my family and me?"

"You know well, dear friend, I have no say in this matter. I can only present my view. If all goes well and the court gives due credit to your cooperation, I am sure our queen would like to express her gratitude. That would not be by throwing you back to the land you betrayed. Without giving you untoward hope, let me say this. We will not want you just to live here as a permanent guest but to be of use by serving our kingdom. As for now, I can only ask you to be patient."

Irrespective of the future relationship between the two kingdoms, Zan could be of great assistance with his experience. Sennefer could think of all the espionage going on in this city. In addition, with the Hittites transporting their differences to Kemet, maybe one day, even their civil war would be transported and staged here.

They had taken the final curve and reached Met's home. Leaving the driver seated in the cart, Sennefer and Zannanzash approached the front door, which was open. They entered and announced themselves. Met's mother, Tiaa, came out from the kitchen and greeted Zan. He introduced Sennefer to her, calling him a colleague in Kemet. Tiaa was her usual motherly self, inquiring after Zan's health. Her husband was away in the market, but she would do her best to be hospitable to the rare visitors. The chat also turned to Met, whom Sennefer had met. The mother was pleased to hear words of praise about her daughter, whose intelligence and presence of mind were now cherished by two elderly officers.

After the small talk and drinks, when the time came to depart, Zan turned to the reason for their visit. This was the Hittite way of politeness, not to break in and immediately announce the banal reason for the visit but first to make it a social affair and "by the way" mention what the visit was about. When he asked for the sack he had left behind, he got a jolt.

"Do you mean that linen bundle with the pieces of clay? But you sent someone to pick it up for you. You must have it by now." Tiaa looked at him with her eyes wide open.

"No. I did not send anybody to pick it up. I think there is a mistake."

"Two days ago, at about this time, when I was home alone, two soldiers came here and said Zananzash had sent them to bring the object he had left behind, as he was not yet able to move much. The men were from the army."

Zan asked, "How do you know they were from the army?"

Tiaa shrugged. "That is what they said. They were soldiers. They were wearing leather straps across their torsos and carrying tall, chest-high rawhide shields. In their hands, they held leather straps."

Sennefer interrupted to explain to Zan: "They do not carry spears on civil missions."

"I had no doubts." Tiaa shrugged. "At any rate, they were polite and only doing their duty, following their orders, and I had no cause to challenge them."

In the ensuing silence, Sennefer stood and smiled at Tiaa. "There is some mistake here. I cannot imagine how the army could get involved in this affair, even if by mistake. But never mind, dear lady. We will make inquiries and find out where that bundle is now." He turned to Zan and said, "I plead for patience."

As he took his leave, Zan stammered some nice words for Tiaa's husband and her daughter. Assisted by her and his colleague, he limped towards the cart. He was in a daze.

Driving back home with empty hands, Sennefer broke the glum silence. "I suspect it could have been the military. They would never act on behalf of a civilian, much less a foreigner. They act only under orders from the military authority. These men were impostors. Whom did you tell where the documents were stored?"

"No one except Tiaa. In fact, I made it a point not to reveal where they were when the prince visited me and was sifting through the first batch I presented to him. It is true. I did tell him there were more in reserve, but I did not tell him where. The girl was present, but I spoke in Nesite. She did not understand a word."

"Think again. Did this subject pop up any time after that in a moment of pressure or elation?"

"My friend, it is my profession to guard secrets, even state secrets, in this case for my own well-being. Do you imagine—"

"Please do not mistake me, dear Zananzash, but even the best horse can stumble one day. Think again."

Zan shook his head and lowered it. He pushed his tongue against his cheek. This was not a moment to parade professional pride as a master of secrets. A self-interrogation could be the only help.

After a pause, he said, "After the skirmish with the two men, we were in a hurry to leave the place before Suppilamus returned. The prince reminded me to pick up the tablets for which he had come. I was limping towards the kitchen for that purpose and mentioned once again that the second batch was stored somewhere. Now that I was secure, it was a moment of relief for me. Only the prince and I were present."

"Where were the others?"

"Teremun and the girl were off to fetch the cart parked down the road."

"And the other man, Teremun's friend?"

"Bak? Oh, he was…" Zan fell silent.

"Try to visualize the whole scene. The way you moved towards the kitchen, with the prince waiting, either seated or standing. Also, precisely word for word what you told Hartapu."

Zananzash nodded and closed his eyes. After a long while, he spoke up again.

"Hey, I imagine… No, I clearly saw the fellow standing at the front door to help me out and get into the cart when it arrived. He was there when I turned my back to move towards the kitchen. Of course, he could have heard me, for I spoke a bit loudly, calling out over my shoulder from the kitchen. I spoke in Nesite. But do you think…"

"Why not? I heard from Teremun he is conversant in your language."

"Come to think of it, he was also sitting in the driver's seat when we stopped at the girl's home. Her mother checked my wound, and when she fixed the bandage, she asked me in your language, 'Have you everything with you, or did you forget something?' I understood what she meant. To be careful, I just said, 'The bundle? Not now,' and she nodded. He must have associated this with the tablets."

"We will check this out with Teremun. We must know more about that fellow Bak and see if he was, indeed, behind this mischief. Despite this setback, I want you to remember your contribution so far, even without these additional documents, has been commendable. Rest assured, I will speak to the queen about your future."

After a while, Zan started thinking aloud. "It is not just that I cannot show you these documents proving I am not a liar. Nor can I point my finger at poor Tiaa, who knew nothing about the text or the value of the documents. She is definitely not involved. It could be only... I hope, I do hope, it is, indeed, real soldiers and not the Red Hoods posing as soldiers. If the correspondence in the tablets falls into the hands of the Hittite king, I would be charged with treason and hunted down. You must understand my situation, not to mention my prospects of finding shelter in your kingdom."

After a further long lament, Zan was exhausted. They rode on without exchanging another word but sharing the black moment.

If only Sennefer had procured the last documents and shown that the fear of the Assyrians was stated in the correspondence, the queen's battle could have been won. Now, with the conference due in a few days, how would he answer to the queen? Tell her of documents that possibly did not exist and were only imagined by Zan? How could such a phantom stand as proof? He racked his brain for some way to find the miscreant and the booty. His mind kept yelling at him: *Those tablets were the best part of the proof! There could have been nothing better!*

What should he tell the queen? Should he tell her the truth and point out that the matter must be investigated? Would that help before the conference? The burning question remained: who stole the documents?

It could have been the Red Guards posing as soldiers. Or was this the work of a spy, someone listening in all the time, someone among the friends? Atrocious!

Who could outplay a foe amid friends?

Only a friend among foes.

Chapter 12

CONFERENCE

The date for the third conference had been set. The news from Sennefer had reached her just a few days before. It was, indeed, a grave setback for Nefertari. The additional documents of Zananzash clearly explaining the fear of the Hittites were now gone, the evidence purloined. The suspect called Bak, who had snuck onto the prince's team, had absconded. Conveniently, he was reported to have gone to his village due to a family tragedy. It was a safe bet he would never appear again. It would be a long shot to expect the recovery of the documents at all, much less procuring them in time. Talking about them would be of no avail. It would only set up the good man Zan as a liar, an intrigant who took his colleague Sennefer for a ride. Nefertari would stand exposed as gullible and naïve for supporting her wobbly position with hearsay. It would be wise for her to drop even the mention of such mysterious, unseen, and missing information altogether.

Originally, after assembling all her thoughts, the queen had wanted to visit Hathor's temple on this day for an ultimate prayer before the meeting, but she had postponed the visit after the news she had received from Sennefer. It would be audacious to think the gods could wait, but the strange fact was, in contrast to mortals, they could be approached anytime. Anyone could pray to a god at any time, regardless of the festival days and hours, which were celebrations and not appointments. Giving an audience was the habit of royalty.

She had decided to spend the next hours alone without any interruption. She had given instruction to Bennu to ward off anyone, no matter what reason they might bring up for needing an "urgent" audience to seek her advice or permission. She could rely on the seasoned lady-in-waiting, who had never failed her even in the most sundry of duties.

Reminded of the audience, she wondered about Paser. She had expected him to appear for a "consultation" so he could take stock of the situation. At the last encounter, she had suggested to him more news in the offing in due course. Either he was engaged otherwise and had no time to come digging or he needed no more information. Whereas she was thinking day and night about the forthcoming meeting, for him, the conference was a routine affair of a life filled with consultation, debates, influencing others, and enforcing one's views.

But Paser had signaled resistance to her views. Consequently, she had to prepare herself with whatever weapons she had so far. Strange. Weapons for a war for peace—that could be called her Peace Offensive! Was that not an oxymoron? Whatever. She had chosen to fight, so fight she would.

Gradually Nefertari's mind entered a debate of its own. She was set to fight her case to the end, but the debate began about the means. In retrospect, she wondered if she had been too attached to the means of documents, written stuff, one after another advocating her case.

At the outset, she had been convinced beyond any doubt by that young man from Hatti when he had read out the translation of the curious message from Puduhepa in a strange language. The very fact that a Hittite had read it out had given validity to the message.

This time, how would the men react? In the conference, the documents would be reproduced and summarized by her. Her arguments would be based on her interpretation of the text. Would that lend more authenticity to them? Paser would try to counter her arguments, calling them outdated and worn-out thoughts. What if Paser should call up homegrown military experts, committed and eloquent, to present their expert appraisal? Two of the three men in the conference, Shishi and Amun-her, were men of action, not given to ifs and buts nor to glyphs and words. They would be more impressed by military experts with a crisp delivery of their opinions.

Was she at a disadvantage?

Not at all. She had at her disposal two veterans, two worthy and senior officials from the other side, both suited to give their testimony orally in support of her position. On whichever side of the royalty in Hatti the officials Zananazash and Suppilamus could be, they concurred on the point of the fear their land posed. Neither of the two had any reason, bias, or ill will for such an assertion. Their identical conclusion could have nothing to do with their personal interest in securing refuge in one case or in saving one's skin in the other. No collusion on this point could be suspected. These men could take the stand, swear, and support what she presented etched into clay.

She sat erect, looked up, and took a deep breath. Yes, she would play out these two "state guests," who, like two doves, had flown into her shelter, to face the court and speak under oath to their own gods. That course of action would be her next line of defense—rather, offense— if the court was not impressed by her own effort.

She took one last look at what more she had in her possession. Among the tablets, there was the last document, which categorically denied Kemet as the major worry for Hatti and the aim of war preparations there. That was her weapon for her own war with words. Anything more? Anything else?

She was disturbed by someone clearing their throat at the door. It was Bennu. How dare she...

"What *is* it, Bennu?" Nefertari could not hide her irritation.

"I am sorry to disturb you, your majesty, but there is a courier who has to deliver an important message and return forthwith. He says he has to hand it to you in person."

"Show him in."

The herald walked in with quick steps. Used to travel and hardship, he was agile on his feet and did not show signs of fatigue. He seemed even to have washed himself prior to this personal encounter with the queen. On her direction and without any further comment, with both hands, he gently placed a clay envelope on the table. He bowed to it and then to the queen and stood erect for dismissal. She nodded and waved him away. Bennu would handle the matter of rewarding the man for his service.

The material of the message told her its origin: from the north, of course, where papyrus was unknown. She broke open the seal and drew out the tablet. The insignia announced its sender as Puduhepa. This time, she had chosen to write in Akkadian, most likely in response to Nefertari's request.

Nefertari skipped the customary initial rigmarole and headed for the core of the message. After much browsing, she found the essential lines. There they were, in clear language: *"Very soon, the cherished pharaoh will be receiving from my gracious spouse an offer of an agreement of peace to be negotiated between the monarchs of the two great powers for their mutual benefit."*

She read the passage before and after this sentence. She read the sentence again and again. She took the time to read the whole text of the message from top to bottom. A misinterpretation was not possible. The dear lady had chosen simple and unmistakable words. Nefertari looked up and stared ahead in disbelief as her gaze got fuzzy with tears of joy. *Thank you, Hathor!*

* * *

Nefertari was ready for combat.

However, she was constantly aware that whatever her odds were, hubris was the last friend she needed on this occasion. Diplomacy and convincing arguments even in the face of a challenging opposition were called for. However, she allowed herself a combative mood to foster her courage. She would be alone against the rest of the world, which would be made of three men on this morning at the final conference in the "war room."

On entering, she felt the room she had known as a place of calm discussion and speculation had turned into a place of debate for a decision, even a verbal battleground and place of judgment. Of course, much was at stake. She could not stop her imagination from flying beyond the reality of the moment. The picture of the final judgment hovered in her mind, the day in her afterlife when she would be accompanied by the falcon-headed god Anpu for the judgment by Osiris, standing at the balance. Her soul would be weighed against an ostrich feather. Should the heart balance the feather, she would be beckoned to heaven; otherwise, she would be damned to the underworld. She shrugged off this thought, telling herself she was not appearing here to be judged. It was the case she was representing that would be judged, and the decision of the pharaoh, war or peace, would be supported by the divinity. It would be her words against those of the others.

She need not fear for herself. She had done her best. Hathor was on her side. She felt the goddess's hand on her shoulder, pushing her towards the chair as if to say, "Now, go ahead and do your best."

Ramses began the meeting by restating what had been discussed the previous time, but instead of the topic she had wanted to jump into, he started off with some problem regarding defense measures, in particular, the procurement of provisions for the military in the north. Amun-her brought up his complaints, and there was a long discussion on matters in which she had no interest.

At long last, after she had to stifle a yawn or two, the pharaoh turned to the matter of war and peace. He announced briefly that he had decided to grant asylum to Mursili at the audience scheduled to take place sometime in the next ten days, irrespective of the reaction of the present king of Hatti and his demand for extradition.

"We can satisfy Hattusili's demand for extradition," Amun-her said with a broad grin. "Soon I will be prepared personally to accompany

Mursili along with all our troops all the way to Hattusha, evict that usurper from the throne, and re-install our guest as the rightful king. Hattusili will have his wish of repatriation of his nephew fulfilled."

The quip fell flat. Only Paser graced the prince with a weary smile.

Ramses looked at Nefertari.

"Does our queen Meritmut have anything new to report?"

Nefertari nodded, rose, and cleared her throat. She took her time appraising all the three persons, finally resting her eyes on the welcoming face of Shishi for support.

She said, "It all began with the flight of the previous king, Urhi-Teshub Mursili, after losing his hold on his kingdom to his uncle. That family affair erupted and has involved and affected us because of a request for asylum in our land. This situation was neither initiated nor desired by us.

"A simple solution to the problem could have been to surrender him. In our previous meeting, this convenient measure was discussed. Such a step was ruled out as it would be against the principle of our land and our commitment to humanity. Our ancient traditions cannot be compromised.

"Besides the matter of principle, let me point out one more reason. Such a favor to Hattusili would have been seen as weakness. As in the case of blackmail, this would only encourage more demands from that man in Hattusha."

From the corner of her eye, she caught Ramses nodding with emphasis.

She went on: "When we refrain from restoring peace by doing him a favor at the cost of our principles and at the risk of facing more demands, the alternative has to be the contrary, namely inviting belligerence, even declaring war. I am not suggesting but only echoing this notion, for I hear there are well-founded indications, even verified information from our military experts, that the new king in Hatti is planning an all-out assault on our land."

Nefertari paused. She raised her chin and threw her gaze at Paser and then at her son. Paser was watching Amun-her, and the latter stared at his feet. She looked back to Ramses. Shishi had a slight frown.

She said, "In affairs of the state, there are times when one feels cornered facing multiple solutions and has to search for the least painful choice. But is that the case here? I looked out further: to a double negation. My quest was to avoid both extradition and war. To pursue peace."

She noticed the hush. Three leading men in frozen silence. With the stage and the mood set, she went into details: the escape of the senior official Zananzash with his documents and the efforts of her team to procure them. She also reported the arrest of Suppilamus, a senior civil servant of the Hittites caught here on a clandestine mission to hunt down the fugitive king. Both Zananzash and Suppilamus had been interrogated and were at hand for further questioning by the court and would take their stand under oath.

"At the outset, I studied, in fact, scrutinized, all these documents presented as clay tablets, which had been verified for authenticity. They were all internal communications of the Hatti kingdom and pointed towards the military preparation of their land under the new king. They do not contradict the presumption of the court on this matter. The Hittites are, indeed, preparing for war. Yet..."

The queen paused for effect and watched the audience stir. "Yet, we may rule out the intention or plan, let alone strategy, to attack Kemet. They do indicate military preparation, but only to defend their kingdom; they do not indicate an offensive intent whatsoever. They appeal to neighboring states for cooperation in renewing the defensive alliance those states already had with the Hatti kingdom. In only one of the documents is our kingdom mentioned. In a message to his viceroy in Qadesh, Hattusili frankly states his fear of our supporting his nephew and consequently marching into his land. He states, at this weak moment, there is no way the Hittites could engage with Kemet, even in defense.

"Of course, the lack of evidence to prove that Hatti is, indeed, preparing for an invasion or even an attack on Kemet could mean nothing. I cannot advocate a hollow argument that the absence of evidence is proof of the contrary. But before I offer real proof, permit me to digress for a moment.

"What can we make of Hattusili? New to the throne, inexperienced, and ill-advised, with many of his experts leaving his land, of course he is nervous and at a loss. He has quite a few foes: his people at home sense his weakness and are becoming rebellious, and his vassals will be joining them to lay siege to Hattusha. As for other powers, he has respect for Kemet after our campaigns and now fears our supporting Mursili and attacking his land outright. We could even threaten him with this measure."

She bent forward and slightly raised her voice. "But who is the *real* threat for Hattusili? Whom does he fear *most*?"

She paused.

"It turns out that we ignored one other obvious enemy."

Nefertari paused again. Paser was sitting erect and watching her like an alerted falcon.

"The enemy is the Assyrian," she declared, raising her voice and pointing at a tablet.

She picked it up from the table. Amun-her bent forward.

"In a message from the viceroy of Qadesh to King Hattusili, the viceroy stresses that the flight of Mursili would be a matter too trivial for the pharaoh to begin a war with Hatti, and he closes his remarks with this line: 'As we discussed, there is a danger from elsewhere, especially after Hanikalbat.'

"What does that mean? The viceroy is mentioning the region where Mitanni was located, the region we call Naharin. He is referring to the conquest of Mitanni by the Assyrians some ten years ago when they seized the land from the Hittites and razed the whole region to the ground. What remains now is only the void called Hanikalbat.

"The significance of this remark has been substantiated and confirmed. Sennefer interrogated two Hittites separately, namely the official Zananzash I mentioned before and Suppilamus, the arrested senior civil servant of the Hittites. Two senior officials, so-called 'table-men' of the royal court of their respective kings, with different loyalties and motives. They were interviewed only fifteen days ago on separate occasions by

Sennefer without any setups and traps. Both the officials voluntarily claimed, even averred, that the scourge of the Hittites is Shalmanazzar."

She let that name sink in. She drew a deep breath, lowered her voice, and said almost as an aside, "With this background, we can attempt a debate. That is, provided the court still feels the evidence is not enough and would like to weigh it against other facts proving Hatti is preparing for war on Kemet." She looked at each face.

"But wait," she said, although no one had moved a muscle. "Now I even have proof of my previous assertion that the kingdom of Hatti is not, I repeat, *not* planning an assault on our kingdom. Only two days ago, I received this."

Nefertari picked up the next tablet and brandished it with a flourish.

"It is a message from Queen Puduhepa of Hatti. It is in response to mine, which I sent to her immediately after our last conference here. I will read out the whole message for you to appreciate the substance and so you don't fail to sense the tone, style, and plea in the message of the queen of the Hittites. It is written in Akkadian, in the customary diplomatic tongue, yet it is meant as a personal message from woman to woman."

Her Shishi smiled.

The queen proceeded, raising her voice for the message.

"This is the message: 'Thus says Puduhepa, the great queen of Hatti, the beloved land guarded by the storm god Tarhunt, unto her sister Naptera, the pharaoh's great wife, the Exalted Lady for Whom the Sun Shines, the mistress of the two lands Kemet and Desheret, guarded by the sun god Amun.'

"This initial address is followed by thanks for my previous message and the several presents accompanying it and an inquiry about the well-being of our family and subjects. Thereafter, the message turns to the momentary situation.

"'My spouse is well in charge of the kingdom and is blessed with the support of our gods. We have no cause to fear any famine, floods, or other penal measures of the gods. My spouse is also warding off miscreants and elements seeking a break-up of authority in Hattusha.

"'Let me now turn to your excellent observation in your message that peace would be helpful for both of our kingdoms. Indeed, the real threat could be from far off, beyond the borders of our kingdom and even beyond those of your kingdom, your two lands. Soon both our kingdoms will be called upon to assert themselves against an enemy seeking expansion at the cost of our vassals for a start and with the goal of further threatening our realms. Even today, it would be wise to show strength at home and beyond, avert belligerence, and deter ambitious warlords from yon. They should be forewarned that they will be facing both our world powers at once should they attempt aggression against either of the kingdoms. To this end, our monarchs could agree on a resolution and commitment affirmed by a treaty of non-aggression and mutual defense, thereby establishing peace towards each other.

"'Very soon, the wise and cherished pharaoh will be receiving from my gracious and peace-loving spouse an offer of a peace agreement hopefully to be negotiated between the two great powers for their mutual benefit.'

"This passage is followed by her customary closing solicitation."

Nefertari stopped and put away the document. For the sake of decency, she did not want to read out the rest unless there was a demand. In this part, Puduhepa had confessed on a wife-to-wife note her personal situation, going into details like how her spouse is worried and sleepless, her prayers to Ishtar, and so on. The document could be read at leisure by anyone in the room. *Enough for now.*

Ramses had been listening, motionless, with an elbow placed on the armrest and his cheek on his fist. He dropped his arm, took a deep breath, and said, "We should thank our queen Meritmut for her active engagement and valuable results. She has made an excellent presentation with evidence supporting her views. As proof, she has produced documents and statements by responsible citizens of the enemy, not mere reports by sleuths and spies nor hearsay and possibly cooked-up stories of gossipmongers.

"Moreover, the personal message from Queen Puduhepa of Hatti carries its own weight and cannot be treated as a personal opinion without any footing. It heralds an official offer for negotiation from Hatti. On the last occasion, after we were warned by Puduhepa about the impending request for asylum, her message was followed by the request of the king for extradition. This time, we could likewise look upon the call for negotiation as real and prepare ourselves for this possibility, too. Are there any more comments on this matter? Even fundamental objections?" He looked at the other two men.

Paser made some signs, stirring in his seat. He said, "The report of her majesty is commendable, and her conclusion is convincing. I see no point in raising doubts only for the sake of a debate. It is one thing to make a peace approach on our own, but it is a different matter when we are offered an opportunity from the adversary. Such a proposal or call should be welcome. It appears the present king of Hatti, fearing the Assyrians, metaphorically follows the footsteps of his nephew by seeking, in essence, refuge and shelter in our power by begging for negotiation for peace and defense. To this extent, we are in a superior position."

Ramses smiled and nodded.

The vizier continued: "We need vassal states in the north to form a buffer between us and the other powers, Hatti and Assur. If we allow these protectorates to be conquered by Shalmanazzar, we will be facing a border with the Assyrians, and any border conflict would erupt in total war. We have to strengthen and retain the vassals as our safeguards. This is where Hatti failed by ceding their protectorate Mitanni to the Assyrians."

Having made his point, the old man turned to his mug for a sip. He might have had more to say, but Nefertari pounced on the break.

"Our vizier made a wise remark. The fate of Mitanni while we fought at Qadesh reminds me of the story of two lions quarreling over a kill while a third one gets away with the prey. As far as we are concerned, we have to be strong against all powers and guard the minor entities to the north lest history is repeated with the aliens invading us. I can only stress that we need these peripheral kingdoms and must nurture the subjects of these states, too, safeguarding them against border violations from others.

219 |

"As for the other regions beyond, there is no reason to conquer and suppress minor states not subject to us. After conquest and expansion of our kingdom to include them, we would only face the same obligation towards them of nurturing and protecting them as we have for our other subjects. Nor is there a need for military campaigns just to demonstrate power. We can impress others with the peaceful and sovereign attitude and conduct becoming of a major power, as will be the case when our pharaoh grants asylum on principles. A power like ours knows its might and has no need to attack minor states to prove its worth."

She said after a break for emphasis, "Prowess obliges restraint."

Paser nodded. "May lord Amun bless us with peace!"

Carried away by a sense of triumph, with the words flowing of their own volition, Nefertari added with candor, "Lord Amun is on our side if we are righteous and therefore right. The sun god shines over every land, be it Hatti, Assur, or Kemet. Let us remember: the god lets the sun shine to lay bare our efforts and their results—whether it shines on the flourishing crop in the farmer's field or on the perishing corpses in the battlefield."

Rapt attention. Pin-drop silence.

Ramses was the first to recover. He cleared his throat and summed up, "We have enough evidence of the state of affairs in Hatti and the anxiety and uncertainty Hattusili is facing. The message from Queen Puduhepa is more than a confirmation." He looked at the vizier and the prince and prompted, "I would like to hear arguments to the contrary and in clear support of any claim that Hatti is preparing an assault on our land."

Ramses allowed a long hiatus, which announced the end of the discussion.

After a quick glance at Nefertari, he wound up the meeting.

"If there are no more comments forthcoming, we can come to a conclusion. I see no reason not to accept the offer from Hatti, which may be due in a few days. In light of these facts and arguments, we will then seriously consider the official offer for negotiation. "

He leaned forward and raised his hand.

"But we must be clear about two points: for one, the asylum for Mursili shall be non-negotiable. Hattusili shall have no influence now or ever on this petition already presented to our kingdom.

"Secondly, we have nothing to lose, and Hattusili has everything to gain by a treaty of non-belligerence. Therefore, we will set out with resolve and conviction from a position of strength and under our terms. As the call comes from him, he will have to comply with the conditions, and he may neither command nor demand, not even in style. And we set the conditions.

"Make no mistake: I am not averse to a military engagement, whoever the enemy is, Hatti or Assur. But I also appreciate and acknowledge our queen's appeal for peace for our own benefit. Only when peace is secured can we turn wholeheartedly to the reforms in the kingdom and the construction works we have planned for the long run. That is the primary responsibility of a pharaoh."

He was expressing his main interest in improving the daily lives of his subjects and their prosperity, as well as the construction projects for posterity.

He brought the conference to an end, thanking his queen for her favor with the words, "*Dewa-netjer en-etj.* Praise the god for you."

* * *

The audience of Urhi-Teshub Mursili III with the pharaoh Ramses II took place at the palace. Security had been ensured right from the outset, with the king arriving from his domicile along a secret route at an undisclosed hour on an undisclosed day. In the presence of the vizier as the witness, the pharaoh granted him his wish, mentioning the conditions for the hospitality of the pharaoh's kingdoms: no political activity nor support of any turmoil in Hatti or elsewhere. In return, Urhi-Teshub would lead a luxurious life of the nobility, becoming of a retired monarch. He would be provided with sufficient protection to ward off danger. In the near future, he would reside in the palace. After a proper residence had been found in the city, he would be transferred to that place of safety, with all the amenities promised. Visitors would be allowed access after due inspection.

The day before the audience, Hartapu had a chance to meet his father and have a long chat explaining his own plans. Urhi-Teshub understood the young man's aspirations in this regard and gave him his blessings for his venture. The father had neither plans nor means to suggest any better future for his son. For Urhi-Teshub, it was a bitter valediction before the positive news awaiting him at the audience the next day. Hartapu had thought over and rehearsed this scenario for a long while and had mustered the courage to face this farewell from his past.

The day arrived for Hartapu's departure from Kemet. With the sky clear of any clouds, the sun shone as brilliantly as ever, and nature seemed to have come to a rest. Only the birds were flying rather than just chirping.

Under orders from the queen, Sennefer had made arrangements for Hartapu's travel to Tarhuntassa. A special boat had been organized for the trip along the river to the port near Avaris in the delta, escorted by four guards along with the captain and the oarsmen.

The passage from Egypt to the mainland of Tarhuntassa would be on a regular seafaring ship on its way to the island of Alasiya (Cyprus) to let other passengers alight who were heading for Ugarit and Amurru to the east. Thereafter, the voyage would continue for the last hop to Ura on the coast of Tarhuntassa. The guards would accompany the prince all the way and return only after he had found a safe place to stay. Hartapu's arrival was a secret.

Anat would accompany her groom. Sennefer had to play a major role in her departure. As her uncle, he had had to console and encourage the parents for days. After protests and tears, they were rational enough to acknowledge the day had arrived for their dear daughter, the little baby of yesterday, to spread her wings and take flight with her chosen partner.

When Hartapu approached the quay, not far from the spot where he and Anat had had their first rendezvous, he saw Sennefer standing with

Anat at his side. Sennefer greeted him. Swinging his arm in a dramatic gesture, he pointed at the special boat docked behind him and shouted with a broad grin, "Most welcome, Hartapu! The pleasure boat and the crew are ready!"

Two guards came from that direction and picked up the bags Hartapu had put down on the ground. Hartapu's first reaction was, "How are Anat's parents getting on?"

"They are all right. You will understand that they wanted to give their daughter their blessings only at home and preferred to stay back. They were not up to the pressure of seeing their daughter depart. But otherwise, they have accepted the inevitable. They also left home when they were young. Do not worry. I am here to take care of them. I will heal their wounds. After all, I am a healer." the priest's laughter was a bit hollow. Hartapu could guess it was overshadowed by his own sorrow at his little Anat's departure.

Anat had made no bones about her excitement for the voyage ahead, and Hartapu noticed she was enthralled by the riverboat trip to Avaris for a start. He could hardly wait for her later reaction on boarding the big ship for passengers and cargo to cross the sea.

He took a close look at the boat. It was a typical, medium-sized riverboat with wooden planks pegged together and laced with ropes. Also, the hull at the bow and stern was fastened with rope for added strength. Traveling downstream against the wind from the north, as usual, the boat would need only rowing by the oarsmen, with the sails taken down and fastened in crutches.

The water playfully sloshing against the boat and the rhythmic sound of the boat in polite protest seemed to show him the way, pointing out the direction to proceed, to the north, off and away from Kemet. In the glittering reflection of the sun, he mused that the river's flow was also a symbol of the flow of time towards his future—in another land. He would stop being what he was, for who cared who he was?

As if in reply, he heard a voice calling out to him, "Harti, Harti!" It was a female voice.

He turned and saw two people rushing towards him. The tall man was Teremun, and the other one, waving her hand, was…Met!

"*Ii-wey!* It is a great surprise, indeed!" he called out.

When Sennefer joined in the greeting, Hartapu remembered that Anat was a bit left out because the two ladies had never met. He decided to introduce them to each other. They neared each other in slow motion, sizing up each other in suspenseful silence. He noticed the gleam in their eyes and smiles, which voiced appreciation and approval after an appraisal, on both sides, of course, of Anat and Mehetweret. The encounter of the women was, indeed, momentous.

After quite a while, Hartapu got the nudge from the captain that it was time to board.

Sennefer stepped forward and gave Anat a long hug. He kissed her on both cheeks and blessed her by placing his hand on the top of her head. "I'll miss you, Uncle, dearly," she whined. Hartapu ended his chat with his comrades. They had planned a line of communication with Met at the alehouse as the addressee for Hartapu to send his first intimation from Tarhuntassa. His invitation to visit his place one day was well meant and well received, yet all knew it was too early for any concrete plans.

After the introduction of the ladies and the short chit-chat, the conversation turned to the plans Hartapu had and a mutual promise to maintain contact. Once again, the words "Do keep in touch" followed.

The group of five split into two . Teremun, with Sennefer and Met on either side, stepped back, away from the quay. Hartapu and Met got onto the boat and stood facing them.

As the boat moved away at the command of the captain, Hartapu saw Met reach out for Teremun's hand and grab it. Before turning away, she threw Harti one last bewitching smile and waved with the other hand. Hartapu waved to her with fervor. When he turned to Anat at his side, she cocked her head, smiled, and cooed,

"Hmmmm?"

Chapter 13

THE ACCORD

More than a month had passed since the final conference that set the track towards a peace treaty. During this period, Hattusili's official offer for negotiations had reached the pharaoh. This time, the language and style had been well chosen, and even though officious, they bordered more on a plea rather than a demand. No feathers were ruffled.

Nevertheless, Ramses had chosen to take one more independent action besides granting asylum to the royal fugitive Mursili. He had followed Nefertari's suggestion to thank Zananzash by offering him a position in the royal service of his kingdom where he would work under Paser and clean up the mess of the Hittite espionage net in the kingdom. This operation was to begin at once and proceed irrespective of the progress of negotiation for a peace deal. Zan would present a list of all the details of the network to his knowledge, for he was the one who had built it up in Per-Ramesses in the first place, beginning under King Muwatalli. All these elements would be rounded up, declared undesirable individuals, and deported no matter what happened with the parallel negotiation going on with the Hittite kingdom. Zananzash's family would be united and dwell in Per-Ramesses.

Only the decision about Suppilamus was still pending. With Mursili sheltered in the palace and beyond any danger, this officer would be harmless if set free. Yet he was held in custody to surprise the Hittites during the negotiations: at the right moment, he was to be offered as a goodwill gesture and returned to their kingdom unscathed, with a ban prohibiting him from setting foot in Egypt ever again.

After all the effort Nefertari had put into this project before the conference, what mattered now to her was the realization of an accord that ought to be binding and assure long-lasting peace. But as she had partly hoped and was even anxious about, Ramses had asked her to cooperate further in this venture by working with Paser from now on. Ramses had explained he trusted her female instincts in the forthcoming discussions with the Hittites, all the more as she had proved effective at reading the mind of the erratic opponent Hattusili in his "apprenticeship" as king.

"We were all *young* and inexperienced when we began," Ramses had scoffed and chuckled in their private moment. Considering his otherwise polished language even when alone with his spouse, it had sounded like an unusual insult of the veteran Hattusili when he had stressed the word "young."

It would not be becoming of a queen to join the fray when it came to long, drawn-out diplomatic tussle on a low level, but Nefertari wanted to get into the details behind the scenes. On the one hand, she was full of energy and curiosity to contribute to the minutiae safeguarding the interests of the kingdom, and on the other, she also felt the urge to be constructive and not just stay aloof as a supervisor or a well-wisher.

This morning, Nefertari had her first appointment with Paser to get an initiation in the affairs of the state, a lecture on how to prepare for a negotiation. She was to meet him in a special room in the southern wing on the other side of the palace. It was a storehouse of documents known as the Room of Scrolls—a library devoid of books.

The large room with high walls was not an inviting reception hall but a region for contemplation and discussion in hushed voices. It had few windows and was dimly lit with skylights. The room was to be guarded against sunlight and heat, not so much for the comfort of the occupants as for the health of the documents. Carpets and reed mats had been laid out for the needs of the typical scribe studying and copying the scrolls spread around. Several scribes were busy with their study. At the far end of the hall, large tables and chairs were set out for other visitors.

As she entered, she saw one of the scribes with an apprentice. The latter was idly looking around and not much interested in his master's scrutiny of a text in hand. She walked the narrow path between the mats while her nose got used to the strange smell of bygone years and the murmurs of the mummified bodies of rolled-up papyri. She reached the vizier, hunched over a large scroll spread out on a table. He bowed and greeted her with a broad smile.

Paser seemed to have no more qualms about cooperating with the Hittites. He seemed to have no passion or prejudice. It was all about reason and rationality in his world. On the previous encounter in the conference, Nefertari had wondered why he had not protested and commented on the military experts warning of war by the Hittites. Had he already given up his stance and begun mistrusting his own sources? She could not believe her plea in the court had been so impressive that neither he nor her son had mumbled a word of protest.

Anyway, that was bygone, and she had no use for retrospection. Now it was the joint effort of theirs, and she was again a newcomer to the whole field, with the wise man leading her the rational way. From now on, they were colleagues and not competitors.

They receded to a small adjoining room with two chairs and a table to speak without disturbance.

He smiled and pointed towards the hall from which they had come.

"Your majesty, I chose the Room of Scrolls for our first encounter in this venture, as I found it most appropriate. After all, the outcome of our effort in the following days and months shall be a scroll like all those over there. That shall be the aim, result, and evidence of our achievement.

"You know well the Hittites are fond of peace treaties to secure or ascertain their position in relationship with their vassals. Although what they have now proposed may be the first of its kind between two major powers, we can treat the past treaties with minor kingdoms as models."

As an afterthought, he added, "In effect, looking at these serious documents with the eyes of a commoner, they could come down to nothing more than the result of a bargain in the market." He laughed.

Nefertari shrugged and joined the laughter. "For your information, my vizier, I only have a faint idea of haggling in the market. All I know is what goes on in the palace, mainly between women. It is the same story of haggling, intimidation, threats, give and take, and compromise."

His countenance became serious. "Well, you will find parallels. Nevertheless, let me make some general comments in earnest. May I?"

"Yes, do go ahead."

"First of all, long before the first encounter with the other side, we must have a clear picture of the treaty—that is to say, what we expect and want, what we aim to achieve. We must define our positions. Besides that, we must also define our interests. In addition, several items will remain non-negotiable. For instance, our pharaoh considered our position about offering asylum to the fugitive as non-negotiable, and the matter is now out of the picture, off the table. Such items must be made clear to the other party right at the beginning. In the course of negotiation, after all the bargaining, at some stage, both sides will have to settle for and accept a compromise. On our part, we may concede and sacrifice one position or the other, but we must guard our interests. Otherwise, any agreement would be a betrayal of our kingdom.

"With this in mind, I beseech you to take a look at all the peace treaties of the Hittites that we have at our disposal. You will come to know how they are framed, although neither the style nor the contents shall be of binding relevance to our case. Of course, those treaties are all one-sided, with the major power Hatti laying conditions and limitations binding on the minor states and not the reverse. But they will give you an idea as to how the aims of the two parties were reached and realized in a single document. They are all finalized versions in Akkadian, copied from their tablets; there are no drafts available. Studying them would be good preparation before the negotiation begins in a few days."

They returned to the table in the hall. Paser showed her the heap of scrolls he had set aside at one end and receded to the other side, seating himself in a corner. Nefertari sat down on a chair and began poring over them. She did not notice the lapse of time. It took hours to find the information and absorb it.

They could be classified into two kinds. The first kind was those between Hatti and its vassals. The treaties could hardly be considered bilateral. They were almost unilateral, amounting to a decree disguised as an agreement. The opening section or the preamble mentioned only the king of Hatti and not that of the vassal. The treaty ended with an oath, *rikishtu* and *mámítu* in Akkadian, binding before both humanity and divinity for the vassal. But for the Hittite king, it was only binding before mankind.

The second type was the treaty with vassals of greater autonomy, the so-called protectorates; they did not pay tributes to Hatti. In the preamble of this type, both parties were mentioned. The oath with divine witnesses was binding and applied to both parties.

The agreement between Kemet and Hatti would be between equals and was to be designated a treaty in the real meaning of the term. Such a parity treaty must be properly balanced in content, style, and text and could not be modeled on the impositions of Hatti on its vassals and protectorates.

After registering this difference, Nefertari began sorting out the scrolls she had not yet gone through. When she looked up, she noticed Paser had left the table. As she looked around, she saw him re-entering the hall through a side door.

He smiled and placed three more scrolls before her.

"I found these, too. They will be of interest to you."

One of the scrolls beckoned, rolling away from the others and stopping right before her hands. "You see?" He chuckled.

She unfurled it. It was a treaty between Hatti and its protectorate Mitanni. *Back to Hanikalbat!*

* * *

The next day, they met again, this time in the presence of the pharaoh in the conference room. Ramses had discussed the whole matter with his vizier many times, but this was one final conference before the negotiation, which would be attended only by Paser. It was a concise chat to refresh the goals and conditions that had been set by the two men at the outset. But Paser brought in a new aspect this time.

"Yesterday, our queen raised a fundamental question. It concerns the treaty between the kings Suppiluliuma of Hatti and Shattiwaza of Mitanni assuring support and security to its protectorate Mitanni, agreed upon some hundred years ago. Only ten years ago, the king of Hatti at that time, namely his brother Muwatalli, committed a serious breach of this treaty. When Mitanni was attacked by the Assyrians, he ceded the land without a fight, and there was no sign of complying with the word of Hatti. It was a betrayal. Our queen pointed out this fact and raised the question: can we trust them?"

Nefertari nodded and said to Ramses, "The irony is that they sacrificed their own protectorate to resist your advance in the north. In addition, in this accord with a protectorate, the witnesses called upon are their own gods. For Hatti, they are the various storm gods and tutelary gods and goddesses of various places, and for Mitanni, they are gods like Mitra, Indra, Varuna, and Nasatya. But there are also gods of both parties who have been included, Ishhara, the goddess of oaths, as well as Ishtar, Anu, Antu, Enlil, and Ninlil. Ignoring the divine witnesses by the Hittites amounts to a violation of the lowest category."

Nefertari proceeded after a pause: "The treaty they have now proposed will be between equal powers. There shall be no talk of protection proper, as in the case of a protectorate, yet it will be implicit, as it will deal with mutual defense and bilateral support. Now, with this record of Hatti with Mitanni, with Hattusili as the commander of the troops at the time of the breach, how can we trust the Hittites? It does not matter whether we would ever need their support when attacked by an enemy. Trust is what matters in the negotiation."

Ramses nodded. "You have raised an important point. At that battle, Muwatalli let go of his protectorate despite the treaty with that kingdom. This poor record is quintessential to our negotiation. Let us see how they try to explain that betrayal, or 'mistake,' as they might say. No matter. We can dangle this argument of a betrayal before their eyes every time the negotiation falters due to their untoward demands. It is, indeed, a serious aspect."

Paser said, "There is another item we can discuss in advance. All the treaties of Hatti deal with the matter of succession to the throne of the vassal or the protectorate. In our case, I am sure this matter will come up for both partners. Hattusili is bent upon dispelling the specter of Mursili or his progeny ever claiming the throne in Hattusha. He would like us to decline in the treaty by writ any support to Mursili on this matter, and he may even go further and ask us to assure the support of his being the king—so, too, his dynasty. There I see a problem."

"I do not see a problem there. Can you explain?"

"It is a matter of reciprocity in a bilateral agreement. I am not sure if we, on our part, would need likewise assurance and support of a foreign power to secure your position as pharaoh and that of your successors, your majesty."

Ramses rocked with laughter. "Now I see your point. A pharaoh is not a usurper like Hattusili, trembling at the thought of his position, his wobbly throne. A pharaoh is called to the throne by Lord Amun and the gods; they bestow on the pharaoh the ability and power. He is also a divine presence in the land. Of course, we will decline any support by way of a treaty from the hands of mortals, especially from those in Hatti, who do not seem to respect their own gods." He laughed again.

"Therefore," Paser said with a smile and a nod, "we can raise some other demand in its place that should also be of long-lasting importance to our land."

"That is a good point. We must think about it."

The location for the negotiation had been chosen to be Per-Ramesses. There had been no tussle over this matter, for Hattusili had too much trouble at home to assure a prolonged peaceful space in his town. The negotiation was to be held in the southern wing of the palace, secure from mischievous and curious elements and any harm to the visitors. The attendees would be Paser and his team of selected diplomats, officers, interpreters, scribes, and servants and their counterparts from Hattusha.

On the very first day, a provisional agreement would be reached, a truce for non-aggression between the kingdoms during the whole period of negotiation so as not to hinder or delay it by any means. The discussion went from there into detail about the observance of protocol and the communication between the capitals. There would be a special confidential messenger service set up to operate between the two capitals so that Hattusha was kept informed of the results on a weekly, at times, even on a daily, basis. Their diplomats in Per-Ramesses would await advice, approval, and instruction from the king in Hattusha.

The vizier would keep the pharaoh and the queen abreast of the progress by ad hoc meetings where any questions could be raised, and the course of the negotiation adjusted or corrected.

* * *

1258 BCE

Six years passed before a peace treaty could be cobbled together and declared finalized.

The reason for the long duration was neither merely the snail's pace due to forming opinions, indecision, consultation, and haggling, nor the enormous time needed to pass the information to and fro between the far-flung capitals. The negotiation had stalled often, with long respites due to the turmoil in Hatti. Unrelated to the deliberation in Per-Ramesses, more than once, there had been nearly a breakout of civil war in the Hittite kingdom, with rising unrest in the capital pertaining to the acceptance of Hattusili as the rightful successor to the throne. This not only took the attention of the royalty in Hattusha but also caused prolonged interruptions due to disruptions of the communication lines.

At long last, after plenty of discussion, posturing, break-ups, and squabbles over details ever so minute, the two powers had reached a historic peace treaty, now approved and sealed by both parties and to be made public in both capitals, Per-Ramesses and Hattusha. The final outcome was, in effect, the result of unwavering and sustained effort on both sides.

The treaty had essentially the same form as all the previous ones of Hatti. But here, the preamble mentioned both the monarchs as brothers. It was an indication of respect and cordiality as well as a reference to the equal status of the two endorsers. This was followed by sections describing the purpose of the treaty and the future relationship between the powers. Here, again, the terms "peace" and "brotherhood" were stressed.

The purpose of the treaty was clearly stated as to end hostilities, mutually respecting the possessions of the other power. Moreover, an agreement on a defense alliance was reached, according to which, if a third party should attack either of the participants, the partner will come to its aid as an ally by sending its infantry, bowmen, and chariots. The third party could be a separate power or even the subjects of the affected partner. The paragraph dealing with succession remained lopsided, with only an assurance to Hattusili that his right and that of his line of succession to the throne were guaranteed. Ramses eschewed any such assurance by Hatti.

The final section dealt elaborately with fugitives in the future. In general, refugees seeking protection in the kingdom or office in the royal service of a power would be returned to their respective land of origin but without any reprisal towards the subject's relatives. This agreement,

233 |

initiated by the Hittites, was, of course, bilateral, pertaining to subjects from either kingdom.

In exchange for all these additional demands of paramount importance to Hattusili, the Hittite had to make several concessions on his side. Although wary of any claim by Mursili to return to power in Hattusha, Hattusili had to accept the asylum given to the fugitive as an accomplished fact. In order to avoid any misgivings, Paser had exacted, on Nefertari's insistence, a separate personal assurance in writing by Hattusili to Ramses that the pharaoh could keep the fugitive Urhi-Teshub as his guest with all the amenities he deemed fit for him but denying him any recognition as the ruler of Hatti or any attempt to wage war against Hatti.

As the treaty would apply only after it became valid and not retroactively, all shelter and royal appointments granted before were not affected, thereby guaranteeing the position of others like Zananzash in Egypt. Also, an agreement was reached to allow Prince Hartapu, who had no part in the quarrel between the monarchs of Hatti, free access to all parts of Hatti provided he laid no claim to the throne in Hattusha. This concession also applied to the descendants of Mursili in general. Trade routes and access to all the ports of Hatti and its vassals and protectorates, like Amurru and Ugarit, were allowed for Kemet at no levy. The ports could be practically used as those of Egypt.

In the closing lines, Hattusili gave his oath, calling as witnesses all the gods, as done in the previous treaties. The pharaoh only mentioned Amun, thanking the god for the guidance and support in this momentous agreement, for he was acting as the god's representative.

The language of the treaty was Akkadian, the *lingua franca* of the time. The Egyptians wrote up their version, and the Hittites had their own version. They were written down on silver plates, silver being the most precious metal in Egypt. In the interest of fairness, the two versions were exchanged.

Thus, the Egyptians received the Hittite version, which was transcribed into hieroglyphs and put up on the walls, like those of the temples in

Thebes and Karnak. The Hittites received the Egyptian version, which was copied onto clay tablets.

The proclamation of the treaty was not only a political affair. It was crowned by a festival of three days in all major cities of Egypt. In Per-Ramesses, the Amun temple was the site for the celebration, with rituals conducted throughout the day. Thanks to his special contribution in this matter, Sennefer had been promoted to the chief priesthood of the temple complex. This occasion was also his first performance in his new office.

After the third of the exciting but strenuous days, Sennefer retired to his quarters full of elation and reminiscence. Back home and all to himself, he cast off his attire and sat down on his favorite mat. He looked around. He was too tired but at the same time too excited to concentrate on anything in his neglected household. He was not alone: his mind was crowded with people and thoughts. In this moment of joy, all those who had worked and contributed to this cause rejoiced like him, too, in effect, *with* him. He was, indeed, one among them.

Despite his modesty, this time, he allowed himself to think of all the efforts he had taken on his part, beginning with the request for the oracle by the queen. She had supported him all along, and he had also done his best to support her with all his abilities as a priest, shaman, and agent. In addition, he had assisted in maintaining peace and harmony in his sister's family.

Faces and voices shot past his mind. He thanked the goddess Hathor for her advice and encouragement. The queen had, indeed, embodied her in her valiant effort.

The original treaty in the Egyptian version was to be deposited in Hattusha in the temple of the storm god of heaven, known by the Hurrian name Teshub, and his consort, Hepat, the sun goddess of Arinna.

To enter that temple, one had to pass the prominent main gate, called the *hilammar*. On entry, the visitor came to a large courtyard used for public gatherings for ritual ceremonies and enactments of mythical stories during festivals and celebrations. From there, the stroll to the temple proper was not straightforward as in temples of other cultures. It was a winding one, comparable to a maze, making access for the devotee a passage demanding effort, as in search of disclosure. Along the way, the devotee did not know what was around the corner, and with nothing foreseen, he had to practice patience—as in life.

After the long, labyrinthine march, one reached the shrine proper. Only then could one face the life-size figures of the two deities, Teshub and Hepat, in gold and silver, standing in a well-lit enclosure with windows all around. This was reminiscent of ancient times, when a place of worship was always in the open air.

The shrine was surrounded by various offices and rooms for storage of food, clothes, and equipment pertaining to worship. Also, the archives of the kingdom were among the stores. This was the depository for precious documents like the peace treaty, in the holiest of places of the kingdom, to be watched over, sheltered, and protected by the divinity.

At first, the silver plates with the wording of the treaty arriving from Per-Ramesses were brought to the temple and set up at the wall in the courtyard after passage through the *hilammar*. The first religious ceremony, beseeching and invoking the gods for their blessing to grant the treaty an eternal life, was conducted here, before the public, with enough pomp to drive home the significance of the peace negotiated with Egypt.

After the ritual, a herald translated and read out the salient features for the audience, and a dignitary followed this with an explanation of the treaty's significance. As agreed upon with the counterparts in Egypt, a copy of the treaty on clay tablets would be read out once a week at a chosen time yet to be announced in the coming months for the benefit of those who were not present on this occasion.

After the event at the *hilammar*, the silver tablets were ceremoniously brought all the way to the depository in the shrine in a procession, accompanied by the royalty and the nobles, and deposited in the archives.

* * *

Two men, a generation apart, sat chatting a few days after the accord had been reached, somewhere neither in Per-Ramesses nor Hattusha. Far from either city, seated in Tarhuntassa, they were celebrating the treaty together. They formed a strange pair, indeed. One was an Egyptian, the other a Hittite.

Watching the other man draining his mug, the younger man said, "But for your queen in Kemet, the treaty may never have materialized."

His father-in-law gulped down his drink and shook his head. "True, partly true. How about the prince of Hatti? Did he have nothing to say in this matter?

"In a way, yes, if you like." Hartapu shifted in his seat and smiled.

Rai'a said, "Modest as ever, young man? These are the moments I would like to put you on an anvil and—"

He raised his hand.

Anat had joined the company. "Oh, no, Dad. Do you really want to hit him with your hammer?"

Rai'a laughed. "No, dear, only spank him and get him into shape." He turned back to Hartapu. "Just take the credit, young man, where it is due. *You* began the whole boat rocking or the whole rock rolling. *You* got those clay pieces with strokes and wedges for the queen to believe in her mission, right?"

Hartapu nodded and said, "In fact, only the other day, I sent her majesty a message congratulating her on realizing her mission, with goddess Hathor's help. I also passed on your salutations and the news that you have settled down here and we are now a family of five."

Bennu came out through the door with her grandson.

"Did I hear anvil and hammer? Rai'a, are you missing your old servants back home?"

"No. The hammer and anvil were my partners. They earned my bread." He laughed.

Working in the royal service, Hartapu had been promoted recently and been assigned the key post of *gal meshedi,* The Chief of the Bodyguards of the king. This was a senior post given only to a close relative of the ruler, of King Kurunta in this case. It indicated the absolute loyalty to the crown demonstrated by Hartapu's grandfather Muwatalli, who had appointed his own brother Hattusili to that post in his days.

They were seated at the front of their vast mansion, big enough for the whole family. It was located on the outskirts of the palace of Tarhuntassa yet near enough for Hartapu to be available at short notice for the palace guard. The parents had settled down in Tarhuntassa to lead a life of leisure. At Bennu's suggestion, Rai'a was sporting a beard to appear wise and go with the local men of age. They were protected and looked after by the young couple. With peace in their hearts, they were now celebrating peace in the world.

Instead of calling for a servant, Rai'a rose to fetch another mug of beer himself; he peered into the other mug and grabbed it, too. Looking down on Hartapu, he said slowly in a calm voice, "Harti, I wish I had a son like you."

Hartapu smiled and tried to return the compliment,

"And I wish I had a—"

Bennu was quick to cut Hartapu short. She laid the child on his lap and said, "Harti, you do have a wonderful son, and your son has in you a great father. What more do you want?"

Chapter 14

IN PEACE

After sealing the treaty and its celebration, it was for the future to prove the merit and endurance of the agreement. It had to prove itself to be resilient, with the future monarchs of both the powers willingly abiding by it, whatever the external threat might be.

Nefertari had been warned by Paser how diplomacy in this matter would demand patience and perseverance on both sides. No wonder—she had found the snail's pace of the progress towards the maturing of the treaty at times enervating. The process itself tested the willpower of the two sides, especially of the two disparate monarchs. It demanded foresight, patience, and commitment to the cause.

She hoped her contribution had its value in initiating this process and someday, someone might even mention it openly in her presence. In this victorious and optimistic mood, she was glad to hear that her dear Amun-her, her first-born son and heir, would like to spend some time with her for a chat. He had been involved in the deliberations leading to the treaty, and she imagined he was coming to offer his felicitation.

True to her expectation, the crown prince began the chat with, "My venerable mother, I have come to congratulate you on your success in bringing about a permanent peace with the Hittites. You have noticed how both sides are rejoicing at this achievement. Of course, they have yet to learn and appreciate your contribution."

"Oh, thank you, dear. I must be fair about the birth of this treaty. But for the acceptance of my proposal by your father and the court in general, the proposal would not have made any progress. In fact, help also came from the queen on the other side, who picked up my suggestion for everlasting peace and heralded its approval by her spouse. Thus, in effect, it turned out to be an official offer of Hittites—to our advantage."

"What do you mean by that?"

"Well, they picked up the initiative from our side and dressed it up as their own official offer. Your father pointed out that with this move, they came begging for peace. So, we were in a stronger position right at the beginning of the negotiation."

Amun-her nodded and laughed. "At any rate, it was your foresight, mother, which brought up the idea of a peace treaty in the first place. Now your effort has been crowned with success."

He resumed his thoughtful posture, resting his elbows on his knees, lowering his head, and staring at the ground. Then he raised his head for a second.

"I am glad for you, my dear mother. Have you thought of me?"

"Oh, I am sorry, dear. I did not ask how you are getting on. I heard there has been great progress in building up our defense in the north."

"Yes, I have been at it all the time. We are now well equipped and can defend ourselves against any major power. But what for? With the new treaty taking effect, we do not have to fear the Hittites anymore, and with them as our allies, not even the Assyrians or Babylonians. Who is now left as a threat?"

"You cannot look at it that way. Supposing— "

"Mother, please understand what I am getting at." Amun-her cut her short. He paused to lick his lips and clear his throat. "I acknowledge that you excelled with your effort and achieved your goal, which was plainly peace.

"How about me? I wanted to become a seasoned warrior to be a worthy pharaoh one day, like my father. Do you ever care or try to understand how important war is to me? If I am the crown prince and will one day sit on the throne of a pharaoh, I must prove to myself, my siblings, my subjects, the world, and above all, the gods that I am worthy of that position. I must prove myself with my leadership and success at the front, as my father did and his father and his father. I cannot just climb the throne with nothing to show, no past as a guardian of our people, no experience or credentials as a warrior, leader, and protector.

"Do you think the subjects would honor a man who is no more than a symbol, a decoration, with nothing on record? Thanks to your peace treaty, I lost my chance of proving my worth as a commander and fighter with campaigns and conquests."

Amun-her was out of bounds. He went on. "Have you thought over what you have done to me? And to my father, your own beloved spouse?

"You seduced him into believing he ought to lay down his sword for the sake of peace. You reduced him to a mere figurehead, an aging monarch celebrating and reveling over his past campaigns of no consequence, plain reminiscence. Indeed, he had been nursing grandiose dreams of expanding the kingdom to the extent our ancestor the pharaoh Thutmose did ages ago. In those days, the Lower Kingdom reached out across the Sinai. This was a dream my father had wanted to achieve again, a dream shared with his father, Seti, may the gods bless his soul. This was also the dream I shared with my father, the conquest of what was a part of our kingdom.

"Your peace treaty prohibits our laying claim to those forgotten lands to the north; instead, it is laying chains on our ankles and wrists.

That dream of ours has been shattered, gone forever.

Nefertari shrugged. It was time for a rebuttal.

"It is a strange way to defend the cause for war, justifying your own intention and ambition." Nefertari chuckled. "War is not a game to savor.

241 |

As commander, you ought to know well far better than I do that war has as its primary objective to deliver death and destruction.

"Have you ever thought of us women, forced to send their husbands, brothers, and sons to the front, not knowing if and in which state they will ever return? Have you ever thought of the lot of the widows and orphans as destitute beggars after facing the loss of their dear ones and life support, what you would call a mere 'casualty'? Have you ever thought of those survivors, with their lives disrupted, their families annihilated, even being marched off in chains and neck stocks as war booty to a far-off place to drudge and perish in the mines? Yet we women are expected to send our men to the front, marching in a death row—in the name of what? In the name of conquest and glory?"

Amun-her shook his head. He seemed to search for the right words, for the right weapon. He shrugged and tried to belittle the argument.

"That is life, Mother. I ask myself and ask you, are we men any better with women? Now, listen."

He had narrowed his eyes and bent forward.

"I have to thank my father and my mother for being born. I have to thank you more, for you carried me for months, nursed me after my birth, and took it upon yourself to be a mother, fully aware that childbirth is a dangerous event. You risked your life for me and then five more times for my siblings. What do we men do? Don't we just take part in the pleasant phase of conception and then joyously send women to their possible death by getting them pregnant? It will be expected of me, too, to send my beloved wife to the 'front' for the sake of an heir. That is life, too. Where is the difference?"

Nefertari had never known him to be so articulate. But she noticed he was leading her to slippery ground with sophistry. It was not syllogistical; it was simply silly.

"My dear son, please do not bring up such twisted arguments. Progeny is needed lest mankind should perish. War is not a means to prosper and procreate. War is a necessity only when forced upon us when we need it to survive. Let us not digress.

"Turning back to the peace treaty, this was not just your lay mother's idea nor her invention or design to get attention. It was approved on wise grounds by the pharaoh and the vizier. I must add they did so in the face of other pointers. Listen, a few days before the conference, Paser told me of your military experts having proof of Hatti planning an assault on our kingdom. But in the conference, there was no mention of that, not even by you. Utter silence. Where was your eloquence in the right place at the right time?"

Amun-her leaned back and fell silent for a change. His aggressive mood was gone, extinguished. He began fidgeting with his fingers after puckering his lips. She might not know the manifest command of the northern army of the kingdom, but otherwise, she knew her son inside out. His behavior reminded her of the little boy who had been caught lying once again.

"All right, Mother. Because it is you, I will explain after all these years." There followed a sigh. She could watch his chest heave.

He took a deep breath and said, "After the information we received from Hatti, the notion among us all was that the Hittites were making all kinds of preparations for war. Noticing all of you were avoiding war for one reason or the other, I made up the story. I told Paser that according to our military experts, the indication was more than just some saber-rattling. It was a real preparation to attack us with assault weapons."

"You lied, didn't you?"

"A bad word, Mother. Do not call your own son a liar. I am admitting that I exaggerated the truth, projecting my own thoughts into what was going on and misquoting my experts. That was in a private chat with the ever-curious vizier. Nothing official. But mind you, I did not repeat nor press the matter at the conference."

"Who was behind the thievery of the second batch of documents of Zananzash? Was that your order?"

"Yes, I admit it. I had an informant who found out there were more documents and where they were hidden."

"Was that a man named Bak?"

"Yes. Thereupon I sent my men to get the documents in the name of that Hittite so that I could know if they would support my view of aggression towards our land. It was not the case."

"They were the proof I needed to show explicitly that the Hittites were on the defensive against the Assyrians. You sabotaged my evidence by your robbery, my son, with the help of real soldiers on a stealth mission sent by you as the commander."

"At that time, the tablets were not in your possession as evidence, dear mother. I only borrowed them from an alien traitor who was volunteering information to us anyway—only they were picked up without his knowledge. Anyway, I did not display them, and they had no consequence on the outcome of our conference. Later, I had them returned to the owner intact and with apologies for the mistake."

He grinned.

Nefertari got furious as never before.

"With awkward arguments, you try to rationalize your own betrayal of the kingdom and your family. How could I ever pardon this mischief?"

The erupting wrath was about to go beyond her physical control as she rose.

"Amun-her! You were adding up things like a gossipmonger in the market, or worse, like a conspirator. You were passing on invented information to our vizier with the sole purpose of influencing him and beginning a war. You had documents stolen to obstruct any support for my case. On purpose, you were also consciously working against my effort, your mother's honest effort. All that in your senior position as commander of the army. What a grand, loyal son I have reared. How could I ever forgive you?"

She stood with her hands akimbo and glowered down upon him. Amun-her leaned back in his seat, raising a hand to head level as if to ward off a slap.

He swallowed hard. "I admit my mistake and beg to be forgiven, Mother. I also confess exaggerating an opinion to better my position. I deplore my words to Paser. Please remember, I never brought up this assertion officially in the conference. In fact, all along, I was only following your advice when I was young: 'If fortune does not come your way, you ought to help yourself and correct the outcome with your own effort.'"

The audacity of her son was getting out of hand. She could not let that pass. But she was breathless and speechless.

He was not.

He proceeded with a shrug. "But does all this change my position now? You won. I lost."

She sighed and said, "I was praying to the goddess Hathor for strength and support, and you were out to stab me in the back."

There was a pause until he licked his lips and said, "Please listen, Mother. Even if I am treading on delicate grounds after hurting your feelings, please have patience and listen to me. Earlier, you declared that war is prompted by the egotism of monarchs in the name of fame and glory. Now you accuse me of lying to avoid peace and begin a war. It could be true. We are all mortal, human, and fallible, dear mother. I am no better."

She shook her head. "You are seeing the whole international affair from your own personal, even selfish perspective, my son."

There was a pause. He took a deep breath. He seemed to be mustering courage for the next salvo.

"*Selfish?* You may charge me with seeking war and adventure just to prove myself, as I have been trained to be a warrior and command my troops. You may accuse me of being egotistic. You may even deplore my father and grandfather for following the same wrong motive: egotism. But how about *you*, Mother? With my conscience in doldrums, may I still hold a mirror to yours, please?

"How was it with you, dear mother? My conjecture is you wanted, you needed recognition. Were you not also discontented with serving only as a symbolic first queen of the pharaoh? Were you not also eager to be of service to the pharaoh in his reign? Were you not glad to make yourself available in the name of the peace you avowedly hold so dear as a virtue to our kingdom? You need not have gotten involved in the situation, but you strove hard to secure peace with our eternal enemy, our archenemy, the Hittites.

"I may be wrong, but I do think you felt excluded from the design of statecraft and politics, from ruling. You were tired of being just a decoration. You wanted, you needed recognition. You achieved your goal. Also, you had a selfish motivation, which you are now dressing up as following a noble cause now that you do not feel left out. Understand my position. Now I am the one who is being left out.

"Are we not all just egotistic souls wanting to project ourselves before others and eager to leave a legacy?"

Abruptly he rose and made a deep bow, but then he rose to his full height. With his head aloft and a full-blown chest in triumph, he marched off through the door. Nefertari sat still, staring at the void in the exit, but her mind's eye was fixed on the emptiness within her. She shook her head and whispered, "My son."

* * *

1255 BCE

After a week, Nefertari was busy in her chambers, writing a reply to the recent message from Puduhepa relating to the aftermath of the treaty and the positive spirit in her land ever since. Although the ladies had never met, the way Puduhepa addressed her as her sister spoke of the trust accomplished by their venture. From now on, Puduhepa would no longer be just a harbinger of news.

Nefertari was formulating her words for the text when her back stiffened as she felt a hand on her shoulder. Stunned, she looked up and saw Shishi standing behind her, all smiles.

"Engrossed in your script, dear?" he asked.

After a long, welcome hug and kiss, she asked with a bow in feigned formality, "What brings me the honor of a visit from my master?"

He spoke of the celebratory mood he was still perceiving everywhere. She pointed to the papyrus sheet and said, "I was writing a reply to Puduhepa in this regard. I heard the mood over there in Hatti is also jubilant. You may like to know she now calls you her dear brother and sends you her best wishes." She laughed and added, "At times, she even makes me feel jealous."

"That honor she gives me is a consequence of the beginning formulation in the treaty insisting on peace and brotherhood. Her husband and I are named brothers, although I never met him and do not have a high regard for him, either."

"You need not always have a high regard for a brother. They are there whether you like it or not. This could happen in the best of families."

"You have a point. Neighbors and brothers are given, not chosen. I will accept him as a step-brother."

Playfully, he reached her necklace, groping for the *ankh* attached to it. "Still in love with this symbol?"

"That was your present before you went on your campaign. In fact, it was a promise that you would return hale and hearty."

"I kept my promise, didn't I? Now you have kept your word and delivered it, too."

"My promise?"

"Yes, dear. On that occasion, you assured me that when I returned, there would be peace and happiness. We now have peace and happiness, and you showed me the way to achieve it."

"Don't flatter me, dear." Nefertari threw him a coy smile and blushed. She bit her lip and added, "But at what cost?"

"I don't follow you."

"I am not sure all are happy with this agreement of non-aggression."

He frowned and shook his head. "Ah, forget the warmongers. War is a necessity, not a game or a pastime. Now I am free to concentrate on the welfare of the subjects, and don't forget the monuments to posterity. In fact, it is in this connection that I came over to pass on some good news."

"Really?"

"Do you remember the construction work we started for the two temples, one in my name and another in yours?"

Nefertari thought for a second and asked, "Is it not on a site far south up the river, right through the Upper Kingdom all the way to the border with Tanehsu?"

"Yes. Right there. I am leaving next week for an inspection of the site and the work in progress. I wondered if you would like to join me and take a look. I have plans for an elaborate depiction and description of your life and contribution to the reign on that and other sites."

"About *me*?" She laid her finger on her chest and laughed.

He had strolled towards the statue of Hathor. Looking at it, he said, "One of the proposals from the artists was to put up a wall painting of me at the battle of Qadesh with Lord Amun's support and help. Another one was of an event twenty years later of you receiving a scroll of papyrus from the goddess Hathor. The accompanying script on the wall would describe the peace treaty, which, to this day, is one of your major accomplishments and contributions to my reign."

"Oh, no."

Ramses swung around, raising his eyebrows. "Why not? What is the matter?"

"It is very gracious of you, dear. As for joining you on your trip, as you know, I am not feeling well of late. The travel all the way to the other end of our kingdom would be quite a strain for me now. I have asked for the healers to call on me. I hope I can make the journey. I am not sure. Please understand." She looked at her hands. Luckily, they were not shaking.

She thought of the fragrance of the invisible jasmine in the garden and took a deep breath before her next remark.

"Moreover, I beg you never to mention in public any of my contributions, what you call achievements, to the affairs of the state, please. Whatever I was allowed to do by you, whatever I was blessed to do by the gods, I did for my people, for our kingdom—not for my personal glory."

She came close to him with a smile and whispered as she stroked his cheek, "I did it for *you*, Shishi."

* * *

Ramses had conceived a colossal project at the border in Meha (Abu Simbel), in the region the natives called Wawat. The decision had been taken to construct two temples at the border: the first, the temple of Ramses, dedicated to his personal deity, Amun, and the second, the temple of Nefertari, dedicated to her personal deity, Hathor. At the entrance, large statues of both Ramses and the queen, some six times life-size, were to be carved out of a sandstone cliff.

As planned, the inauguration for the monument proceeded for several days, beginning with the formal religious ceremony followed by the secular festivity for the subjects. It was, indeed, a gorgeous festival, with the royal pair representing the divinity as well as the glory of their kingdom radiating beyond the border of the Upper Kingdom in the south. The royalty and the public would remember the ceremony and the celebration for ages to come.

This occasion was an appropriate pendant to the success in the peace mission pertaining to the Lower Kingdom in the north, where Per-Ramesses lay. For Ramses, it was a public assertion of his intent to reign in his lands with peace and power, promoting prosperity for his subjects. Nefertari also saw in this act his approval of their desire to treat war and aggression only as means to preserve peace and not to glory. There were other methods like this peaceful one to demonstrate the grandeur of a kingdom. For the royal pair, this inauguration was also to be the celebration of their joint venture.

Unfortunately for Nefertari, the auspicious occasion was shadowed by her ill health. Even at the outset, she had not been sure it would permit her to be present at all the ceremonies. They would be quite exacting, conducted in a row for days in the arid climate of the deep south. She had been wise to take her daughter Meritamen to be of help in representation. On many occasions, her daughter had to substitute for her when she was ill.

After all the ceremonies were over, Ramses had to return to Per-Ramesses with Paser. As Nefertari had become too weak for travel, her daughter stayed behind to take care of her, assisted by several healers. They planned to return later in a leisurely voyage down the river in a more comfortable boat.

One morning, the chambermaid found Nefertari stretched lifeless in her bed, holding in her hand the *ankh*, the symbol of life and love. But her soul had left her body. The queen rested in peace.

The message had reached Per-Ramesses. Paser was seated before Ramses, sharing a long silence as they swallowed the news, which was irrevocable. No healers could be of help, for this was the will of the gods. Paser had tried to stitch together some consoling words, but they had all gotten stuck in his throat. He was speechless, like the pharaoh. The vizier had known and cherished Nefertari ever since she had been about eleven. That jumpy and hilarious little girl who turned later into a brilliant woman of strong will and disposition—who had even taught him quite a few things in statecraft—was no more.

Ramses broke the gloom of silence in a deep and husky voice. "She is a noble woman, Lady of Grace, my first and only love. She is—was more foreseeing and wiser than I. Always at my side, she was my true companion, guide, and solace. And now? I am alone, and she is alone. The gods have called her back, but they want me to stay on. What for?" He hit his thigh with his fist. "She will never return."

After searching for the right words for a long while, Paser said, "You have a long reign ahead, your majesty. Lord Amun wants you to stay on, for you have many tasks for the future and much to accomplish."

Ramses did not seem to hear. He said, "For her sake, the sun shone. Will he shine on to lead my way now that I am alone and groping in darkness, now that I am lonely and lost without her?"

On nearing him, Paser saw Ramses shudder and grit his teeth. The sunlight from the windows highlighted his desperation. His majesty's eyes glistened. The vizier laid a hand on his shoulder. The pharaoh turned his head away and lowered it with a deep sigh, his fingers pressing his eyes.

Paser heard him whisper, "Meritmut, my glorious companion, my real queen."

Then he burst out with a cry: "Why did you call her away, my god?"

END

Author's Note

"A peace is of the nature of a conquest; for then both parties nobly are subdued and neither party loser."

—SHAKESPEARE, *HENRY IV, PART II* (ACT IV, SCENE 2)

In this narrative, I have done my best to stick to known facts and details. Eight Egyptian and Hittite personae, four on each side, are historical characters.

The reign of Ramses II was one of the pinnacles of ancient Egyptian history. He ruled for another forty years after Nefertari's demise. He died after reaching an age around ninety, but the crown prince, Amun-her-khepeshef, died a few years after his mother. The successor to Ramses was Amun-her-khepeshef's stepbrother Merenptah.

Hartapu is mentioned by scholars as succeeding Kurunta as the king of Tarhuntassa. Hartapu adopted the same title as that of his predecessor and uncle, "Great King and Hero." Three years ago, in 2019, a stele of Hartapu was found near the site of Türkmen-Karahüyük. It had been inscribed in the Luwian language in memory of his conquest of Phrygia. It has been pointed out by scholars that the royal line of Hartapu persisted far after the demise of the Hittite empire. However, the precise location of the capital Tarhuntassa has not yet been determined.

The peace treaty was honored by both sides for decades. It lost its significance only with the collapse or implosion of the Hittite empire some eighty years later. This course of history reminds me of the dissolution of the Soviet Union in the last century after nearly fifty years of the Cold War with the West. The Egyptian version in hieroglyphs can be found in Thebes on the walls of the Ramesseum and at the temple of Karnak. The Hittite tablets are to be seen in the Museum of the Ancient Orient in Istanbul, Turkey, and in the State Museum of Berlin, Germany. A copy of the ancient treaty is displayed in the United Nations Headquarters in New York City.

Personae

Amun-her-khepeshef — Crown prince of Egypt, son of Nefertari and Ramses.

Anat — Daughter of Ria'a and Bennu.

Ankhef — Foster father of Mehetweret.

Bak — An Egyptian assistant of Teremun.

Bennu — Lady-in-waiting of queen Nefertari.

Hartapu — Hittite prince, son of Mursili III.

Hattusili III — Present king of the Hittites, uncle of Mursili III.

Mashanda — An assistant of Suppilamus.

Mehetweret (Met) — A waitress in an alehouse.

Nefertari Meritmut — Queen of Egypt.

Paser — The vizier of Ramses.

Puduhepa — Queen of the Hittite kingdom.

Ramses II — The Pharaoh.

Rai'a — A smith, Bennu's husband, Anat's father.

Sennefer — The shaman.

Suppilamus — An envoy from Hattusili on a secret mission.

Tarkondemos (Demos) — A Hittite envoy from Tarhuntassa.

Teremun — A Hittite supporter of Mursili III.

Tiaa — Foster mother of Mehetweret.

Urhi-Teshub Mursili III — Fugitive king of the Hittites.

Zananzash (Zan) — Fugitive officer from the Hittite kingdom.

Glossary

Ankh — A symbol for "life" or "breath of life": a cross with a loop at the top.

Deben — A weight made of copper.

Desheret — The "Red Land," the desert part of Egypt stretching beyond the banks of the Nile.

Hasawa — Multi-skilled Hittite professional involved in rituals, midwifery, and healing.

Hyksos — Egyptian name *hekau-khasut*, "rulers of foreign lands," foreigners who ruled Egypt from 1648–1550 BCE.

Iunum — The original name for the Greek city of Heliopolis.

Ishhara — The Hittite goddess of oaths.

Kemet — The "Black Land" on the shores of the Nile, also used as the indigenous name for Egypt.

Nesite — Official language of the Hittites.

Per-Ramesses — The capital, meaning "House of Ramesses" (also spelled PerRamessu and Pi-Ramesses).

Teshub & Hepat — Storm god and goddess of the Hittites (Hurrian names).

Waset — The original name for Thebes.

Wawat — In Nubia, the region between the first and fourth cataracts.

About The Author

Naveen Sridhar is a scientist and an author living in Germany. He has a Ph.D. in chemistry and chemical engineering. He was born in India and migrated to Germany at an early age for studies in Berlin. Widowed in 2017, he has two sons.

Besides his profession, he was also an entertainer, and in 2011, he wrote and published *A Complete Guide to Ventriloquism: Principles, Practice, and Performance.*

His other published works:

Candlelight in a Storm: Born to be a Berliner

Starlight in the Dawn: The Poetic Priestess Who Chose to Fight

Made in the USA
Monee, IL
15 July 2022

99600519R00156